D1531846

ENGLISH LANGUAGE

for Cambridge International AS & A level

Dr Julian Pattison
Duncan Williams

OXFORD
UNIVERSITY PRESS

Great Clarendon Street, Oxford, OX2 6DP, United Kingdom

Oxford University Press is a department of the University of Oxford. It furthers the University's objective of excellence in research, scholarship, and education by publishing worldwide. Oxford is a registered trade mark of Oxford University Press in the UK and in certain other countries

British Library Cataloguing in Publication Data
Data available

978-0-19-830012-0

2 3 4 5 6 7 8 9 10

Paper used in the production of this book is a natural, recyclable product made from wood grown in sustainable forests.
The manufacturing process conforms to the environmental regulations of the country of origin.

Printed in China by Printplus

Acknowledgements

The publisher would like to thank Cambridge International Examinations for their kind permission to reproduce past paper questions.

Cambridge International Examinations bears no responsibility for the example answers to questions taken from its past question papers contained in this publication.

The publishers would like to thank the following for permissions to use their photographs:

Cover image: Cienpies Design/Shutterstock

p11: Image Bank; **p12:** Velkol/Bigstock; **p15:** Hulton Archive/Getty Images; **p20:** Roberto Schmidt/AFP/Getty Images; **p21:** Everett Collection/Rex Features; **p22:** Steve Collender/Shutterstock; **p31a:** Superstock/Glow Images; **p31b:** Universal Images Gtoup/Getty Images; **p42:** KPA/Heritage Images/Glow Images; **p46:** Everett_Glow/Glow Images; **p51:** Rex Features; **p57:** Maxx Studio/Shutterstock; **p61:** Lassen/Poodles Rock/Corbis; **p62:** Nicholas Bailey/Rex Features; **p64:** Rajasthan Tourism; **p66:** Heritage Images/Corbis; **p73:** cTermit/Shutterstock; **p75:** Daily Mail/Associated Newspapers/Rex Features; **p78:** Boudikka/Shutterstock; **p93:** KSL/Fotolia; **p94:** Asianet-Pakistan/Shutterstock; **p106:** Moviestore/Rex Features; **p112:** Imagebank; **p113:** Rex Features; **p137:** FCG/Shutterstock; **p140:** Tim Haggarty; **p148:** Time & Life Pictures/Getty Images; **p146a:** OUP Picturebank; **p146b:** tgellan/Bigstock; **p154:** CBsigns/Alamy; **p155a:** Contrasaddict/iStockphoto; **p155b:** Kabby/iStockphoto; **p155c:** Konurk/iStockphoto; **p158:** Brooks Kraft/Corbis; **p169:** Joe Biafore/iStockphoto; **p170:** Imagebank; **p172:** Imagebank; **p182a:** lp3/iStockphoto; **p182b:** Mau Horng/Shutterstock; **p192:** Sion Touhig/Sygma/Corbis; **p194:** Cartoon Stock; **p197:** Moviestore Collection/Rex Features; **p202:** Eric Purcell; **p216:** Betsy Streeter; **p223:** S Harris; **p225:** Cartoon Stock; **p236:** Image Bank; **p253:** Photos 12/Alamy; **p262:** Mikhail Pogosov/Shutterstock; **p257:** The Paducah Sun, Stephen Lance Dennee/AP Images; **p265:** SoulCurry/Shutterstock; **p277:** Medusa81/Bigstock

Artwork by Phoenix Photosetting

The author and publisher are grateful for permission to reprint extracts from the following copyright material:

Chimamanda Ngozi Adichie: excerpt from *Americanah*, © 2013 Chimamanda Ngozi Adichie reprinted by permission of HarperCollins Publishers Ltd. and Alfred A. Knopf, an imprint of the Knopf Doubleday Publishing Group, a division of Random House LLC, all rights reserved.

Chimamanda Ngozi Adichie: excerpt from *Half of a Yellow Sun,* © 2006 Chimamanda Ngozi Adichie, reprinted by permission of HarperCollins Publishers Ltd.

Jean Aitchison: excerpts from 'The Language Web' and 'The Power and Problem of Words', The 1996 BBC Reith Lectures, 1997, copyright © Jean Aitchison 1997, published by Cambridge University Press, reprinted by permission.

Jennifer Allen: from the article 'Speak Easy', frieze magazine, issue 137, March 2011, see www.frieze.com for further information, reprinted by permission.

Kingsley Amis: excerpts from *Lucky Jim,* copyright © Kingsley Amis, 1953, reprinted by permission of The Wylie Agency (UK) Limited and The Orion Publishing Group Ltd, London.

BBC Worldwide Ltd: excerpt from the transcript of *Africa,* reprinted by permission of BBC Worldwide Ltd.

Lillian Beckwith: *The Loud Halo,* copyright © The Beneficiaries of the Literary Estate of Lillian Beckwith 1964, reprinted by permission of Curtis Brown Group Ltd, London on behalf of the Literary Estate of Lillian Beckwith.

Tim Berners-Lee: excerpt from *Weaving the Web,* copyright © 1999, 2000 by Tim Berners-Lee, reprinted by permission of HarperCollins Publishers and Tim Berners-Lee.

Katherine Boo: excerpt from *Behind the Beautiful Forevers,* reprinted by permission of Portobello Books.

Raymond Carver: 'Little Things' (first published as 'Popular Mechanics') from *What We Talk About When We Talk About Love: Stories,* copyright © 1974, 1976, 1978, 1980, 1981 by Raymond Carver, reprinted by permission of The Random House Group Limited, The Wylie Agency (UK) Limited and Alfred A. Knopf, an imprint of the Knopf Doubleday Publishing Group, a division of Random House LLC, all rights reserved.

Raymond Carver: 'The Father' from *Will You Please Be Quiet, Please?* (1976), copyright © Raymond Carver, reprinted by permission of The Random House Group Limited.

Raymond Chandler: excerpt from *The Big Sleep,* (Penguin Books, 2011), copyright © 1939 by Raymond Chandler and renewed 1967 by Helga Greene, Executrix of the Estate of Raymond Chandler, reprinted by permission of Penguin Books Limited and Alfred A. Knopf, an imprint of the Knopf Doubleday Publishing Group, a division of Random House LLC, all rights reserved.

Robbie Collin: from 'Skyfall James Bond Review', 24 October 2012, *The Telegraph,* © Telegraph Media Group Limited 2012, reprinted by permission.

William Dalrymple: excerpt from *The Age of Kali,* © 1998, William Dalrymple, reprinted by permission of HarperCollins Publishers Ltd.

Farrukn Dondy: 'Run and dance your way to health', from *Deccan Chronicle,* Bangalore, 8 September 2012, reprinted by permission.

Prof. Peter Elbow: *Vernacular Eloquence: What Speech Can Bring to Writing* (2012), reprinted by permission of Oxford University Press, USA, (www.oup.com).

Express Newspapers: 'Scenes of horror, *The Daily Express,* 20 January 1922, reprinted by permission of Express Newspapers.

William Faulkner: excerpt from *The Hamlet,* © Copyright 1940 by William Faulkner and renewed 1968 by Estelle Faulkner and Jill Faulkner Summers, reprinted by permission of W. W. Norton & Company, Inc., The Random House Group Limited, and Random House LLC.

William Faulkner: excerpt from *The Sound and the Fury,* published by Chatto & Windus © Copyright 1929 and renewed 1957 by William Faulkner, reprinted by permission of W. W. Norton & Company, Inc., The Random House Group Limited, and Random House LLC.

Jonathan Safran Foer: excerpt from *Extremely Loud and Incredibly Close: A Novel,* (Hamish Hamilton, 2005, Penguin Books, 2006), copyright © 2005 by Jonathan Safran Foer, reprinted by permission of Houghton Mifflin Harcourt Publishing Company and Penguin Books, all rights reserved.

John Fowles: excerpt from *The Magus,* published by Jonathan Cape. Reprinted by permission of The Random House Group Limited and Hachette Book Group (Little, Brown and Company).

Janet Frame: excerpt from *To the Is-land,* first published by George Braziller 1982, reprinted by permission of The Wylie Agency (UK) Limited.

George MacDonald Fraser: excerpt from *The General Danced at Dawn,* reprinted by permission of Curtis Brown Group Ltd, London on behalf of The Estate of George MacDonald Fraser, copyright © George MacDonald Fraser, 1974 and HarperCollins Publishers Limited.

Jeffrey Gil: excerpt from 'English in China: The Impact of the Global Language on China's Language Situation', 2005, from http://research-hub.griffith.edu.au, reprinted by permission of the author.

Greater London Authority: extracts from a transcript of a meeting of the London Assembly's Economic Development, Culture, Sport and Tourism Committee, reprinted by kind permission of the Greater London Authority.

Mohsin Hamid: excerpt from *The Reluctant Fundamentalist,* Copyright © 2007 by Mohsin Hamid, reprinted by permission of Houghton Mifflin Harcourt Publishing Company and Penguin Books (UK), all rights reserved.

Ernest Hemingway: excerpt from *In Our Time,* copyright © 1925, 1930 by Charles Scribner's Sons, copyright renewed 1953, 1958 by Ernest Hemingway, reprinted with the permission of Scribner Publishing Group and The Random House Group Limited, all rights reserved.

Dr Sarah Jarvis: extracts from 'Medication side effects - protecting yourself and others', written for health website Patient.co.uk by an expert – Dr Sarah Jarvis, who is clinical consultant for the site, reprinted by permission.

The Honourable Paul Keating: eulogy given at the interment of the Unknown Australian Soldier in 1993 at the Australian War Memorial in Canberra reprinted by permission of the Office of the Hon Paul Keating.

Nigel Latta: article 'Relax and enjoy kids' by Nigel Latta, 3 June 2007, *New Zealand Herald,* reprinted by permission of Nigel Latta.

Continued on back page.

Introduction

Welcome to your *English Language for Cambridge International AS & A Level* book.

This book has been written as a companion to support you throughout your English Language International AS and A Level course.

The book has been divided into two parts: one for the AS Level and one for the A Level. Each part will guide you through the techniques you will need to interpret and produce texts in a variety of styles and for a variety of audiences. There are engaging activities throughout that will allow you to put your new skills to use and sample answers from real students to show how you could use these skills in an examination.

The accompanying *English Language for Cambridge International AS & A Level* website contains a glossary of all of the new terms that are introduced in the book. It also has additional worksheets, activities, and presentations that will support you and your teachers on your journey through the English Language Cambridge International AS and A Level course.

www.oxfordsecondary.co.uk/cambridge-alevel-english

Authors and acknowledgements

Julian Pattison, author of the AS level section, taught English at Merchant Taylors' School, London and then at Wolverhampton Grammar School, where he was Head of English and subsequently Vice-Principal. He holds a Ph.D. in English from the University of New Brunswick, Canada. He has worked as a senior examiner in English and Literature in English for over thirty years.

Thanks to the many teachers in Argentina, South Africa, New Zealand, India, the United States who have all helped shape this book and trialled (unwittingly) some of the assignments. In particular, I am indebted to Eleanor Trafford and the students of the English department, Bradford Grammar School, for the worked examples in Chapter 5. Dilshad Engineer and students of the Bright Start Fellowship International School, Mumbai provided new ideas at just the right moment. Neil Swindells read the proofs and put up with the process – and the book is better for it. Callum Turbet (born 7th January 2013) was a constant point of reference – he has all of this still to come.

Duncan Williams, author of the A-level section, holds a degree in English from the University of Cambridge. After a time teaching EFL in Greece, he worked as a teacher of English Language and Literature at a range of secondary schools in England and Wales.

All of the many teaching colleagues with whom it has been my privilege to work have helped in the writing of this book. The good ideas are theirs, and the shortcomings mine. I am especially grateful to the teachers and students of the English department, Portsmouth High School, for the sample responses in Chapter 14.

Table of Contents

Introduction to Part 1

Getting started

This book is not a traditional textbook because it can't possibly include examples of all the different sorts of speech and writing that you will need to be familiar with in order to tackle the examinations at the end of the course. Rather, it is a companion to help you along the way.

As you read, the book will introduce you to a wide variety of key words that you will need in order to analyse texts that are given to you at that point or that you find for yourself. These terms will be printed in **bold** type the first time you encounter them and will be defined. You need to learn these words and their definitions. There is a glossary on the accompanying website at http://www.oxfordsecondary.co.uk/ cambridge-alevel-english. Throughout, the word **text** is taken to mean any communication in the language, either written or spoken.

Because of my background (middle-aged, British, teacher), you will find some rather British turns of phrase and perhaps some slightly British humour (and spelling) in this book. All of this could be edited to make things more language neutral, but I want you to have some picture of me as a real person – I am trying to build up a relationship with you through the way that I write. I want you to trust my judgments about the subject and, as we are going to be companions for a number of weeks, I'd like you to think we might be friends. In other words, I am constructing a personality on paper and, of course, one of the things about English as a global language is that you have to get used to adapting yourself to the variety in the language as you listen and read. That's the colour of the language, its diversity, its spice, and also the central concern of what is to follow.

Am I ready?

Let's start with some words of congratulation…

If you are reading this book, then you have already done the hardest part of the course!

You may not be a virtuoso violinist or a world-class soccer player, but in terms of language skills you are already an expert. Since you were a baby you have been trying to make an impression on the world, and one of the most obvious ways in which you will have done this is by learning to talk. From the age of about five you will have been talking in your first language (it doesn't have to be English) with great fluency, making only occasional errors. That's quite a trick, particularly because you will have gained these skills without having been anywhere near a textbook.

Not only had you learned to talk by that stage, but you had a sound grasp of how to put the language together in a wide variety of ways. In other words, you had managed to internalize the rules of English, or your first language, with no great difficulty. This is probably the cleverest thing you will ever do – it's certainly one of the most useful.

In his book *The Language Instinct*, Steven Pinker, the experimental psychologist, puts it like this:

> *Language is a complex, specialized skill, which develops in the child spontaneously without conscious effort or formal instruction... People know how to talk in more or less the sense that spiders know how to spin webs. Web-spinning was not invented by some unsung spider genius and does not depend on having had the right education or on having an aptitude for architecture or the construction trades. Rather, spiders spin webs because they have spider brains, which give them the urge to spin and the competence to succeed.[1]*

Elsewhere, Pinker notes that a first-language English speaker will have a strong sense of how words work together, even if he or she has never put together a particular phrase before. Even when sentences appear to be nonsense you are able to speculate about meaning: "The mups glorped spodily", will create a picture in your mind, even though you have no experience of three of the words, because you will have immediately fitted them into sentence patterns that you recognize.

This suggests that we learn language from principles, that there is such a thing as universal grammar, and that learning a first language is not done simply by repeating examples that we have heard. We know instinctively that "Mo nailed posters to the wall" sounds reasonable, while "Mo nailed the wall with posters", is somehow wrong. Without going into the detail of Pinker's argument we can be confident that "Amy poured water into the glass" is a workable sentence, whereas "Amy poured the glass with water" is not, even though it makes grammatical sense and in textbook terms is an exact equivalent of "Dad loaded the car with luggage".

By now, you have a vocabulary of many thousands of words and you can conjure any of them at a moment's notice in order to make an impression on other people. What's more, you can put them together in an infinite number of combinations in order to express your needs and desires to a wide variety of people in different situations.

By the time you were five, you would have found virtually all of the sentences below strange to say; you would have felt instinctively that they weren't quite right:

- Mummy goed out.
- Sammy jump over wall.
- I bigged it.
- It goed round and round.
- I willn't do it.
- He got two arm.
- I see Daddy bike.
- Mine is the bestest.
- Me don't want to do it.
- The mans bettern't do that.

Bearing in mind that small children construct grammatical rules without a textbook, why might the speakers of each of these utterances assume that what they say is correct?

With a moment's reflection, you can see how skilful you are in this subject. Compare this with learning an additional language, with its grammar books and exercises and the errors that you make in quite simple communications, both spoken and written. Somewhere along the way you have managed to accomplish something extraordinary with your first language, seemingly without effort.

Slightly more problematic, perhaps, is your relationship with reading and writing because you probably haven't given that the thousands of hours of practice that you have unconsciously put into listening and speaking. Nonetheless, you probably have little memory of a stage before you could read, where words were just a jumble on the page, and you quite possibly have little memory of your first efforts at handwriting either, though your parents may have kept some examples of your faltering first attempts.

By now, you may have written more on a computer (or a mobile phone or tablet) than on paper and may even find the business of shaping letters by hand quite hard work. In other words, you are a typical 21st-century user of your mother tongue.

Activity 1.1

Test your current competence with the following verbs followed by prepositions:

▶ knock in, knock out, knock down, knock round, knock through

▶ break in, break down, break through, break up.

The chances are that you will be able to see that each of the phrases means something different. You will be able to define most, if not all, of them. Spare a thought, then, for the non-native speaker who has to learn each one individually and then to realize that in British English "knock off" can mean both to steal and to stop work. Phrases like these demonstrate a language at work at its most idiomatic and colloquial, where a native speaker will understand automatically, and a second-language speaker will either have to nod wisely or find a dictionary.

What's involved?

Having reached a high level of competence with a language, it is possible to start thinking much more explicitly about how texts are constructed in order to create meaning. All texts contain elements of content, and that's always attached to issues of how the text can be shaped for maximum effect. If you fall off the back of a boat, it's obvious that you would probably shout "Help!" in the brief seconds you had before you hit the ocean, rather than phrasing the request more formally as "I wonder if someone would offer me assistance". In other words, situations shape texts. The process of discussing how texts create meaning is called **discourse analysis**. You will be looking at a vast range of different sorts of texts during your studies. At the same time you will also be producing your own texts in a variety of styles, and reflecting upon the choices that you make as a speaker or a writer. You will also enlarge your technical vocabulary for critical analysis.

There are four main areas of expertise that you will be developing:

- a critical and informed response to texts in a range of forms, styles, and contexts
- the interdependent skills of reading, analysis, and research
- effective, creative, accurate, and appropriate communication
- a firm foundation for further study of language (in use) and **linguistics** (the scientific study of language and its structure).

During the course you will be asked to engage with a wide variety of different sorts of texts, and you will need to be sure that you have read examples of the following different **genres** (types of writing):

- advertisements
- brochures
- leaflets
- editorials
- news stories
- articles
- reviews
- blogs
- investigative journalism
- letters
- podcasts
- biographies and autobiographies
- diaries
- essays
- speeches (both spontaneous and scripted)
- narrative and descriptive writing

The analysis of spontaneous speech will only really become important if you do the full course to A Level, although you will meet some of the basic ideas at AS Level.

How will I be assessed?

At the end of each phase of the course there will be two examinations. For Cambridge International AS Level you will need to take the following two papers.

Paper 1 Passages
(2 hours and 15 minutes)

In this paper you need to answer two of the three questions given; one is compulsory.

For each question you will need to read the passage given and then write a commentary that discusses ways in which the text creates meaning.

You will then be asked to produce a piece of directed writing that is based on the style of the original extract you read.

Paper 2 Writing
(2 hours)

This paper is divided into two sections, and you have to answer one question from each section.

In Section A you will produce a piece of imaginative writing, where you will need to demonstrate your skill as a producer of narrative or descriptive writing.

In Section B you will demonstrate your skill in discursive and argumentative writing for a specified type of reader (the **audience**) and will be asked to write in a specific genre, such as a letter to a newspaper editor.

To gain a Cambridge International A Level qualification, you will need to add to your scores by taking two more papers.

Paper 3 Text analysis
(2 hours 15 minutes)

You will be given two questions and you must answer both. In one of the questions there will certainly be a transcript of spoken language.

In Question 1 you will be given a passage to read. The question will ask you to re-cast the original for a different purpose or audience. Once you have done that, you will then be asked to compare your text with that of the original.

In Question 2 you will be presented with two linked texts, each of a different type (spontaneous speech/magazine article, for example). You will be asked to compare the language and style of the texts.

Paper 4 Language topics
(2 hours 15 minutes)

You will write two essays, each from a different topic area. There will be a choice of three questions. The topic areas are:

- Spoken language and social groups
- English as a global language
- Language acquisition by children and teenagers.

In the test you will be given some material to work on, but you will also need to discuss material that you have prepared in relation to the topic in order to demonstrate that you have an understanding of a range of issues that the topic might raise. You will need to produce lots of examples from your own experience, and you will have done some research into language communities around you.

The big picture

Every time you come across a text or are asked to create one, you need to think about the circumstances of its production and its effectiveness.

Let's start by thinking about the process of creating a text.

The **writer** or **speaker**

begins with a

purpose (an intention for the text)

and then chooses a

genre (type of writing: for example, a diary, a leaflet).

He/she then thinks about how to shape the text for an

audience (the person/people who will listen to or read this text).

At the same time the writer or speaker needs to consider the

context (the situation in which the audience will receive the text).

Once that is done, the text creator must choose an appropriate **form** (shape and length) and start to consider appropriate words (**style**) in order to create an effective

TEXT.

By looking at the various stages of text production, you are starting to engage with the construction of texts. You will have noticed that although this is a course in English language, we have thus far avoided any mention of things like grammar. That's not because they are unimportant, but because the primary function of the analysis you will be expected to do focuses on patterns of language and the social and cultural contexts in which it is used. Of course, you will need to be able to analyse in detail, but you need to keep the bigger picture in mind as you encounter texts. Your main focus, therefore, is on language in use. So as you read, speak, or listen, you need to be constantly asking yourself the following questions:

- What is this text trying to do? (**Purpose**)
- Who is it trying to communicate these ideas to? (**Audience**)
- Where will this text appear? (**Context**)
- What does it look or sound like? (**Form/Structure**)

And of course all of these things exist side by side in a piece of writing. The model isn't quite a straight line. Perhaps it's more like the diagram on the right.

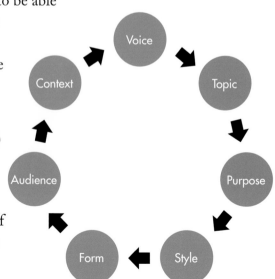

You can go deeper by starting to consider the relationship between the social and cultural contexts in which a text is produced. For example, if you think about greeting a friend at school or college with a casual "Hi, how are you?", both of you know that your friend is not being invited to give a full account of his or her health, mood, and relationships. You both have a common understanding of this sort of exchange, and you obey the rules. This sort of understanding between people is known as **pragmatics**. It means that you don't have to explain absolutely everything to a listener or a reader before you can start communicating with each other.

Here's a silly example. If you travel by train to London from the north of England, you get to Euston station and discover a sign on the escalator to the underground trains that says "Dogs must be carried on the escalator". Having located a dog and picked it up, you then journey on to Charing Cross, where a new message creates further difficulties. By now, "Dogs and heavy shopping must be carried on the escalator". It's clear what the sign means (if you happen to have a dog or heavy shopping with you at the time, you should carry them on the escalator), but there is an assumption about the word "must" that may not be shared by all members of the audience for the text. But to go looking for a dog and some shopping would be perverse – it is fairly obvious from the context what the language is intended to mean. Context is everything here.

For our purposes, it is important to recognize that words can be differently interpreted. For example, when Abraham Lincoln was shot by John Wilkes Booth on 14 April 1865, he didn't die instantly and some of Booth's friends claimed that it wasn't Booth who killed Lincoln: it was the incompetent doctors who tried to save him that really killed him. Booth simply fired the gun.

Activity 1.2

Have a look at the following photograph taken in a café in New Zealand. In what way does it not quite achieve the effect intended by the writer?

At times, when trying to compress a story into only a few words, newspaper headline writers produce statements that can be read in two ways, often with comic effect. Without meaning to, they give completely the wrong impression:

- KIDS MAKE NUTRITIOUS SNACKS
- RED TAPE HOLDS UP NEW BRIDGE
- HERSHEY BARS PROTEST
- DRUNK GETS NINE MONTHS IN VIOLIN CASE
- STOLEN PAINTING FOUND BY TREE
- SQUAD HELPS DOG BITE VICTIM
- END TO FREE SCHOOL LOOMS
- NURSE CRITICAL AFTER OPERATION
- HOT FAT BOY SUES
- PRINCESS DIANA DRESSES TO BE AUCTIONED
- MINERS REFUSE TO WORK AFTER DEATH
- TEENAGER HELD OVER SHREDDER
- LACK OF BRAINS HINDERS RESEARCH

Activity 1.3

Try to explain why these headlines are open to different interpretations. Then pick one of them and write a brief (200 word) article that takes the unintended story as a serious piece of news.

Activity 1.4

Have a look at the following table and see if you can make some statements about how you might present yourself in terms of language in a range of different situations.

Where?	Examples of different uses of language	Constraints/rules
Home and family		Informal Need to maintain order and discipline Affection Family-agreed codes and "in" jokes
School and teachers		More formal Structured/pre-meditated in terms of lesson content
Soccer, Saturday afternoon	Limited topics	Very informal Lower threshold for "bad" language "Male" dominated

See if you can add a few more scenarios from your own experience to the ones given in the left-hand column.

Activity 1.5

Another way of thinking about this is to consider different influences on your own language that determine the ways in which you speak. You should try to think about six or seven different aspects of your own language use.

Factor	Use of language with examples
Education	
Gender	

You can apply the same ideas to yourself in terms of your written work too.

Working with your own experience

Whenever we produce texts we are saying something about our relationships with each other. As soon as you start to talk or write, an audience or reader will start to make judgments about the words used, your accent, your level of education, the complexity of the way you express yourself, and your world view. You construct yourself (in part at least) through your use of language.

By now, you will have learned to write and speak in a variety of styles, and you will be acutely aware that an essay in school written for your teacher is very different to the sort of piece that you might produce by text message, where emoticons and abbreviations are acceptable, or in an email, where you will probably be rather more informal. You are on your way to recognizing yourself as part of a **language community** – a group of people who demonstrate belonging and gain their identity from their language choices. More correctly, you will be identifying yourself as part of a number of communities, all of which share much in common (the vastness of the same language) but have subtle differences between them.

Spend a few minutes now on Activity 1.6. You will quickly establish that, although there are many variations of colour, shape, material, and expense, people tend to wear shoes on their feet and hats on their heads. In other words, the function remains the same, even though the costume is different. The same is true of words in a sentence. Different types of words (verbs, nouns, etc.) perform different grammatical functions, but a writer or speaker's choice of particular examples ("exclaimed" rather than "said", for example), gives a different impression to a reader or listener. In terms of both writing and clothing, we can define this separation as **style**. Understanding this difference and being clear about it will be crucial to your success in this course.

Activity 1.6

People often stake out their claims to belong to a group through what they wear. See if you can identify a number of different youth fashions, and then discuss the differences in style between them.

Conclusion

We have established a number of things in this opening chapter.

- You know what is involved in the course.

- You are aware of your own linguistic history and current competence in the language.

- You have started to think about yourself as a producer and consumer of texts.

- We have recognized that the main purpose of the course is to examine language in use.

- We have established some very broad outlines of terminology that you will need to develop as we move forwards.

References

1. Pinker, Steven. 1995. *The Language Instinct*. London. Penguin Books.

A toolbox for textual analysis

Assembling your toolbox

The purpose of this chapter is to:

- introduce you to the vocabulary that you need to know in order to be able to analyse texts

- demonstrate these terms in action

- make you aware of how thinking about writing by other people can help you reflect upon the thinking process and choices that you make in your own writing

- give you a firm grounding in some of the concepts involved in discourse analysis.

Genre and context

One way in which we start to understand any text that we encounter is by trying to relate it to other similar texts that we have seen before. We immediately start to think about characteristics of this text that are familiar to us. Consider, for example, the mobile phone text message, a seemingly straightforward and simple communication. In fact, the process you go through before you can send one of these is quite complex.

Here's an example of a typical message.

Your process of thought and analysis might go something like this.

Author	Me
Audience	Someone I know quite well as they give me presents and invite me to social events
Purpose	To thank the person
Situation	The day after my birthday
Physical form	Text message seen on mobile phone screen
Constraints/rules	Only a limited number of characters can be used
Content	Greetings and thanks
Level of formality/register	Very casual
Style	Directly addresses the other person
Written language	Doesn't need to be in complete sentences: emoticons and abbreviations are perfectly acceptable
Structure	None, except to remember to keep it short

The left-hand column gives you a list of terms that are useful for the analysis of any text that you come across, and you should get in the habit of reading texts with them in mind. The important point to recognize is that almost unconsciously you make a large number of decisions about any text you either produce or try to interpret. This is **genre classification**, and it is a key factor in being able to make sense of a text. In very formal terms, this sort of text identification is known as **corpus linguistics**, the linking of a text to the "body" of other texts with which it shares central characteristics.

Activity 2.1

See if you can discuss and apply the same ideas from the table above to analysing some other form of text. What, for example, are the rules for messages on Twitter or another instant messaging service?

There are, of course, instances of writers playing tricks with genre, using an established form in order to manipulate a reader. William Carlos Williams wrote the following: "This is just to say I have eaten the plums that were in the icebox and which you were probably saving for breakfast Forgive me they were delicious so sweet and so cold". At first it seems like a casual note, in part because of its lack of punctuation, but once you know that Williams was a famous poet, it changes things considerably.

Activity 2.2

Try comparing the version above with the way that the poem appears in Williams's *Collected Poems*.

THIS IS JUST TO SAY

I have eaten
the plums
that were in
the icebox

and which
you were probably
saving
for breakfast

Forgive me
they were delicious
so sweet
and so cold

All of a sudden, you have to start applying the rules of genre that you know as poetry, not the rules for casual notes stuck to the fridge, and so you have to ask rather different questions of the text from those you might have originally had in mind.

A note on textspeak

Many adults think of textspeak as a sign of the ignorance of the young and of declining standards in written English. However, people have been abbreviating words in writing since at least the 17th century. In the 19th century this sort of writing was called emblematic poetry and everyone considered it innovative and terribly clever. Consider this: "I wrote 2 U B 4", a line from Charles C. Bombaugh's *Gleanings from the Harvest-Fields of Literature*, or his verse below.

> He says he loves U 2 XS,
> U R Virtuous and Y's
> In X L N C U X L
> All others in his i's.

The star-struck lover in 2015? Not at all – this was written in 1867. Technically, abbreviating a word to one letter (U = you) is called a **rebus**, and its use goes back centuries. People have been abbreviating whole phrases into their initial letters for centuries, too, with IOU (I owe you) being first recorded in 1618.

At the time of writing, it seems that all the panic is misplaced. Linguistic researchers are starting to report that, with the arrival of full-keyboard mobile phones and the dominance of predictive text and free messages, it's starting to look like too much trouble to use textspeak anyway.

As you can see, context and audience make a difference to your interpretation of a text. For example, the sentence "You have a green light" is ambiguous. Without knowing the **context** (the identity of the speaker/writer, his or her intent, the situation) it is difficult to infer the meaning with confidence. It could mean:

- that you have a green light while driving your car and can move on
- that you can go ahead with a project (a metaphorical meaning)
- that your body has a green glow
- that you possess a light bulb that is tinted green.

This is an example where context gives the clue, of pragmatics in action.

Activity 2.3

Select three or four texts from a variety of sources and see if you can apply the rules of genre classification to them. Remember that the texts can be quite short.

In classifying these texts, you are demonstrating some of the fundamental skills you need for this course: you are responding to a number of forms, styles, and contexts and thinking about the audience that they are directed towards. You could, of course, also apply these ideas to an evening's viewing on the television – the conventions for news broadcasts are, for example, entirely different from those of a cookery programme.

As you work, it will be clear that you are applying a series of rules in order to place the texts. They will probably be something like this:

- obvious features of form and shape – formal letters or a utility bill might be examples of this
- particular subject matter – a detective story focuses on finding out who committed the crime while a biography focuses on detailing the life of its subject, usually chronologically
- the writer's attitudes or the expected response from a reader – a travel brochure is based on the reasonable understanding that the reader agrees with the writer that taking a holiday to an exotic spot is a worthwhile thing to do

- expectations over time – if you have experienced James Bond films or Bollywood movies, you know what to expect when one comes on the television. In other words, you have a **prototype** (a pre-formulated model) in mind as you read, watch, or listen.

It will also be clear that, as with the Williams poem, there is no such thing as a fixed number of sorts of texts and that "genre" is often a flexible term. Genres can be very wide: when you categorize the natural world, vultures, albatrosses, and chickens all belong to the family of birds, even though each is obviously and very significantly different from the others. Similarly there are vast numbers of different types of experience categorized as "computer games".

Voice and point of view

Every text you come across, unless it is mechanically generated (a bus ticket, for example), will create a relationship with the audience. It does this in part by establishing a **voice**, a personality that comes through as you read or listen. Before we go into the detail, it's important to understand that there are two fundamental ways of creating a voice in a piece of writing. The first is when you aim to tell things from your own point of view, using the word "I". This is called **first-person narrative**. You can also tell things in a rather more objective way, **third-person narrative**, where everything seems to be seen as a camera might take a picture, without prejudice and simply reporting what is seen. Both may involve you in talking about **point of view**, the stance that the narrator is taking in relation to the information he or she wants to tell you.

You can, incidentally, also write using the second person using "you", which is what this book is doing by talking to you directly on paper.

First-person narrative

With first-person narrative, the advantage is that the writing has a sense of immediacy – the reader gets involved with the person that is talking to them right from the beginning. Even a few words are enough to draw you in: "I come from Des Moines. Somebody had to", the opening to Bill Bryson's book *The Lost Continent: Travels in Small Town America*, leads you

---

Activity 2.4

Here are some text openings. Identify the genre of each of them.

- Make wonderful plans to do new things in your life during the next 10 days while Jupiter aspects Pluto ...

- Once upon a time ...

- First, chop the onion ...

- He's placing the ball. I think he's the man hoping to strike it, but first he's having a word with the captain ...

- The manhunt extended across more than one hundred light years and eight centuries ...

- Set on the tip of the peninsula, the hotel's grounds take in the sea, Samana village, and a tropical cliché worth of palm trees ...

Write one of these openings down and then pass it on to another student. The other student should then write a further sentence in the same genre, fold over the paper so the next writer can't see your initial contribution and then pass it on again. Do this five or six times and then read out the result. See if the genre is still in place by the end.

Now you should assess how far the texts you have produced follow the rules for the particular genre.

into thinking that you are listening to someone who has a good sense of humour. Think too about the opening of Herman Melville's 900-page novel *Moby Dick*, where we are invited into an immediate and close relationship with the narrator with the words "Call me Ishmael".

Look at the opening of the novel *The Adventures of Huckleberry Finn* by American writer Mark Twain.

Activity 2.5

What sort of person is talking to you here? What can you work out about Huck from the way in which he addresses you?

Text type: prose narrative, fiction, USA

You don't know about me without you have read a book by the name of *The Adventures of Tom Sawyer;* but that ain't no matter. That book was made by Mr. Mark Twain, and he told the truth, mainly. There was things which he stretched, but mainly he told the truth. That is nothing. I never seen anybody but lied one time or another, without it was Aunt Polly, or the widow, or maybe Mary. Aunt Polly – Tom's Aunt Polly, she is – and Mary, and the Widow Douglas is all told about in that book, which is mostly a true book, with some stretchers, as I said before.

Now the way that the book winds up is this: Tom and me found the money that the robbers hid in the cave, and it made us rich. We got six thousand dollars apiece – all gold. It was an awful sight of money when it was piled up. Well, Judge Thatcher he took it and put it out at interest, and it fetched us a dollar a day apiece all the year round – more than a body could tell what to do with. The Widow Douglas she took me for her son, and allowed she would sivilize me; but it was rough living in the house all the time, considering how dismal regular and decent the widow was in all her ways; and so when I couldn't stand it no longer I lit out. I got into my old rags and my sugar-hogshead again, and was free and satisfied. But Tom Sawyer he hunted me up and said he was going to start a band of robbers, and I might join if I would go back to the widow and be respectable. So I went back.

The Adventures of Huckleberry Finn by Mark Twain

You might recognize that there is quite a subtle mixture of first-person and second-person narrative going on here, and that the writer is aiming for a very particular effect from this. A further point to note, of course, is that Huck is a fictional creation – his voice has been created by Mark Twain – but Twain tries hard to give the reader the impression that the narrator is quite simple, speaks truthfully, and is not very educated. Although the book is a novel, it has disguised its genre to give you the impression that it is an **autobiography** (someone's life directly written or spoken from their own experience). The text is a written text, but it's clear that Huck thinks that he is talking directly to you from the page, almost as though this is a transcript of a live interview. Fairly obviously, as the speaker is involved in the action, his point of view is **subjective** and may be biased or slanted in order to present himself in a particular way.

Here are two more examples for you to talk about.

Text type: prose narrative, fiction, USA

In my younger and more vulnerable years my father gave me some advice that I've been turning over in my mind ever since.

"Whenever you feel like criticizing anyone," he told me, "just remember that all the people in this world haven't had the advantages that you've had."

He didn't say any more, but we've always been unusually communicative in a reserved way, and I understood that he meant a great deal more than that. In consequence, I'm inclined to reserve all judgments, a habit that has opened up many curious natures to me and also made me the victim of not a few veteran bores. The abnormal mind is quick to detect and attach itself to this quality when it appears in a normal person, and so it came about that in college I was unjustly accused of being a politician, because I was privy to the secret griefs of wild, unknown men. Most of the confidences were unsought – frequently I have feigned sleep, preoccupation, or a hostile levity when I realized by some unmistakable sign that an intimate revelation was quivering on the horizon; for the intimate revelations of young men, or at least the terms in which they express them, are usually plagiaristic and marred by obvious suppressions. Reserving judgments is a matter of infinite hope. I am still a little afraid of missing something if I forget that, as my father snobbishly suggested, and I snobbishly repeat, a sense of the fundamental decencies is parcelled out unequally at birth. And, after boasting this way of my tolerance, I come to the admission that it has a limit. Conduct may be founded on the hard rock or the wet marshes, but after a certain point I don't care what it's founded on. When I came back from the East last autumn I felt that I wanted the world to be in uniform and at a sort of moral attention forever; I wanted no more riotous excursions with privileged glimpses into the human heart.

The Great Gatsby by F. Scott Fitzgerald

Text type: prose narrative, fiction, UK

It was 7 minutes after midnight. The dog was lying on the grass in front of Mrs Shears' house. Its eyes were closed. It looked as if it was running on its side, the way dogs run when they think they are chasing a cat in a dream. But the dog was not running or asleep. The dog was dead. There was a garden fork sticking out of the dog. The points of the fork must have gone all the way through the dog and into the ground because the fork had not fallen over. I decided the dog was probably killed with the fork because I could not see any other wounds in the dog and I do not think you would stick a garden fork into a dog after it had died for some other reason, like cancer for example, or a road accident. But I could not be certain about this.

I went through Mrs Shears' gate, closing it behind me. I walked onto her lawn and knelt beside the dog. I put my hand on the muzzle of the dog. It was still warm.

The dog was called Wellington. It belonged to Mrs Shears who was our friend. She lived on tthe opposite side of the road, two houses to the left.

The Curious Incident of the Dog in the Night-Time
by Mark Haddon

You will have noticed that as you read you are hard at work trying to make sense of the voice, to work out whether the speaker is old or young, rich or poor, clever or stupid – the list could go on. And, of course, you have to decide if you want to listen to this voice, whether you trust and like it or not. If you write in the first person, you need to be very aware that readers are conjuring up a picture of you in their minds. The advantage of the voice here is that we are allowed direct access into the thoughts of the person writing. The disadvantage is that we have no means of knowing what other people might think about the events that are being described or whether the narrator is telling the truth.

Third-person narrative

As we have seen, first-person narrative offers you intimacy with the speaker or writer's voice. You can demonstrate this easily by contrasting Haddon's narrator in *The Curious Incident of the Dog in the Night-Time* to the opening of Charles Dickens's novel *A Tale of Two Cities*.

Text type: prose narrative, fiction, UK

It was the best of times, it was the worst of times, it was the age of wisdom, it was the age of foolishness, it was the epoch of belief, it was the epoch of incredulity, it was the season of Light, it was the season of Darkness, it was the spring of hope, it was the winter of despair, we had everything before us, we had nothing before us, we were all going direct to Heaven, we were all going direct the other way – in short, the period was so far like the present period, that some of its noisiest authorities insisted on its being received, for good or for evil, in the superlative degree of comparison only.

A Tale of Two Cities by Charles Dickens

Here Dickens writes as though he is **omniscient**, with an all-seeing eye, someone who is telling the story and has the right to observe events and comment on them in very serious tones. Sometimes the writer creates a voice that comments on the action explicitly, as here.

This is called **intrusive narration**. Narrators who simply let the action unfold are **unintrusive**. If the writer seems to know everything then it can be called **unrestricted narrative**. On the other hand, sometimes writers limit themselves to **restricted narrative**, where the events unfold themselves without the writer seeming to know everything from the start. Remember, too, that writers may be trying to convey an impression of themselves as they write which may not correspond to the day-to-day characters of the writers themselves. You will also notice that a writer can choose to be **objective**, non-judgmental, about what is being said, or can offer a commentary in which they express some opinion, which then makes the writing **subjective**.

Sometimes, factual writing borrows some of the techniques of fictional writing in order to become more vivid.

Text type: prose narrative, non-fiction, India

Prologue: between roses

July 17, 2008—Mumbai

Midnight was closing in, the one-legged woman was grievously burned, and the Mumbai police were coming for Abdul and his father. In a slum hut by the international airport, Abdul's parents came to a decision with an uncharacteristic economy of words. The father, a sick man, would wait inside the trash-strewn, tin-roofed shack where the family of eleven resided. He'd go quietly when arrested. Abdul, the household earner, was the one who had to flee.

Abdul's opinion of this plan had not been solicited, typically. Already he was mule-brained with panic. He was sixteen years old, or maybe nineteen—his parents were hopeless with dates. Allah, in His impenetrable wisdom, had cut him small and jumpy. A coward: Abdul said it of himself. He knew nothing about eluding policemen. What he knew about, mainly, was trash. For nearly all the waking hours of nearly all the years he could remember, he'd been buying and selling to recyclers the things that richer people threw away.

Now Abdul grasped the need to disappear, but beyond that his imagination flagged. He took off running, then came back home. The only place he could think to hide was in his garbage.

He cracked the door of the family hut and looked out. His home sat midway down a row of hand-built, spatchcock dwellings; the lop-sided shed where he stowed his trash was just next door. To reach this shed unseen would deprive his neighbors of the pleasure of turning him in to the police.

He didn't like the moon, though: full and stupid bright, illuminating a dusty open lot in front of his home. Across the lot were the shacks of two dozen other families, and Abdul feared he wasn't the only person peering out from behind the cover of a plywood door. Some people in this slum wished his family ill because of the old Hindu–Muslim resentments. Others resented his family for the modern reason, economic envy. Doing waste work that many Indians found contemptible, Abdul had lifted his large family above subsistence.

The open lot was quiet, at least—freakishly so. A kind of beach-front for a vast pool of sewage that marked the slum's eastern border, the place was bedlam most nights: people fighting, cooking, flirting, bathing, tending goats, playing cricket, waiting for water at a public tap, lining up outside a little brothel, or sleeping off the effects of the grave-digging liquor dispensed from a hut two doors down from Abdul's own. The pressures that built up in crowded huts on narrow slum lanes had only this place, the *maidan*, to escape. But after the fight, and the burning of the woman called the One Leg, people had retreated to their huts.

Now, among the feral pigs, water buffalo, and the usual belly-down splay of alcoholics, there seemed to be just one watchful presence: a small, unspookable boy from Nepal. He was sitting, arms around knees, in a spangly blue haze by the sewage lake—the reflected neon signage of a luxury hotel across the water. Abdul didn't mind if the Nepali boy saw him go into hiding. This kid, Adarsh, was no spy for the police. He just liked to stay out late, to avoid his mother and her nightly rages.

It was as safe a moment as Abdul was going to get. He bolted for the trash shed and closed the door behind him.

Inside was carbon-black, frantic with rats, and yet relieving. His storeroom—120 square feet, piled high to a leaky roof with the things in this world Abdul knew how to handle. Empty water and whiskey bottles, mildewed newspapers, used tampon applicators, wadded aluminum foil, umbrellas stripped to the ribs by monsoons, broken shoe-laces, yellowed Q-tips, snarled cassette tape, torn plastic casings that once held imitation Barbies. Somewhere in the darkness, there was a Berbee or Barbie itself, maimed in one of the experiments to which children who had many toys seemed to subject those toys no longer favored.

Behind the Beautiful Forevers by Katherine Boo

Another technique that a third-person writer can use is to give you partial insight into what one of the characters or participants is thinking, or how he or she is responding to a situation. The voice is external, but we are seeing the situation through the eyes of a character. The opening of Chimamanda Adichie's novel *Half of A Yellow Sun*, set during the civil war in Nigeria, offers a fine example.

Activity 2.6

Focus on three aspects of Boo's style here:
- how it moves straight into the situation
- details of the story that could come from a newspaper report
- vividness of description.

Which is the most important?

Text type: prose narrative, fiction, Nigeria

Master was a little crazy; he had spent too many years reading books overseas, talked to himself in his office, did not always return greetings, and had too much hair. Ugwu's aunty said this in a low voice as they walked on the path. "But he is a good man," she added. "And as long as you work well, you will eat well. You will even eat meat *every day*." She stopped to spit; the saliva left her mouth with a sucking sound and landed on the grass.

Ugwu did not believe that anybody, not even this master he was going to live with, ate meat every day. He did not disagree with his aunty, though, because he was too choked with expectation, too busy imagining his new life away from the village. They had been walking for a while now, since they got off the lorry at the motor park, and the afternoon sun burned the back of his neck. But he did not mind. He was prepared to walk hours more in even hotter sun. He had never seen anything like the streets that appeared after they went past the university gates, streets so smooth and tarred that he itched to lay his cheek down on them. He would never be able to describe to his sister Anulika how the bungalows here were painted the colour of the sky and sat side by side like polite well-dressed men, how the hedges separating them were trimmed so flat on top that they looked like tables wrapped with leaves.

His aunty walked faster, her slippers making *slap-slap* sounds that echoed in the silent street. Ugwu wondered if she, too, could feel the coal tar getting hotter underneath, through her thin soles. They went past a sign, ODIM STREET, and Ugwu mouthed *street*, as he did whenever he saw an English word that was not too long. He smelled something sweet, heady, as they walked into a compound, and was sure it came from the white flowers clustered on the bushes at the entrance. The bushes were shaped like slender hills. The lawn glistened. Butterflies hovered above.

"I told Master you will learn everything fast, *osiso-osiso*," his aunty said. Ugwu nodded

attentively although she had already told him this many times, as often as she told him the story of how his good fortune came about: While she was sweeping the corridor in the mathematics department a week ago, she heard Master say that he needed a houseboy to do his cleaning, and she immediately said she could help, speaking before his typist or office messenger could offer to bring someone.

"I will learn fast, Aunty," Ugwu said. He was staring at the car in the garage; a strip of metal ran around its blue body like a necklace.

"Remember, what you will answer whenever he calls you is *Yes, sah!*"

"Yes, sah!" Ugwu repeated.

They were standing before the glass door. Ugwu held back from reaching out to touch the cement wall, to see how different it would feel from the mud walls of his mother's hut that still bore the faint patterns of moulding fingers. For a brief moment, he wished he were back there now, in his mother's hut, under the dim coolness of the thatch roof; or in his aunty's hut, the only one in the village with a corrugated iron roof.

Half of a Yellow Sun by Chimamanda Adichie

Activity 2.7

What do you learn about Ugwu from the passage? How do you learn it?

Speeches

We have looked at genre and voice and can now think about how they combine in political speeches.

Here is the ending of John F. Kennedy's inaugural address given on 20 January 1961 on becoming President of the United States of America.

Text type: scripted spoken, USA

So let us begin anew – remembering on both sides that civility is not a sign of weakness, and sincerity is always subject to proof. Let us never negotiate out of fear, but let us never fear to negotiate.

Let both sides explore what problems unite us instead of belaboring those problems which divide us. Let both sides, for the first time, formulate serious and precise proposals for the inspection and control of arms, and bring the absolute power to destroy other nations under the absolute control of all nations. Let both sides seek to invoke the wonders of science instead of its terrors. Together let us explore the stars, conquer the deserts, eradicate disease, tap the ocean depths, and encourage the arts and commerce. Let both sides unite to heed, in all corners of the earth, the command of Isaiah – to "undo the heavy burdens, and [to] let the oppressed go free." And, if a beachhead of cooperation may push back the jungle of suspicion, let both sides join in creating a new endeavor – not a new balance of power, but a new world of law – where the strong are just, and the weak secure, and the peace preserved. All this will not be finished in the first one hundred days. Nor will it be finished in the first one thousand days; nor in the life of this Administration; nor even perhaps in our lifetime on this planet. But let us begin. In your hands, my fellow citizens, more than mine, will rest the final success or failure of our course. Since this country was founded, each generation of Americans has been summoned to give testimony to its national loyalty. The graves of young Americans who answered the call to service surround the globe. Now the trumpet summons us again – not as a call to bear arms, though arms we need – not as a call to battle, though embattled we are – but a call to bear the burden of a long twilight struggle, year in and year out, "rejoicing in hope; patient in tribulation," a struggle against the common enemies of man: tyranny, poverty, disease, and war itself.

John F. Kennedy

Can we forge against these enemies a grand and global alliance, North and South, East and West, that can assure a more fruitful life for all mankind? Will you join in that historic effort?

In the long history of the world, only a few generations have been granted the role of defending freedom in its hour of maximum danger. I do not shrink from this responsibility – I welcome it. I do not believe that any of us would exchange places with any other people or any other generation. The energy, the faith, the devotion which we bring to this endeavor will light our country and all who serve it. And the glow from that fire can truly light the world. And so, my fellow Americans, ask not what your country can do for you; ask what you can do for your country. My fellow citizens of the world, ask not what America will do for you, but what together we can do for the freedom of man.

Finally, whether you are citizens of America or citizens of the world, ask of us here the same high standards of strength and sacrifice which we ask of you. With a good conscience our only sure reward, with history the final judge of our deeds, let us go forth to lead the land we love, asking His blessing and His help, but knowing that here on earth God's work must truly be our own.

John F. Kennedy's inaugural address

Now look at the Gettysburg Address, given by Abraham Lincoln towards the end of the American Civil War at the inauguration of the American National Cemetery (1863).

Activity 2.8

What picture does Kennedy aim to give of his new administration?

Text type: scripted spoken, USA

Four score and seven years ago our fathers brought forth on this continent, a new nation, conceived in Liberty, and dedicated to the proposition that all men are created equal.

Now we are engaged in a great civil war, testing whether that nation, or any nation so conceived and so dedicated, can long endure. We are met on a great battlefield of that war. We have come to dedicate a portion of that field, as a final resting place for those who here gave their lives that that nation might live. It is altogether fitting and proper that we should do this.

But, in a larger sense, we cannot dedicate—we cannot consecrate—we cannot hallow—this ground. The brave men, living and dead, who struggled here, have consecrated it, far above our poor power to add or detract. The world will little note, nor long remember what we say here, but it can never forget what they did here. It is for us the living, rather, to be dedicated here to the unfinished work which they who fought here have thus far so nobly advanced. It is rather for us to be here dedicated to the great task remaining before us—that from these honored dead we take

Lincoln Memorial in Washington D.C.

increased devotion to that cause for which they gave the last full measure of devotion—that we here highly resolve that these dead shall not have died in vain—that this nation, under God, shall have a new birth of freedom—and that government of the people, by the people, for the people, shall not perish from the earth.

Gettysburg Address by Abraham Lincoln

When Kennedy was preparing his speech, he got his speechwriters to study Lincoln's words carefully. What connections in terms of style and strategy can you make between the two pieces?

It might help you to see the similarities by using the table that you used to determine the genre of a text (see pages 11–14).

You will probably find that you have identified some of the following:

- **Emotive** language, designed to stir your emotions

- Bold, simple statements

- **Rhetorical questions** –"Will you join in that historic effort?" You the listener are not being invited to reply out loud, so it is a question where the answer is already understood

- Inclusive **pronouns** (we, our)

- Metaphor ("can we *forge* against our enemies …")

- Alliteration

- Repetition/parallels

- Understatement

- Irony

- Escalation in tone (the relationship between diction, sentence structure, etc.)

- **Colloquial** or **idiomatic** language – language that makes you feel that the speaker is talking directly to you and using expressions that are quite informal or local, and turns of phrase that are understood by first-language speakers but cannot be easily defined by looking up the individual words ("brush with death", for example)

- **Allusions** – references to other texts: politicians are particularly fond of the Bible because it makes them sound like prophets)

- **Discourse markers**, terms such as "but" and "now" that move the argument forward and link paragraphs

Almost certainly, your discussions will have touched on the following areas:

- context – cultural, social, and historical

- ideas and issues

- values

- structure

- style and language features

- rhetorical devices.

What's very clear is that both of them are trying to conjure up a presidential voice to match the seriousness of the occasion.

See if you can apply the same principles to the speech on the following page given by the Australian Prime Minister, The Hon P.J. Keating, in 1993 on the burial of his country's unknown soldier, a symbol of all who die in battle but whose bodies, if recovered, are never identified.

Text type: scripted spoken, Australia

We do not know this Australian's name and we never will. We do not know his rank or his battalion. We do not know where he was born, or precisely how and when he died. We do not know where in Australia he had made his home or when he left it for the battlefields of Europe. We do not know his age or his circumstances – whether he was from the city or the bush; what occupation he left to become a soldier; what religion, if he had a religion; if he was married or single. We do not know who loved him or whom he loved. If he had children we do not know who they are. His family is lost to us as he was lost to them. We will never know who this Australian was.

Yet he has always been among those we have honoured. We know that he was one of the 45,000 Australians who died on the Western Front. One of the 416,000 Australians who volunteered for service in the First World War. One of the 324,000 Australians who served overseas in that war, and one of the 60,000 Australians who died on foreign soil. One of the 100,000 Australians who have died in wars this century.

He is all of them. And he is one of us.

This Australia and the Australia he knew are like foreign countries. The tide of events since he died has been so dramatic, so vast and all-consuming, a world has been created beyond the reach of his imagination.

He may have been one of those who believed that the Great War would be an adventure too grand to miss. He may have felt that he would never live down the shame of not going. But the chances are that he went for no other reason than that he believed it was his duty – the duty he owed his country and his King.

Because the Great War was a mad, brutal, awful struggle distinguished more often than not by military and political incompetence; because the waste of human life was so terrible that some said victory was scarcely discernible from defeat; and because the war which was supposed to end all wars in fact sowed the seeds of a second, even more terrible, war – we might think that this Unknown Soldier died in vain.

But, in honouring our war dead as we always have we declare that this is not true.

For out of the war came a lesson which transcended the horror and tragedy and the inexcusable folly.

It was a lesson about ordinary people – and the lesson was that they were not ordinary.

On all sides they were the heroes of that war: not the generals and the politicians, but the soldiers and sailors and nurses – those who taught us to endure hardship, show courage, to be bold as well as resilient, to believe in ourselves, to stick together.

The Unknown Australian Soldier we inter today was one of those who by his deeds proved that real nobility and grandeur belongs not to empires and nations but to the people on whom they, in the last resort, always depend.

That is surely at the heart of the ANZAC story, the Australian legend which emerged from the war. It is a legend not of sweeping military victories so much as triumphs against the odds, of courage and ingenuity in adversity. It is a legend of free and independent spirits whose discipline derived less from military formalities and customs than from the bonds of mateship and the demands of necessity.

It is a democratic tradition, the tradition in which Australians have gone to war ever since.

This Unknown Australian is not interred here to glorify war over peace; or to assert a soldier's character above a civilian's; or one race or one nation or one religion above another; or men above women; or the war in which he fought and died above any other war; or one generation above any that has or will come later.

The Unknown Soldier honours the memory of all those men and women who laid down their lives for Australia.

His tomb is a reminder of what we have lost in war and what we have gained.

We have lost more than 100,000 lives, and with them all their love of this country and all their hope and energy.

We have gained a legend: a story of bravery and sacrifice and with it a deeper faith in ourselves and our democracy, and a deeper understanding of what it means to be Australian.

It is not too much to hope, therefore, that this Unknown Australian soldier might continue to serve his country – he might enshrine a nation's love of peace and remind us that in the sacrifice of the men and women whose names are recorded here there is faith enough for all of us.

Prime Minister P. J. Keating speaking at the burial of Australia's unknown soldier

Structure, form, and cohesion

One of the things to look out for in a piece of writing is its **structure**, the shaping of the writing. This can also be called **form**. An obvious example of this lies in jokes. Although they may seem rather trivial examples of texts, you still have to learn the rules in order to be able to tell them effectively. And, as the audience for a joke, you need to know when to laugh.

Example 1

Knock knock
Who's there?
Howie
Howie who?
I'm fine, how are you?

Example 2

An Englishman, Irishman, Welshman, and Scotsman are captured while fighting abroad, and the leader of the captors says, "We're going to line you up in front of a firing squad and shoot you all in turn. But first, you each can make a final wish."

The Englishman responds, "I'd like to hear 'God Save The Queen' just one more time to remind me of the old country, sung by the London All Boys Choir. With morris dancers dancing to the tune."

The Irishman replies, "I'd like to hear 'Danny Boy' just one more time to remind me of the old country, with Riverdance dancers skipping gaily to the tune."

The Welshman answers, "I'd like to hear 'Men Of Harlech' just one more time to remind me of the country, sung by the Cardiff Male Voice Choir."

The Scotsman says quickly, "I'd like to be shot first."

Example 3

Will you remember me in a week?
Yes
Will you remember me in a month?
Yes
Will you remember me in a year?
Yes.

Knock knock
Who's there?
Forgotten me already?

In the second example a rule of jokes is being deliberately broken (it's almost always three men because three allows the situation to be set up, confirmed, and then changed). In this case, there have to be three speakers first in order to establish firmly what a nightmare the Scotsman will face if he has to put up with the others' last wishes. It's no accident that Goldilocks has to deal with three bears, or that there are three little pigs who are attacked by the wolf in the children's story.

Activity 2.11

Make a list of jokes and try to establish the rules that make them work.

Rhetoric and spoken language

Since ancient times, public speakers have been aware that words need to be particularly and specifically shaped for maximum effect. Modern politicians, like their Roman predecessors, are very fond of building a sentence with the same pattern of repetition in sets of three (technically called a **tricolon**). It helps them escalate the tone of a speech, and is a clue that they are expecting a round of applause or a cheer. Take for instance the excerpts from Barack Obama's election victory speech below.

> It's been a long time coming. But tonight, because of what we did on this day, in this election, at this defining moment, change has come to America.

The tone is escalated still further by the repetition of combinations of words, as below with "who still" (technically called **anaphora**).

> If there is anyone out there who still doubts that America is a place where all things are possible, who still wonders if the dream of our founders is alive in our time, who still questions the power of our democracy, tonight is your answer.

Barack Obama's election victory speech, Chicago, November 2008

In both cases Obama implies a question through his rhetoric and then answers it for himself – **epiphora** – in order to elicit a response from his audience.

In your own writing you will need to develop a strong sense of the rules, conventions, and structures of a variety of different sorts of writing. It's perhaps best to see the issue in terms of playing a sport. If there is no net in a tennis game or no lines on a soccer pitch, then some of the challenge of the game disappears and it's much less fun for the spectators. Similarly, you wouldn't expect to buy a house or a boat unless you were convinced that it had a coherent design and structure, suited for the purpose you have in mind.

One way of doing this is to make sure that everything fits together logically. It may be, however, that the patterns are not immediately apparent. That doesn't necessarily make the text less effective: it just means that the reader or writer has to work harder to make sense of the structure, and the process of reading is more strenuous. As we saw earlier in this section, you have to be taught the rules of a joke before you can begin to appreciate the fun.

The business of linking words into phrases, sentences, paragraphs, and then into a whole text is called **cohesion**. A number of principles can be suggested, some of them to do with content, some to do with language.

To be cohesive a text often demonstrates:

- explicit links with what has gone before, linked by relationships of time, result, or contrast: "I went early. However, John partied all night with our friends."

- features that can't be interpreted without some reference to what has gone before. This is called **co-reference**. It can look backwards (**anaphoric reference**): "The rioters approached. They seemed angry." Here the word "they" can't be understood without the word "rioters" from the previous sentence. The reference can also look forward (**cataphoric reference**): "Listen to this: there's going to be a new James Bond film."

- **ellipsis**, there is no need to re-explain something that is commonly understood. We saw this as pragmatics earlier on: "What time does the match start?" (There is no need to specify which match.)

- repetition: "The doctor arrived. The doctor was cross."

- relationships between word families (**lexical relationship**): "The *boats* steamed into harbour. At the front was a *battleship*."

- comparison: "My homework was *terrible*. Hers was *worse*."

These are tricks you can use in your own writing. However, you need to be careful not to use these devices without careful thought. The following sentence, dreamed up by the linguist Nils-Erik Enkvist (quoted by David Crystal)[1], is cohesive to the point of excess but nonsense nonetheless:

A week has seven days. Every day I feed my cat. Cats have four legs. The cat is on the mat. Mat has three letters.

Actitvity 2.12

Here's a recipe that has been jumbled up. Using both your understanding of textual coherence, your understanding of food preparation, and, of course, your common sense, try to put it into the right order.

Text type: instructional, UK

3 rounded tablespoons of mayonnaise. Place in a large mixing basin and add the scrubbed and coarsely grated carrots, the apples, peeled, quartered and coarsely grated, and the scrubbed and finely shredded celery. 4–5 tablespoons oil and vinegar dressing. ½ a white cabbage heart. Meanwhile, in a small basin, thin down the mayonnaise with the cream.

Rinse the cabbage leaves under cold water and remove any outer damaged leaves. 1–2 sticks celery. Leave to chill for 15–20 minutes. 4 tablespoons of single cream. Pour over the salad and toss well to mix before serving. Cut in half, cut away the core, and then shred the cabbage finely. 2 dessert apples. Coleslaw. Toss the salad with 4–5 tablespoons oil and vinegar dressing. 2–3 new young carrots. Time taken 30–60 minutes.

Now examine the recipe using the cohesion terminology you have learned in order to discuss its structure.

With luck, you will have established quickly that it's best to have the ingredients first, followed by a coherent account of the process that needs to be undertaken.

Things get slightly more complicated when you are dealing with a piece of imaginative writing. Ernest Hemingway was known for being able to condense a lot of meaning in a story into very few words. Here's one of his stories. It is printed complete but in the wrong order.

Text type: prose narrative, fiction, USA

1. All the shutters of the hospital were nailed shut.

2. When they fired the first volley he was sitting down in the water with his head on his knees.

3. There were pools of water in the courtyard.

4. They tried to hold him up against the wall but he sat down in a puddle of water.

5. One of the ministers was sick with typhoid.

6. Two soldiers carried him downstairs and out into the rain.

7. There were wet dead leaves on the paving of the courtyard.

8. Finally the officer told the soldiers it was no good trying to make him stand up.

9. They shot the six cabinet ministers at half past six in the morning against the wall of the hospital.

10. It rained hard.

11. The other five stood very quietly against the wall.

In Our Time by Ernest Hemingway

Activity 2.13

Work with a partner to reconstruct Hemingway's original story. Try to explain why you decide on a particular order, both in terms of the logic of the story and of the various cohesion clues that the story contains.

What you will certainly notice by the time you agree on your final version is that you have made decisions about the structure of the narrative that also have implications for its meaning. If you clustered all the references to weather at the beginning, you were emphasizing the atmosphere. If you used sentence 9 as the opening, you probably wanted to place the political implications of the narration firmly in the foreground of the reader's thinking. You might also have wanted the shock value of the immediacy of sentence 9.

At the end of this chapter, you can see the actual order in which Hemingway wrote the narrative.

What we have seen is that writers are not simply committed to telling stories in chronological order. Matters of theme, character or atmosphere may be just as important. Take, for instance, the opening of Donna Tartt's *The Goldfinch*.

Activity 2.14

Compare your version with Hemingway's original. What different effects might your version have on a reader?

Text type: prose narrative, fiction, USA

While I was still in Amsterdam, I dreamed about my mother for the first time in years. I'd been shut up in my hotel for more than a week, afraid to telephone anybody or go out; and my heart scrambled and floundered at even the most innocent noises: elevator bell, rattle of the minibar car, even church clocks tolling the hour, de Westertoren, Krijtberg, a dark edge to the clangor, an inwrought fairy-tale sense of doom. By day I sat on the foot of the bed straining to puzzle out the Dutch-language news on television (which was hopeless, since I knew not a word of Dutch) and when I gave up, I sat by the window staring out at the canal with my camel's-hair coat thrown over my clothes – for I'd left New York in a hurry and the things I'd brought weren't warm enough, even indoors.

Outside, all was activity and cheer. It was Christmas, lights twinkling on the canal bridges at night; red-cheeked *dames en heren* scarves flying in the icy wind, clattered down the cobblestones with Christmas trees lashed to the backs of their bicycles. In the afternoons, an amateur band played Christmas carols that hung tinny and fragile in the winter air.

Chaotic room-service trays; too many cigarettes; lukewarm vodka from duty free. During those restless, shut-up days, I got to know every inch of the room as a prisoner comes to know his cell.

The Goldfinch by Donna Tartt

Tartt's intention is to introduce you to the narrator, and his jumpiness about 'innocent noises', and his admission that he'd 'left New York in a hurry', suggest that there is a mystery involved that has a 'dark edge' and is associated with his 'fairy tale sense of doom'. The contrast between the picturesque jollity of what's going on in the streets and the claustrophobic atmosphere of the hotel room (compared to a 'cell'), with the inside and outside paragraphs alternating, suggests feelings of guilt, particularly when we hear of his upset at not being able to understand the news. It's going to take another 700 or so pages for us to find out how he got into the situation – but plainly the writer (Tartt, not the narrator) has decided that we can know about what happened at the end before we know the beginning of the tale. It's a crafty trick to get a reader involved.

Here's another opening to a novel, set during the New Zealand gold rush of 1866.

Text type: prose narrative, fiction, New Zealand

In which a stranger arrives in Hokitika; a secret council is disturbed; Walter Moody conceals his most recent memory; and Thomas Balfour begins to tell a story.

The twelve men congregated in the smoking room of the Crown Hotel gave the impression of a party accidentally met. From the variety of their comportment and dress – frock coats, tailcoats, Norfolk jackets with buttons of horn, yellow moleskin, cambric, and twill – they might have been twelve strangers on a railway car, each bound for a separate quarter of a city that possessed fog and tides enough to divide them; indeed, the studied isolation of each man as he pored over his paper, or leaned forward to tap his ashes into the grate, or placed the splay of his hand upon the baize to take his shot at billiards, conspired to form the very type of bodily silence that occurs late in the evening, on a public railway – deadened here not by the slur and clunk of the coaches, but by the fat clatter of the rain.

Such was the perception of Mr. Walter Moody, from where he stood in the doorway with his hand upon the frame. He was innocent of having disturbed any kind of private conference, for the speakers had ceased when they heard his tread in the passage; by the time he opened the door, each of the twelve men had resumed his occupation (rather haphazardly, on the part of the billiard players, for they had forgotten their places) with such a careful show of absorption that no one even glanced up when he stepped into the room.

The strictness and uniformity with which the men ignored him might have aroused Mr. Moody's interest, had he been himself in body and temperament. As it was, he was queasy and disturbed. He had known the voyage to West Canterbury would be fatal at worst, an endless rolling trough of white water and spume that ended on the shattered graveyard of the Hokitika bar ...

The Luminaries by Eleanor Catton

Activity 2.15

Try to write a paragraph (use the one on *The Goldfinch* as a model for tone) that analyses the structure of this passage and the hints that it is giving you about what is to follow. Pay particular attention to:

- changing perspective (don't forget about the paragraph in italics)

- how the scene's atmosphere is created (clothes, location, weather, for example)

- the historical detail that puts the narrative into a particular period

- contrasts between the 'stranger' as an observer and the twelve men already in the smoking room. What do you make of him being named very formally as Mr. Walter Moody, for example?

Lexis and diction

These terms are often used to describe exactly the same thing. **Lexis** deals with the study of words; a lexicographer is someone who compiles dictionaries.

Dictionaries

Dr Johnson completed the first proper dictionary of English in 1755. It took him nine years to complete, and he chose his words from printed, respectable sources, mostly literary. It's not surprising then that he defined his own job jokingly as: "Lexicographer: a writer of dictionaries, a harmless drudge, that busies himself in tracing the original, and detailing the signification of words."

The first full American dictionary, *An American Dictionary of the English Language*, was published by Noah Webster in 1828. For both Johnson and Webster, writing a dictionary was a means of guiding people towards correct and tasteful use of the language.

These days, dictionaries reflect the language in use and do their best to keep up to date, a battle they are destined to lose! By the time you read this you may be able to look up the words "omnishambles", "dumbphone", "selfie",

Dr Johnson and Noah Webster

and "flexitarian" in a good dictionary. (See end of chapter for explanation of these terms.) On the other hand, they may have already been consigned to the linguistic graveyard.

The standard dictionary of British English is the Oxford English Dictionary, which you could see as being like a bridge that needs to be painted all the time. No sooner has the job been done than things change. By the time you buy a dictionary it's already out of date.

Obviously, with every text you encounter you need to think about the word choices that a writer, also called a text producer, makes, and this often gives you important clues about the writer's attitudes and values, as well as the genre and voice that is being created.

We all carry around in our heads lists of suitable words for talking about different things. There is, for example, a large vocabulary of words for talking about food or drink. This is called a mental **lexicon**.

Sometimes there are high incidences of language related to the same topic in a piece of writing. For example, you would expect a newspaper article about soccer to be loaded with terminology that is relevant to the game (goals, referee, and so on). This can help you to establish the genre of a text. The grouping together of words from one specific area is called a **semantic field** or a **lexical field**. If you want to comment on this when writing about a text, you need to do more than notice a clustering of words. You need to comment too on the level of formality or informality and its significance for the piece as a whole. In doing so, you are also identifying the tone and the mood of the writing.

More interesting is the fact that all of us put these words into mental hierarchies and orders, ranging from the very formal to the informal. Think, for example, of words we might use for describing someone who is mad. In a hospital we might describe them as: neurotic, psychotic, insane, maladjusted. In a courtroom they might be seen as: insane, of unsound mind, or not in full possession of their faculties. They could also be demented or unhinged. But when a friend is behaving eccentrically we might use: potty, bananas, crackers, daft, loony, batty, cuckoo, or mental.

With each different audience, the choice of words is different. Informal use of language is often called colloquial, and it is often very specific to language communities.

Activity 2.16

Choose a subject area that you know well and put together a lexicon of terms related to it, ranging from the formal to the colloquial. You could choose sport or perhaps an abstract quality such as courage or intelligence.

Think, too, about the hundreds of different ways you have of saying "no", ranging from the apologetic ("if it was up to me") to the evasive ("let's talk about it later") to the highly informal ("you must be joking"; "fat chance").

Classifying words

You don't need to know a lot about what are formally called **parts of speech**, referred to by more modern linguists as **word class**. You will be familiar with all of them already.

Nouns	Abstract nouns focus on states of mind, concepts, and ideas such as *courage* or *progress*. (Think back to the opening of *A Tale of Two Cities*.) Concrete nouns describe solid events, characters, and places: *kitchen* and *kettle* are examples.
Adjectives	These are words that describe nouns: for example, the *black* cat.
Verbs	Stative verbs (*to think, to believe*) indicate a writer's desire to describe states of mind. Dynamic verbs (*to watch, to eat*) place emphasis on what's currently happening.
Adverbs	These are words used to describe verbs: for example, she was walking *slowly*.
Prepositions	These words describe the place of an object: for example, *in, up, with*.
Interjections	Examples of these are *yes, wow*, and *awesome*.
Conjunctions	The words are used to join words and clauses: examples are *and, however, when*, and *but*.
Pronouns	These take the place of a noun to avoid repetition: "The puppy is very naughty. *He's* only five weeks old." There are also possessive pronouns: "The puppy likes *his* walk in the afternoon."
Modifiers	These are the adjectives (applied to nouns) and adverbs (applied to verbs) that add to descriptions and help to shape a reader's response to a text. If there are lots of them, the text could be described as highly modified and quite ornate. If there are not very many, then a text might be thought of as quite cold or sterile.

A difficulty in English is that words slip in and out of their various classes depending on their use in the sentence.

Using the word "round", David Crystal gives the following useful examples of word conversion according to context:

- In the sentence *Mary bought a big round table*, it serves as an adjective, like *red, big, ugly*, and many more.

Activity 2.17

Just to remind you about the various functions of these parts of speech, you could play Mad Libs. You simply take a piece of text, remove the relevant parts of speech and then ask someone else for words that will fit in, without sharing the original.

You will find the results bizarre, funny, or just plain ridiculous.

Here's an example. Fill in the spaces.

"....." (exclamation), he said ..... (adverb) as he jumped into his convertible .... (noun) and .... (verb) off with his .... (adjective) wife.

- In the sentence *The car skidded round the corner*, it functions as a preposition, like *into, past, near*, and many more.

- In the sentence *The yacht will round the buoy soon*, it functions as a verb, like *pass, reach, hit*, and many more.

- In the sentence *We walked round to the shop*, it functions as an adverb, like *quickly, happily, regularly*, along with many more.

- In the sentence *It's your round*, it functions as a noun like *turn, chance, decision*, and many more.[2]

Word conversion often works to help us fill in a gap in the language. When people started to want to look things up on an Internet search engine, it was natural that if the search engine was called Google, then "to google" must be a verb.

Words can be broken down into bits (slow/slowly). You do not need to do this but you should know that this element of language study is called **morphology** and that individual elements of words are called **morphemes**.

Style, register, and tone

When you think about words in texts you also need to think about how to characterize them. You could do this by using a series of adjectives such as:

- formal/informal
- descriptive/factual
- general/specialist
- modern/**archaic** (old sounding)
- simple (short)/complicated
- formal/informal
- evaluative/analytical
- literal/metaphorical.

The focus needs to be on the way language is chosen for particular situations. Think about the language used in the legal world, between a mother and her baby, in a biology research lab, in a news report, or on a sports field. Text producers need to be acutely aware of the **register** of language that is appropriate (often seen in terms of levels of formality or informality) for the current situation and for the genre they are attempting to produce.

A police report, for example, records details of a crime as objectively as possible.

Case Number: **VT 05/04/14/3462**

Incident: **Vehicle Theft**

Reporting Officer: **Constable Ranjit Singh**

Date of Report: **05 April 2014**

At about 10.40 hours on 5th April 2014, I met with Ms. Vanessa Price at 61 South Chorley Drive regarding a vehicle theft. Ms. Price said she parked her car by a parking meter outside Chorley Leisure Centre at about 09.45 hours and went into a nearby shop to return a faulty torch she had purchased the previous day. She said that when she returned to the leisure centre at about 10.00 hours, she discovered her car was missing.

Ms. Price described her car as a maroon, 2005 Mitsubishi Eclipse with a black convertible roof. The car registration number is KM54 UHT. She estimated the value of the car at £6,500 and said there were no distinguishing marks on the bodywork.

Ms. Price told me she locked the car, but she does not have the keys. She now believes she may have left the keys in the boot lock after removing the faulty torch from the boot. Ms. Price said she gave no-one permission to take her car.

I conducted a survey of the crime scene but found no items of evidence. I saw no broken glass in the area, and there were no items to retrieve or photograph.

I obtained a sworn statement from Ms. Price and provided her with the case number and Information Leaflet 99/07 ("What to do when your car is stolen"). I entered the vehicle into the station database as a stolen vehicle. I also searched the area but was unable to find the vehicle.

This is written very formally, with no contractions such as "can't" or "didn't" and without colloquial words or idioms (the car was "stolen", not "pinched" or "nicked"). There is no attempt to be stylish or to vary the sentence structure. The writer is careful to be impersonal, and does not introduce either Ms Price's thoughts and feelings or his own. Dates, times, and details are recorded as precisely as possible.

Activity 2.18

We can explore this by taking a text and transforming it into another genre. With the police text as your model, re-write this children's nursery rhyme using a tone and register that would be suitable for a crime report:

Little Miss Muffet,
She sat on a tuffet,
Eating of curds and whey;
There came a great spider,
Who sat down beside her,
And frightened Miss Muffet away

You can distinguish between different registers or styles by characterizing them as outlined in the table below.

	Typical features
Ultra-colloquial	• Often street language used by the young with new words, or older words adapted to mean something new • Non-standard pronunciation ("gonna", "innit") • Non-standard grammar, with some function words ("of" or "to") missed out • This is sometimes called "vernacular" language
Colloquial	• Words that belong to private rather than public life, often with idiomatic expressions • The language used between friends and family • When spoken, it allows hesitations, pauses, and imprecise expression; grammatical rules are not always followed • It is often described as "conversational"
Modified formal	• Plain words and expressions where a choice to be more formal is made, so "child" not "kid", "dismiss" not "fire", "why" not "how come". • Will prefer to talk about real things rather than abstract terms • Some abbreviations or contractions ("can't", "won't") both in speech and writing • It will flow easily and is the normal language of the working world and will normally obey the rules for "standard" English
Formal	• May use a lot of abstract nouns; this is the language of scholarly discussion • One-word, precise terms rather than short phrases ("discover" not "find out") • Complex or varied grammar • The passive voice (for scientific papers, for example) • When written, it conforms carefully with the conventions of "standard" English • No colloquial language or slang unless it is explicitly drawn attention to for a specific purpose
Ultra-formal	• Formal address ("Ladies and Gentlemen") • Archaic forms of language (long words, often derived from Latin), grammar, and syntax ("Please be seated")

Adapted from *Grammar, Structure and Style* by Shirley Russell [3]

All of these can, of course, be used in either speech or writing, but the vernacular is often hard to understand when written, while the ultra-formal is most often reserved for formal spoken occasions or legal documents. It is worth noting, too, that particularly in speech, people often move between different registers with great fluency, and that the boundaries between them are often very fluid. As we noted earlier, your own spoken language will vary considerably depending on whether you are at home with your family, with your friends, or contributing in class.

Skilled writers often play with levels of register and tone to create meaning. In the next passage, Sathnam Sanghera, a British Asian writer, is helping his parents pack (or rather unpack to avoid excess baggage charges) in preparation for their forthcoming trip to the Punjab to see family.

Text type: autobiography, UK

With Mum gone, my editing became more brutal. Two of the three prayer books went. The teabags and Rice Krispies went. But then, underneath the cereal boxes, I came across something more surreal than even the coconuts: two 2kg boxes of East End vegetable margarine – 'made with 100% vegetable oil, no animal fat'. Incredible. Mum had allocated a fifth of her allotted luggage weight on her flight from Birmingham to Amritsar with a five hour stop in the [...] metropolis of Tashkent to ... margarine.

I laughed, made a mental note to tell Laura about it later, and tried to think of a possible explanation. Maybe she was planning to make chapattis along the journey to my father's village? Perhaps there was some superstition relating to margarine? I flicked through my mental database of Punjabi folklore.

It was good luck to mutter *Waheguru* before you embarked on any task.

It was bad luck to wash your hair on a Saturday or a Tuesday.

It was bad luck to look at the moon.

It was bad luck to sneeze when setting off on a journey (a nightmare when you have allergies, like I do).

It was bad luck to step on money.

It was bad luck to leave one shoe resting on another.

It was bad luck to point your feet at a picture of a guru or a prayer book.

It was bad luck to spill milk.

It was good luck to scoop up the placenta of a cat that had just given birth.

It was bad luck for a nephew or niece to be in the same room as an uncle from their mother's side of the family in a thunderstorm.

No. I couldn't remember anything margarine-related ...

But picking out the boxes with the intention of storming into the living room and remonstrating, I found they were lighter than I'd expected. They rattled too. Phew. Mum was using the boxes as containers. She hadn't lost the plot completely. I opened one and found it contained medication. Mum's herbal pills for her migraines; non-herbal pills for her arthritis; antidepressants; vitamin supplements; paracetamol. The second one was heavier and contained five boxes of tablets. The brands emblazoned across them meant nothing to me. But the name on them did. Jagdit Singh. Dad.

I thought this peculiar because my father is rarely ill. He has diabetes, but the condition is managed well. I had a fuzzy memory of him once being prescribed sleeping pills. But I thought that was a temporary thing. Indeed, I couldn't remember a single time that he'd complained of feeling sick. Couldn't recall him ever having a lie down during the day, for that matter. Ferreting around the box for a clue, I found an envelope addressed 'TO WHOM IT MAY CONCERN.' I was a 'to whom it concerned', so I opened it. It was a note from Dad's GP, Dr Dutta.

> This patient has been registered on my panel since 1969 and was re-registered in 1993. In fact, he is known to me from 1969. He suffers from paranoid schizophrenia. (He is often confused and cannot communicate facts and his wife has to assist him.) He is on regular treatment of injection and tablets (which he often forgets), and his wife has to keep an eye on his medication. He also suffers from diabetes for which he is having regular check-ups and treatment. He is visiting his family in India and he is going for a short visit.

Blinking at the words, I thought: ... *Schizophrenia.*

And then: *Christ.* That's what my sister Puli must have too.

The Boy with the Topknot by Sathnam Sanghera

You will have noticed that the writer maintains a detached, ironic humouring of his parents (think about his use of the word "remonstrating", for example) in order to increase the shock value of the doctor's formal letter, a complete change of tone, register, and genre, that reports in a detached, clinical manner. As the tone changes, so too does the seriousness of the piece, with the writer suddenly realizing that he has to re-discover his family relationships in completely different terms.

As we have seen, word choice often creates the tone of a piece of writing, but you can take your analysis still further by looking at a text and describing it in terms of the frequency of different word classes. Such analysis will often help you to recognize some of the genre characteristics of a text. You will quickly discover the following:

- Conversation has a very high density of verbs.

- News reporting and other sorts of informative writing tend to have a high density of nouns because they are content driven.

- Because adjectives are linked to nouns, texts with high frequency of nouns tend also to have high levels of adjectives. So informative writing will have high densities of both nouns and adjectives.

- As adverbs are linked to verbs and typically describe situations relating to actions, processes, and states, there will tend to be more of them in conversation and fiction.

- Literary writing, particularly when describing, has a high density of both adjectives and adverbs.

Adapted from the *Longman Student Grammar of Spoken and Written English*, p 23.[4]

Activity 2.19

Look closely at the passage and then discuss Sanghera's presentation of himself and his relationship with his parents.

Activity 2.20

Read the following text. Using the points above, try to make a statement about the genre type. How would it read without the adjectives and adverbs?

Text type: prose narrative, drama, UK

It is spring, moonless night in the small town, starless and bible-black, the cobblestones silent and the hunched, courters'-and-rabbits' wood limping invisible down to the sloeblack, slow, black, crowblack, fishing boat-bobbing sea.

Under Milk Wood by Dylan Thomas

You might remember that in the opening section of this book, we thought about style in terms of clothes. Let's go back to that comparison. On occasion, it is expected that men will wear suits – a job interview might require this. At other times – a beach party for example – jeans and a T-shirt will be perfectly acceptable, and to turn up in a suit would embarrass other people or make someone look ridiculous. So there are matters of appropriateness at stake. It would be sensible to say that the register and lexical field (or general expectation) of one sort of event would be the suit, while the register of the other would be jeans and a T-shirt, the tone of one formal, the other informal.

But it's more complex than that. There are many different variations within the "suit" register (colour and cut being just two) and there are many variations possible for jeans – skinny, boot cut, hipster, etc. Any written text can be seen in the same way. There are appropriate registers for each genre, but at the same time there can be variations in layout, vocabulary choice, and sentence structure. In any text there will be a lexis associated with the subject matter (think of a newspaper report of a soccer match) but the style may be very different.

Activity 2.21

Choose a few examples of writing from the same register and try to determine what the common elements are. Then examine the variations that are acceptable as the style of each piece. You could make use of the film reviews in Chapter 4.

Activity 2.22

Go back to the extract by Katherine Boo (pages 18 and 19) and examine it again in terms of register, taking particular note of the ways that it mixes the registers of a newspaper report with those of fictional narrative.

Grammar

Let's start with a definition. **Grammar** is a term that covers two aspects of language:

- the structure of individual words and their function

- the arrangement of these words within a sentence (this can also be called **syntax**).

When most people think about grammar, they have in their minds rather dusty books that publishers produce for foreign language teaching. There is also a slight fear that discussions about grammar are full of pitfalls, where people are simply just waiting for you to make a mistake (often called a **solecism**). A certain type of person will wait for an error and take pleasure in pointing out that you have got something wrong. These people are called **prescriptivists** (although they probably don't know it) because they are very keen on the rules. They will be keen to tell you that you should never begin a sentence with "and" or "but". But they will never clearly explain (see this sentence) why this is such a bad thing. They will tell you that you should never end a sentence with a **preposition** (a word like "up" or "down") and would presumably prefer Churchill's joke sentence "These are things up with which we will not put" to the more natural sounding "These are things we won't put up with".

Most of these rules come from an 18th century desire for the English language to behave like Latin (which, of course, it doesn't). So teachers may still encourage students not to split **infinitives** (the root of a verb in English, for example, "to split"), even though the model is faulty because in Latin infinitives (facere, amare) can't be split as they consist of only one word. But the prescription goes on.

The most famous split infinitive comes from the opening of the popular TV series *Star Trek*. In the voice-over during the opening titles we hear:

> Space: the final frontier. These are the voyages of the starship *Enterprise*. Its five-year mission: to explore strange worlds, to seek out new life and new civilizations, to boldly go where no man has gone before.

Boldly to go? To go boldly? Not quite such an exciting mission, is it?

So for our purposes, prescription is not the way forward. You need to see yourself as a **descriptive** grammarian, someone who describes what is actually going on in a text. However, you will also need some sense of the general rules for the language, without too much detail – a map of the territory.

Activity 2.23

Try re-writing the following sentence without the split infinitive, and you will see how the "rule" falls at the first fence – it leads you into ugly, unclear writing.

I expect our output to more than double next year.

David Crystal suggests in *How Language Works*[5] that of the 3,500 features of English grammar, only about 1 per cent of them are ever the focus of grammatical prescriptivism. But then there are some who always want to find fault, although they would never, of course, argue as the Rolling Stones song does that they "can't get no satisfaction" over these matters because that's a double negative and must be avoided at all costs. This is despite the fact it has a perfectly respectable history in the language from Chaucer onwards as an intensifier: "I couldn't not buy that dress in the sales – it was a bargain".

If I say, "I would of loved one of them apples what you did bought yesterday", you would understand what I had said. Nonetheless, you would be aware that I had not communicated my thoughts in a pleasing or particularly clear, effective way. If, on the other hand, I had come up with the linguist Chomsky's demonstration phrase, "Colourless green ideas sleep furiously", you would have been confident that this is a sentence, a coherent unit of sense with a verb that tells you when the events happened, even though the sentence makes no sense.

You could test this by rearranging the words: "Furiously sleep ideas green colourless". Intuitively, however, you knew that the first of these sentences was better than the second, and this shows that our understanding of grammar exists independent of any sense of meaning.

In many other languages, sentences are constructed by changing the beginnings or endings of words to give readers a clear sense of their function in a sentence. In Latin, "Cesarem occidit Brutus" and "Brutus Caesarem occidit" both mean that Brutus killed Caesar. We don't have that choice in English. In English grammar, word order is central.

Activity 2.24

What's the difference in meaning between these sentences?

- I only put on my shoes when she asks.
- I put on my shoes only when she asks.
- Only I put on my shoes when she asks.
- I put on only my shoes when she asks.

Slippery language

We can all agree that the word "everyone" is not plural: "Everyone is here so let's start," said the tour guide (singular verb). Watch how it transforms itself. "As we are moving into the dust-free area, everyone should leave his or her coat here," she continued. Suddenly it starts to feel wrong: there may be women in the audience, so "his" won't do for everyone, but to put "his or her" in the sentence sounds ugly. So the chances are that suddenly "everyone" becomes plural. "Everyone should leave their coats here" sounds much better. Here is language adapting itself for the needs of the times as we don't have non-gender pronouns (we are stuck with him/her, his/hers), although there have been attempts to use "s/he" in writing.

But it's still more complex. Suppose our tourists have gone to the café at the end of the tour and asked Chris (male) to order the drinks and bring them back from the counter. You get "Everyone hoped that Chris would bring his drink across on a tray." And if Chris happens to be a girl, then the sentence is even more awkward. The sentence remains: "Everyone hoped that Chris would bring his drink across on a tray" because traditionally the masculine pronoun dominates and everyone is doing the hoping. But if you say "Everyone hoped that Chris would bring her drink across on a tray" it's clear that we are only talking about Chris's drink. It's so much easier to break the rules and avoid the difficulty. Let's just hope that everyone enjoyed their drinks.

Cheers.

The Simpsons and the English language

You may have wondered how a new word comes into the language. Often, English finds a need for a word and simply borrows it from another language ("pizza" and "bungalow" are good examples). These are called **loan words**. At other times, it works by association – a little white thing on a desk that scurries around as it points to bits of the screen looks something like a mouse, so a mouse it is.

To actually make a word stick in the language is quite hard. In 1996, the writers of the television show *The Simpsons* had a go. In the episode "Lisa the Iconoclast", they came up with the words "cromulent" and "embiggen", words that sound as though they should exist. The high school principal says of Homer's audition for the job of Springfield town crier: "He's embiggened that role with his cromulent performance". "Cromulent" which means fine or acceptable hasn't really taken off, but by 2013 "embiggen" was starting to have a life of its own in science papers in relation to string theory (don't ask!) and also with tablet computers where you can stretch or enlarge a picture with your fingers. Perhaps its time has come.

The Guardian, 16 October 2012

When words are put together, the rules that govern them are usually called grammar. In technical terms, the whole business of word order is more properly called the **syntactic structure** or **syntactic rules** of a sentence. Some of you will have come across "syntax errors" when trying to program a computer. When that happens, the computer can't read what you are trying to say and stubbornly refuses to let you move to the next stage. With a less exacting reader or listener in a "real" language you can, of course, simply carry on, but at times syntax errors mean that others have to struggle to work out what you mean.

Sentence structure

The fundamental structure of a sentence is quite straightforward.

Morphemes (words constructed out of bits that create various meanings, e.g. (sad/sadly/sadness)

↓ ↓

Create **phrases** (units of meaning without verbs with tense and number)

↓ ↓

They, in turn, build into **clauses** (groups of words organized around a verb)

↓ ↓

Clauses are then used to build **sentences**

The most basic form is the **simple** sentence. You need one verb and you need to demonstrate **tense** (*when* something happened) and **number** (how many people were doing the thing).

> The elephant ate grass.

You can add to this in all kinds of ways, but as long as it only has one verb, it is a simple sentence.

> The grey elephant slowly ate green grass, old leaves, and apples.

We have increased the amount of detail by expanding some ideas into phrases (it's now a grey elephant), but added nothing to the fundamentals of the sentence.

You could, of course, add another clause (a group of words with another verb with tense and number), although the elephant remains the central focus.

> The elephant ate grass and wandered off into the forest.

The presence of two verbs turns this into a **compound** sentence with different clauses bound together by linking words (**conjunctions**) such as "and" or "but". It could easily be two sentences.

Much of the time we want to say something slightly more complicated, so we need to add more verbs.

> The elephant ate apples that had been left by the visitors.

"Had been" adds another verb, but the elephant is still the main subject of the sentence. We could miss out the bit about the visitors. This means that we have started to work on **subordination**, noting that some bits of a sentence support the main meaning but cannot exist without the **main clause**: "had been left by the visitors" has both tense and number, but there is something missing so it can't stand as a sentence on its own.

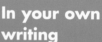

In your own writing TIP

Joining contrasting statements? Words like "although", "however", "but", "though", and "nevertheless" are useful here.

In your own writing TIP

It's worth having a record of the major words that you use to begin subordinating clauses.

after	if	that	where
although	in order that	though	whereas
as	once	unless	wherever
because	provided that	until	whether
before	rather than	whatever	while
even if	since	when	
even though	so that	whenever	

If a sentence has subordinate clauses (underlined) then it can be described as a **complex** sentence:

> The elephant, <u>which was getting rather old</u>, ate green grass, and old leaves, and the apples <u>that had been left by the visitors</u>.

And then, of course, you can add another main clause if you like and you will have come up with a **complex-compound sentence**. Here the subordinate clauses are underlined; the main clauses are in italics.

> *The elephant,* <u>which was getting rather old</u>, *ate green grass, old leaves and the apples* <u>that had been left by visitors</u>, *and wandered into the forest.*

Once you start to see how the different elements of sentences build up, then you can start to be more confident about your own writing. Using only simple sentences can be rather jerky, although that in its own way can create an effect on a reader. So an ability to write a variety of types of sentence is an important skill to have: it will make your writing sound more like your speech.

You should remember the introductory phrase or clause too as a means of getting you into the substance of a sentence.

- When Tom got up, he put on his brown suit.
- Although he didn't like his suit, Tom felt he ought to wear it for the interview.
- As he was walking towards the bus stop, he had a terrible thought.
- Unfortunately, he had mistaken the day of the interview.
- Over coffee, he told his girlfriend what had happened.

You can get yourself into a real mess with grammatical discussions, so it's often best not to try. However, you can often make points about the length of sentences or about syntactic variations without having to use the technical terms. Think, for example, about how the words placed in an unusual order may change your view of their content, the context, or the speaker.

- With this ring, I thee wed. (Church of England wedding service)
- When nine hundred years old you reach, look as good you will not. (Yoda, *Star Wars Episode VI: Return of the Jedi*).

Verbs and tenses

As with so many aspects of this course, noting the effect of a language choice is more important than being able to analyse it in precise detail. So there is no need to get caught up in a discussion of the complexities

> **TIP**
>
> **In your own writing**
>
> The most important point is, of course, that you should be clear. At times you may feel that your sentences need to be complicated because you want to say something quite complex. Often, that's precisely the moment when you need to stop and sort out your thoughts into smaller units.

of describing the various tenses in English (and there are many of them). However, you will mainly come across writing in two tenses: the present and the past.

The present tense

There are fundamentally two variations on this.

You can write in the simple present tense.

> She wants to be an astronaut.

You can also use the present continuous tense.

> He is walking to the shops.

In this next extract, Hilary Mantel, a contemporary novelist, uses the present tense to bring alive an episode from history – Cardinal Wolsey's fall from grace during the reign of Henry VIII.

Activity 2.25

What, in your view, does Mantel get from writing predominantly in the present tense in the following passage? You should think about how she is trying to give a modern reader a sense of being a witness to events that happened many centuries previously.

Text type: prose narrative, fiction, UK

Esher: the cardinal dismounts under the shadow of old Bishop Wayneflete's keep, surmounted by octagonal towers. The gateway is set into a defensive wall topped with a walkway; stern enough at first sight but the whole thing is built of brick, ornamented and prettily inlaid. 'You couldn't fortify it,' he says. Cavendish is silent. 'George, you're supposed to say, "But the need could never arise."'

The cardinal's not used the place since he built Hampton Court. They've sent messages ahead, but has anything been done? Make my lord comfortable, he says, and goes straight down to the kitchens. At Hampton Court, the kitchens have running water; here, nothing's running but the cooks' noses. Cavendish is right. In fact it is worse than he thinks. The larders are impoverished and such supplies as they have show signs of ill-keeping and plunder. There are weevils in the flour. There are mouse-droppings where the pastry should be rolled. It is nearly Martinmas, and they have not even thought of salting their beef. The *batterie de cuisine* is an insult, and the stockpot is mildewed. There are a number of small boys sitting by the hearth, and, for cash down, they can be induced into scouring and scrubbing, children take readily to novelty, and the idea of cleaning, it seems, is novel to them.

My lord, he says, needs to eat and drink *now*; and he needs to eat and drink for … how long we don't know. This kitchen must be put in order for the winter ahead. He finds someone who can write, and dictates his orders. His eyes are fixed on the kitchen clerk.

Wolf Hall by Hilary Mantel

With this technique you are right in the middle of the action and the drama of Cardinal Wolsey's flight from London is described as though a camera is scanning across the scene. We see the events through the eyes of Thomas Cromwell, Wolsey's agent, as though he is a camera lens. At the same time, we are aware that the camera is not neutral as we are aware of his preoccupations and concerns. This is not first-person narrative (see page 14) but it shares some of its characteristics – what Cromwell says, for example, is not given speech marks.

In recent years in British English, teenagers have adopted the habit of talking in the present tense about things that happened in the past. This isn't wrong and it does give a listener a sense of being intimately involved, but to older ears it comes across as rather too immediate.

> "So I'm walking down the street and my friend comes up to me. And she says 'I want to go to the cinema.' So I say 'What shall we go and see?' So she says…"

Other writers and speakers mix present and future tenses to give a sense of vision, hope, and expectation for the future, as Martin Luther King, leader of the African-American Civil Rights Movement, does here. He also uses **imperatives** (command forms of verbs, "Go back" in this case) and repetition to create a sense of mission and purpose.

In your own writing **TIP**

It may be as well to avoid present tense narration. It grabs hold of a reader's attention but is hard to sustain.

Martin Luther King

Text type: scripted speech, USA

Go back to Mississippi, go back to Alabama, go back to Georgia, go back to Louisiana, go back to the slums and ghettos of our northern cities, knowing that somehow this situation can and will be changed. Let us not wallow in the valley of despair.

I say to you today, my friends, that in spite of the difficulties and frustrations of the moment, I still have a dream. It is a dream deeply rooted in the American dream.

I have a dream that one day this nation will rise up and live out the true meaning of its creed: "We hold these truths to be self-evident: that all men are created equal."

I have a dream that one day on the red hills of Georgia the sons of former slaves and the sons of former slave owners will be able to sit down together at a table of brotherhood.

I have a dream that one day even the state of Mississippi, a desert state, sweltering with the heat of injustice and oppression, will be transformed into an oasis of freedom and justice.

I have a dream that my four children will one day live in a nation where they will not be judged by the color of their skin but by the content of their character.

I have a dream today.

Extract from the speech "I have a dream" by Martin Luther King

The past tense

The conventional way of talking about the past is to use the simple past tense, possibly in combination with the imperfect tense which is used for continuing actions in the past.

> I was walking to school one day, when a tree fell down in front of me.

Two actions have finished taking place, but the second of them, expressed in the simple past, interrupted something that was currently happening.

The advantages of past tense narration are:

● things are already finished – you, the writer, know how things are going to turn out

● you can include comments that reflect upon the situation ("It was the best of times; it was the worst of times").

On the whole, once you have decided on a tense for your discourse, stay with it unless there is a very good reason to change. Controlling a "mixed" piece of writing demands great skill and you have to be very clear about the sequencing of your material.

Active versus passive voice

You will sometimes come across reference to the passive voice (note that it is a voice, not a tense). It is often used in scientific writing ("the results are given in Table 1") as it can give a sense of impartiality and can often be a genre clue. Putting something in the passive makes the person who did the thing sound less involved and makes the receivers of the action more important by turning them into the subject of the sentence.

● The boy broke the window. (active)

● The window was broken by the boy. (passive)

● The dog chased the cat. (active)

● The cat was chased by the dog. (passive)

Without going into the technicalities, you should simply notice that in your own writing it is usually best to avoid the passive voice unless you are aiming for a very particular emphasis. In the sentence "President Kennedy was assassinated in 1963", for example, it is clear that the writer is making a point about Kennedy as a victim and that there has been a deliberate decision not to include the name of his assassin.

Punctuation

Some years ago, the British journalist Lynne Truss wrote the most unlikely of things – a bestselling book about punctuation called *Eats, Shoots and Leaves*. It takes its title from an old joke.

> A panda walks into a café. He orders a sandwich, eats it, then draws a gun and fires two shots into the air.

"Why?" asks the confused waiter, as the panda walks towards the exit. The panda produces a badly punctuated wildlife manual and tosses it on the table.

'I'm a panda," he says, at the door. "Look it up."

The waiter turns to the entry in the manual, and sure enough, finds an explanation.

"**Panda**. Large black-and-white bear-like mammal, native to China. Eats, shoots and leaves."

The story makes a point: punctuation is important if it helps the reader and clarifies things along the way. By inserting a comma, the whole meaning changes. The last sentence looks like a list, and therefore the words "shoots" and "leaves" convert themselves to verbs. Note, too, that we can now add to our analysis of jokes (page 26) that they are normally told in the present tense.

You will already know how to write in sentences (capital letter at the start, full stop/period at the end) but it might be useful just to spend a few moments on some of those punctuation marks that perhaps seem slightly more mysterious.

Mark	Name	Definition
,	comma	Use this for separating things out in a list or for helping to demonstrate that some bits of a sentence are subordinate to others. At times, commas are vital to the sense of a sentence. Try the following without the commas. "She took her inspiration from cooking, her family, and her dog." "I'd like to thank my parents, J.K. Rowling, and Dan Brown."
–…–	dashes	You use these when you want to put an "aside" into a sentence and make it slightly stronger than two commas. The text between the dashes could be missed out of the sentence if necessary. "My new car – the one you can see from the window – is in need of a wash."
:	colon	Use this to introduce a list or an example. "There are three things you need to know: firstly…"
;	semi-colon	Use this to join two linked thoughts together. For example, "Godzilla is a misunderstood creature; beneath his raging desire to set people on fire and eat them lies a gentle giant." Both aspects of this are obviously important, and they are linked. Technically speaking the semi-colon is linking independent clauses because there is a main verb with tense and number in each half. You can also use it to separate items in a complex list, where commas may not be strong enough to do the job. In effect, it acts as a super-comma, where you need commas to be doing something else in the sentence. "I would like to thank my colleagues at our headquarters, London; the team on site in the factories in England, France, and Switzerland; and our customers around the world."

As you read texts, it is useful to reflect on how punctuation is being used. Sometimes it's just a matter of fact, a way of keeping the writing clear and unambiguous. At other times it is working with other aspects of the text to create meaning and significance, and it's in these instances that you should try to comment upon its purpose and effectiveness.

Metaphorical language

During your earlier years at school you will have become very familiar with the idea that text producers often like to describe one object in terms of another in order to make it vivid to an audience. You probably won't need reminding that this can also be called **figurative** language and that it stands in opposition to **literal** language, which simply articulates facts.

In simple terms, we have four types of figurative language.

- Simile: "His face was like a wedding cake that had been left out in the rain" (the word "like" shows us this is a simile).

- Metaphor: "He ploughed through his pile of homework" (ploughs are used in fields). In this case one thing becomes the other and there is no need to say "like a plough through a field".

- Personification: "The sun smiled on them when they were on holiday". This gives human attributes to something which does not have human feelings or abilities.

- Symbolism: particularly in literary texts, for example, apples tend to stand for innocence or temptation (as in the story of Adam and Eve) while spider's webs are a symbol of entrapment or hard work.

But these definitions merely help you to spot the devices, not to see how crucial metaphorical language is to virtually all communication. In your language studies you need to recognize that the mere observation of examples of figurative examples is of little importance. Rather, you need to be aware of figurative language as central to the various ways in which speakers of a language formulate a view of the world.

The difficulty is that much of the time we don't actually recognize that we are dealing with non-literal language. When people say "to coin a phrase" they don't dwell on the idea for long enough to recognize that at one stage this idea had a link with the minting of new currency. These are called **dead metaphors**: they have been overused to the point that no one even notices their presence. They can, however, become very vivid by accident if a text producer starts to join them together incorrectly without realizing that they have metaphorical significance.

This happens most often when a text producer runs together two idiomatic phrases, and they are called **mixed metaphors**.

- I'm going to stick to my laurels. (Kate Winslet, actress)

- We need to grasp the nettle by the horns.

- Senator McCain suggests that somehow, you know, I'm green behind the ears. (Barack Obama, US President)

In recent years, attention has been turned more to the way that unconscious metaphors inform our world view. Lakoff and Johnson[6] have suggested that in academic life argument is often spoken about as a journey: we "make progress", we take it "step-by-step", we ask if people can "follow" what we say. At other times, we see such discourse as being a container: the argument, like a bucket, has "holes" in it and "leaks", and can be criticized for being empty. Sometimes, the metaphors are all to do with war: claims are "indefensible", arguments are "attacked", "demolished", and can be "shot down".

Companies often have a mission statement and talk about having a "vision". Users of language like this are trying to make their daily business into something rather more mysterious than it actually is or to motivate their sales staff; they want to see their business as having the significance of a religion, not of a trade. When economists talk about money, they talk about cash flow, about it circulating in the economy, about it being the life blood of capitalism. For them, cash is injected, funds haemorrhage from a failing business. In thinking like this, they frame the whole discussion in terms of the economy being like a human body. If you see a number of metaphors, each of which builds on the same basic idea, then these are called – unsurprisingly – **extended metaphors**.

We also show a great capacity for thinking about the same thing in entirely different terms. For example, at times we see the human mind as being like a machine. My mind isn't "operating" today, I'm a little "rusty", I've "run out of steam". But at other times, the mind is like a precious vase. She's feeling "very fragile" and has to be "handled with care". She was "shattered by what happened" and went completely "to pieces".

Activity 2.26

Below are 10 sentences that demonstrate that we often think of time as a commodity, something that can be traded, or a limited resource.

1. I don't have the time to .... you.

2. How do you .... your time these days?

3. You need to .... your time carefully when you revise.

4. I .... a lot of time on my project when I was off school.

5. I don't .... time to ..... for that.

6. You don't ...... your time ....

7. You're .... of time.

8. He's living on .... time.

9. This machine will ..... you hours each week.

10. .... some time for your hobbies.

Insert the following words where appropriate: put aside, have enough, use, running out, spend, give, profitably, budget, spare, lost, save, borrowed

---

Occasionally, you can see someone trying to come to terms with something unfamiliar by framing a metaphor. Below, Tim Berners-Lee, the inventor of the world wide web, reflects on how his initial ideas moved from being modelled on the idea of an electronic reference book, towards the now familiar idea of a web.

Tim Berners-Lee

When I first began tinkering with a software program that eventually gave rise to the idea of the World Wide Web, I named it Enquire, short for 'Enquire Within upon Everything', a musty old book of Victorian advice I noticed as a child in my parents' house outside London. With its title suggestive of magic, the book served as a portal to a world of information, everything from how to remove clothing stains to tips on investing money. Not a perfect analogy for the Web: but a primitive starting point.

What that first bit of Enquire code led me to was something much larger, a vision. The vision I have for the Web is about anything being potentially connected with anything. It is a vision that provides us with new freedom, and allows us to grow faster than we ever could when we were fettered by the hierarchical classification. It leaves the entirety of our previous ways. It leaves our previous fears for the future in addition; it brings the workings of society closer to the workings of our minds.

Unlike Enquire Within upon Everything, the Web that I have tried to foster is not merely a vein of information to be mined, nor is it just a reference or research tool. Despite the fact that the ubiquitous WWW and .com now fuel electronic commerce and stock markets all over the world,

this is a large, but just one, part of the Web. Buying books from
Amazon.com and stocks from E-trade is not all there is to the Web.
Neither is the Web some idealized space where we must remove our shoes,
eat only fallen fruit, and eschew commercialization.[7]

We can see here that Berners-Lee chose to move his metaphor towards
something more natural (he uses the phrase "organic growth", for
example), where there is a clear sense that everything is interconnected.
The words "vein" and "mined" show he must have thought, too, about
the metaphor as being one of natural resources being excavated.

Having said that, there is of course the limitation of the metaphor
that a spider weaves a web, that there is one central creator at work,
and a central purpose, something that is plainly no longer the case.
Along the way, the vividness of the metaphor has faded and become
irrelevant. But in another way it hasn't. A number of governments,
recognizing the power of the Internet, have attempted to control it
and place themselves in the position of being the predatory spider, just
waiting for the victims to fly into the net. Early on in the history of
the Internet, it was spoken of as an information "superhighway", until
many with slow download speeds realized that they were stuck in the
slow lane. In short, the choice of metaphor often dictates the way that
we think about an aspect of the real world.

The important thing for your purposes is to recognize that many
metaphors are not merely on the surface of a text, simply devices for
making writing more vivid. Instead, when you examine them closely,
you often get much closer to the deepest attitudes and values of a
speaker or writer, to the way that their mind shapes their world.
While you read, it is worth taking the time to see if you can identify
metaphorical patterns emerging, rather than simply noting examples.

Spoken and written language

Although at this level our concern is mainly with written language,
some of the texts you will encounter will give the impression of
having some characteristics of spoken language in order to create a
particular voice or tone. You have to remember, too, that speech itself is
enormously varied. The distinction between everyday talk and scripted
speech is, of itself, worthy of discussion.

The key differences between everyday speech and written language are
outlined in the following table.

Spoken language	Written language
It usually involves more than one person and is interactive.	Although it will have an audience in mind, the presence of the audience is not needed at the moment of composition, so it can be a monologue.
It is immediate: the audience hears it as soon as it is said (although with many types of recording available it can be repeated).	There is a time lag between production and reception.
It has a loose structure which allows for rephrasing, repetition, and clarification.	It is more carefully and more consciously planned.
It can be appreciated by more than one person at a time.	It is usually only read by one person at a time, at a time chosen by the reader.
It can change register easily.	It will probably stick fairly rigidly to one register and genre.
It can rely on other clues such as facial expression, tone of voice, and listener feedback to aid meaning and understanding.	Once it has been written and printed, it is fixed. It is therefore the natural medium for records, tables, lists, and notes.
As the speaker knows who is listening, it is suitable for expressing personal attitudes.	It cannot make too many assumptions about the reader as it may be read by wide varieties of different audiences.
It can rely quite heavily on the common understanding between speaker and listener and thus can be more vague because the context of the utterance often explains what is meant.	It can be received and interpreted at the reader's own pace.

Representing spoken language in fictional writing

You will already know about the formal conventions of presenting speech in a story such as speech marks, but the table above will have made you more aware of the problems of trying to give the impression that characters are talking spontaneously in either a novel or a script. The difficulty is that when we talk informally in real life, there is often only a loose sense of purpose, and we often pause (with an "um" or an "er" to fill the space), or go back on ourselves to clarify things. A lot of the time, we don't speak in full sentences either.

In contrast, when people in a novel or a soap opera talk, they are doing so in order to move the plot forward in some way, and they don't interrupt each other or talk over each other, as quite often happens in real conversation. You may have noticed, for example, that characters in soap operas never talk about what they saw on the television last night, or what they had for lunch. A popular British soap opera *EastEnders* is set in working-class London, and yet no one ever swears, and so its writers constantly have to work around real-life speech features that would, in fact, give their script authenticity.

Activity 2.27

Make a brief transcript (around 200 words will do) of a soap opera familiar to you and discuss the various factors that make you aware that the characters are not speaking spontaneously.

What's more, speech conventions are very much dictated by the particular variety of English that you speak as well as your education, age, and social class. If you ever want to include speech in your own writing, you need to be absolutely confident that you have a grasp of the idioms and speech patterns of the speaker in order to make it sound authentic. That probably means that you should only attempt it if the character speaking comes from the same country as you and has roughly the same background, or if you know someone from the same background as your character sufficiently well that you can imitate the sorts of things that they would say.

Represented speech can also, of course, be used for local colour, as Emily Brontë does in *Wuthering Heights* with the servant Joseph by trying to represent his broad Yorkshire accent.

> "T' maisternobbut just buried, and Sabbath not o'ered, und t' sound o' t' gospel still i' yer lugs, and ye darr be laiking! Shame on ye! sit ye down, ill childer! there's good books eneugh if ye'll read 'em: sit ye down, and think o' yersowls!"

This could be translated as:

> "The master just recently buried, and the Sabbath not over, and the sound of the gospel still in your ears, and you dare be larking about [having fun]! Shame on you! Sit down, bad children! There are good books enough if you'll read them: sit down, and think of your souls!"

The next extract offers the clever trick of being able to address itself to "you" by including an audience for the speaker as a character in the book. Writing where there is only one speaker can be called a **monologue**. The writer, Mohsin Hamid, carefully sets up his narrator (note that it is a character in the novel, not Hamid himself) in what could be a casual meeting in a café in Lahore. This allows him to build a narrative voice that borrows much from natural speech.

TIP

In your own writing

A word of warning: don't ever try to represent speech in a story unless you are absolutely confident that the speaker will sound authentic. It's always dangerous to write about characters who speak in a markedly different way from the way that you yourself speak.

Text type: prose narrative, fiction, Pakistan

Excuse me, Sir, but may I be of assistance? Ah, I see I have alarmed you. Do not be frightened by my beard: I am a lover of America. I noticed that you were looking for something; more than looking, in fact you seemed to be on a mission, and since I am both a native of this city and a speaker of your language, I thought I might offer you my services.

How did I know you were American? No, not by the color of your skin; we have a range of complexions in this country, and yours occurs often among the people of our northwest frontier. Nor was it your dress that gave you away; a European tourist could as easily have purchased in Des Moines your suit, with its single vent, and your button-down shirt. True, your hair, short-cropped and your expansive chest – the chest, I would say, of a man who bench-presses regularly, and maxes out well above two-twenty-five – are typical of a certain type of American; but then again, sportsmen and soldiers of all nationalities tend to look alike. Instead, it was your bearing that allowed me to identify you, and I do not mean that as an insult, for I see your face has hardened, but merely as an observation.

Come, tell me, what were you looking for? Surely, at this time of day, only one thing could have brought you to the district of Old Anarkali – named, as you may be aware, after a courtesan immured for loving a prince – and that is the quest for the perfect cup of tea. Have I guessed correctly? Then allow me, sir, to suggest my favorite among these many establishments. Yes, this is the one. Its metal chairs are no better upholstered, its wooden tables are equally rough, and it is, like the others, open to the sky. But the quality of its tea, I assure you, is unparalleled.

You prefer that seat, with your back so close to the wall? Very well, although you will benefit less from the intermittent breeze, which, when it does blow, makes these warm afternoons more pleasant. And will you not remove your jacket? So formal! Now that is not typical of Americans, at least not in my experience. And my experience is substantial: I spent four and a half years in your country. Where? I worked in New York, and before that attended college in New Jersey. Yes, you are right: it was Princeton! Quite a guess, I must say.

What did I think of Princeton? Well, the answer to that question requires a story. When I first arrived, I looked around me at the Gothic buildings – younger, I later learned, than many of the mosques of this city, but made through acid treatment and ingenious stonemasonry to look older – and thought, *This is a dream come true*. Princeton inspired in me the feeling that my life was a film in which I was the star and everything was possible. *I have access to this beautiful campus*, I thought, *to professors who are titans in their fields and fellow students who are philosopher-kings in the making*.

The Reluctant Fundamentalist by Mohsin Hamid

Activity 2.28

- What impression do you get of the narrator here? How, precisely, does he speak? What are his most pressing concerns?
- How does Hamid create the character of the American? Start by thinking about how it is clear that, although the American does speak, the narrator chooses not to report it directly.

Another variant of this is to allow a story to develop with some authorial intervention but let the speech itself move the narrative forward as in this short story.

Text type: prose narrative, fiction, USA

Early that day the weather turned and the snow was melting into dirty water. Streaks of it ran down from the little shoulder-high window that faced the backyard. Cars slushed by on the street outside, where it was getting dark. But it was getting dark on the inside too.

He was in the bedroom pushing clothes into a suitcase when she came to the door.

I'm glad you're leaving! I'm glad you're leaving! she said. Do you hear?

He kept putting his things into the suitcase.

[...] I'm so glad you're leaving! She began to cry. You can't even look me in the face, can you?

Then she noticed the baby's picture on the bed and picked it up.

He looked at her and she wiped her eyes and stared at him before turning and going back to the living room.

Bring that back, he said.

Just get your things and get out, she said.

He did not answer. He fastened the suitcase, put on his coat, looked around the bedroom before turning off the light. Then he went out to the living room.

She stood in the doorway of the little kitchen, holding the baby.

I want the baby, he said.

Are you crazy?

No, but I want the baby. I'll get someone to come by for his things.

You're not touching this baby, she said.

The baby had begun to cry and she uncovered the blanket from around his head.

Oh, oh, she said, looking at the baby.

He moved toward her.

For God's sake! she said. She took a step back into the kitchen.

I want the baby.

Get out of here!

She turned and tried to hold the baby over in a corner behind the stove.

But he came up. He reached across the stove and tightened his hands on the baby.

Let go of him, he said.

Get away, get away! she cried.

The baby was red-faced and screaming. In the scuffle they knocked down a flowerpot that hung behind the stove.

He crowded her into the wall then, trying to break her grip. He held on to the baby and pushed with all his weight.

Let go of him, he said.

Don't, she said. You're hurting the baby, she said.

I'm not hurting the baby, he said.

The kitchen window gave no light. In the near-dark he worked on her fisted fingers with one hand and with the other hand he gripped the screaming baby up under an arm near the shoulder.

She felt her fingers being forced open. She felt the baby going from her.

No! she screamed just as her hands came loose.

She would have it, this baby. She grabbed for the baby's other arm. She caught the baby around the wrist and leaned back.

But he would not let go. He felt the baby slipping out of his hands and he pulled back very hard.

In this manner, the issue was decided.

Little Things by Raymond Carver

Activity 2.29

- What effect does Carver achieve by shaping an audience's reaction almost entirely from what the characters say?

- How does he create an impression of the characters?

- What are the effects of not putting speech marks around the utterances?

- Why does Carver not characterize the speech with adverbs ("she said, angrily.")?

- What is the effect of all the simple sentences?

- What is the effect of the narrator's interventions? Look particularly at the framing of the opening and closing paragraphs and then think about the structure of the story.

- How would you describe the tone and register of the story?

Conclusion

We have come a long way and it's time to think about what you now know.

You should have a much larger range of terminology and concepts, a more varied set of tools, for describing language and its effects.

You should also be able to see that there is a logical way to tackle any text you come across, which can be conveyed best in stages as outlined below.

Stage 1: Contextual analysis	
Genre of text	What sort of text are you dealing with? What are the established characteristics of this genre that you already know about? Is this a "typical" example?
Social context	In what context is this kind of text normally produced? What constraints/obligations/rules does this impose upon the text? Where might this sort of text be found? What constraints does its context place upon it (a fashion magazine article may, for example, be surrounded by advertisements)?
Purpose	What is the writer aiming to do here?
Reader/listener	What role is required of the reader/writer/speaker/ audience in this text?
Cultural values	What cultural values are shared by both the text producer and the audience of this text? Is this a variation on the normal relationship between producer/recipient in texts of this genre?
Formal text features	What shared understanding of this genre of spoken or written English is required to understand this writing or speech fully?
Stage 2: Linguistic analysis	
Register and tone	What are the significant features of the text in terms of formality/informality? Do they vary within the text?
Diction and grammatical features	What features are prominent and worthy of comment? This could also include features of figurative language, alliteration, etc.
Text patterns	Can you see any patterns in the text? If so, what is the reason for them?
Text structure	How is the text organized into units of meaning? What is the reason for this organization in terms of text type, audience, and intended effect?

Above all, you will recognize that this sort of discussion is firmly based on ideas about *language in use*, not on feature-spotting as you go through the text sentence by sentence.

If you step back from the detail of this for a moment, you will also realize that you now have a strong sense of the main ideas that are central to formal discourse analysis which:

- focuses on language beyond the simple analysis of word, clause, phrase or sentence

- looks at patterns of language in texts and considers the links between the language and the social and cultural contexts in which it is used

- recognizes that the use of language presents different views of the world and different understandings and perceptions

- examines the relationship between the participants – speaker/listener or reader/writer

- considers how language creates and influences identities and relationships

- examines how views of the world and identities are constructed through different varieties of discourse and linguistic techniques.

Hemingway's original story (see page 28)

They shot the six cabinet ministers at half past six in the morning against the wall of the hospital. There were pools of water in the courtyard. There were wet dead leaves on the paving of the courtyard. It rained hard. All the shutters of the hospital were nailed shut. One of the ministers was sick with typhoid. Two soldiers carried him downstairs and out into the rain. They tried to hold him up against the wall but he sat down in a puddle of water. The other five stood very quietly against the wall. Finally the officer told the soldiers it was no good trying to make him stand up. When they fired the first volley he was sitting down in the water with his head on his knees.

Dictionary terms

"Omnishambles" describes a situation that has been comprehensively mismanaged by a string of blunders and miscalculations (see page 31). "Dumbphone" refers to a mobile phone that can only be used for making calls and sending texts, as opposed to a smartphone that does much more. "Selfie" – the 2013 word of the year and already in common use – is a picture taken of yourself on a smartphone. A "flexitarian" is someone who is mostly vegetarian but sometimes eats meat.

References

1. Crystal, David. 2007. *How Language Works*. London. Penguin Books.

2. Russell, Shirley. 2001. *Grammar, Structure and Style*. Oxford. Oxford University Press.

3. Crystal, David. 2007. *How Language Works*. London. Penguin Books.

4. Biber, Douglas, Conrad, Susan and Leech, Geoffrey. 2002. *The Longman Student's Grammar of Spoken and Written English*. Harlow, UK. Longman.

5. Crystal, David. 2007. *How Language Works*. London. Penguin Books.

6. Lakoff, George and Johnson, Mark. 1980. *Metaphors We Live By*. Chicago, IL, USA. University of Chicago Press.

7. Berners-Lee, Tim. 2000. *Weaving the Web*. New York, NY, USA. Harper Collins.

Language issues

How is language used?

In this chapter we are going to look at some of the wider issues raised by language study. To do so, we will be looking at:

- the language of advertising
- ways in which language can unconsciously convey attitudes and values, particularly in relation to gender
- language change and variation
- English, the Internet, and electronic communication
- diaries, autobiographies, and biographies.

We have already noted that language doesn't exist in a vacuum – it is shaped and modified by the society that uses it from day to day. The study of this shaping of language is called **sociolinguistics**. Broadly speaking, it aims to examine ways in which cultural values, expectations, and contexts influence how language is used. You have already seen aspects of this at work, identifying yourself as part of a speech community and recognizing that you constantly practise **code switching** (adapting your language to fit the situation you find yourself in). Your work on register in the last chapter will have given you some awareness of how ethnicity, religion, status, gender, education, and country of origin all influence the way that someone uses a language.

Advertising

One of the most potent uses of language is to persuade people, and advertisers do this as their profession. Over the years, they have honed their skills in order to persuade you to buy certain products. These days, advertisements that simply give you information about where a product comes from (see right) are rare:

On the whole, adverts need to have an emotional appeal; they appeal to your needs or your fears. Most commonly they focus on your need to:

- have something new
- be accepted
- not be ignored
- change old things
- be secure
- become attractive.

Alternatively they can focus on your fear of:

- accidents
- death
- being avoided.
- getting sick
- getting old

Some advertisements have it both ways, combining your desire for something new with your fear that you might be thought less of because you don't have the latest trainers, or that your friends might be avoiding you because you don't use the right shampoo. You are often being sold a "lifestyle" rather than the product itself, and advertisers work hard to appeal to your pre-existing attitudes and values in order to make you want what they have to sell. Therefore, advertisements work on the basis of **presupposition**, an understanding of what an audience brings with it to the text. For example, hair is thought to be more glamorous if shiny; holidays to exotic places are thought to be prestigious and desirable.

Linguists have increasingly turned to exploring the attitudes and values (often called **ideologies**) of texts in recent years. In their analyses, they talk about how the text is presented and the angle or perspective the writer or speaker is working from. This is called **framing** (in the same way that you might "frame" an argument in an essay), a useful term to use when discussing a wide range of texts. Texts also emphasize some concepts or issues (the desirability for silky hair, for example), while playing down other aspects, such as price. This is called **foregrounding** and **backgrounding**. If you were trying to persuade your parents to buy you a new computer, for example, you might well foreground its importance for your studies and success at school, while carefully avoiding (backgrounding) your concealed aim, which is to play computer games for 10 hours a day.

You will probably have noticed that one aspect of advertising centres on the use of "buzz words". These are hooks to reel you in – few people can resist reading on if the word "free" appears in big print. Often the key words are adjectives that might be applied to the product: better, crisper, less fattening, smoother, tastier, tastiest. The adjectives might be applied to the consumer after they have sampled the product too: thinner, healthier, happier.

Activity 3.1

Gather a range of advertisements and discuss the various ways in which they are framed to appeal to you. You should examine:

- presuppositions
- foregrounded elements in terms of attitudes and values
- backgrounded elements
- ways in which images work with words to create an impression and to hold your attention.

For major companies, an image (think of the golden arches used by McDonalds or the Coca-Cola logo) is central to brand identification, but this is often linked to a brief phrase (a **slogan**) that is instantly identifiable with their product. Companies long for you to apply make-up "because you're worth it" and to "reach out and touch someone" on the telephone before you leave for the gym. Once there, "just do it" in your branded sports gear before donning your suitably expensive jeans ("Quality never goes out of style") and enjoying a hamburger on your way home ("I'm lovin' it"), with perhaps some of "America's Favorite Ketchup".

Activity 3.2

Look again at the advertisements you chose for Activity 3.1. Your task now is to examine the language. Look for:

- use of different types of word class (adjectives may feature strongly) and register
- use of phrases (combinations of words without a verb) as opposed to full sentences
- slogans
- use and effectiveness of asking the reader/viewer a question
- relationships between the attitudes and values that are being sold and the language used.

An analysis of this type moves us beyond description of the surface features of a text. It aims to provide an explanation of why a text may be as it is and what it is aiming to do. In looking at the relationship between language, social norms, and values, an analysis attempts to describe, interpret, and explain the relationship between text and audience. By doing so, it also helps a reader/listener to recognize and perhaps challenge some of the hidden (implicit) social, political, and cultural values that underlie the surface discourse.

Activity 3.3

Now go back to your genre table (Chapter 2, page 11) and do an analysis of the texts you have found. You will need to look for patterns that all the texts have in common and also at ways in which there are sub-genres (car advertisements, for example) that share the major characteristics of the main genre but have distinctive features of their own.

One of the things that you may have noticed is that many advertisements – particularly for washing powder or beauty products – make assertions about the benefits of their products by saying things that cannot readily be proved.

This use of fake scientific lexis is often used to give the advertisement a formal register, and this can be combined with dubious survey evidence

("9 out of 10 cat owners that expressed a preference …"). The aim is to impress the innocent, and to suggest that a product has some particular, almost magical, properties. Cosmetics are a particular example: one, for example, claims to contain rare diamond dust particles and to have been tested on astronauts in outer space (it's good to know that they worry about their skin). Another says it has been developed after laboratory tests using a SIAscope on skin for a Spectrophotometric Intracutaneous Analysis.

Another feature you will notice in advertising hype (in other words, exaggeration) is the idea that you personally are in some way important to the company. Words like "exclusive" feature largely, as does the implication that you are in some way privileged or a VIP. Package tours can offer you "Hidden Spain" or "Unknown Portugal", although if these holidays are advertised in national newspapers, the offer is hardly for something hidden or unknown, particularly if you will be going as part of a group.

Activity 3.4

Have a look at the following advertisement for a holiday in Rajasthan and then comment on the techniques that the writer has used to persuade you that this holiday would suit you. Think specifically about:

- the potential purchaser the writer has in mind and the way he or she is addressed

- the attitudes and values that are implicit (that is, not openly stated) in the writing.

Text type: advertisement, India

Royal Rajasthan On Wheels

Rajasthan is the magnificent land of numerous kingdoms, majestic forts and palaces, diverse cultures, varied landscapes and vibrant colours. Experience the land of regal splendour with Royal Rajasthan on Wheels, the contemporary royal living. The Royal Rajasthan on Wheels is the regal delight where every moment is woven together into an everlasting and immemorial experience to be lived and cherished forever. The makers of the Palace on Wheels have rekindled the charm of luxury with utmost consideration of your comfort and modern amenities at the Royal Rajasthan on Wheels. This tour is extensively planned to take you through the whispering sands of desert, the intriguing sagas of forts and palaces, and the adventurous escapades to the wilds; while you

The Incredible State of !ndia

witness the luxuries on the train in a truly royal fashion. This train is newly built and designed in a contemporary royal style. You will be delighted with the magnificent interiors, sumptuous meals, expensive wines, and personalised service.

It stands on its tracks; a gleaming sealed carriage, every bit is royal. The air-conditioning works silently, creating a space where only the excitement of the history of the Rajput kingdoms permeates through, clearly captured in a contemporary mode. In all, there are fourteen saloons, each equipped with two twin-bedded and two double-bedded chambers, with attached baths that have running hot and cold water and showers. The modern conveniences have been thoughtfully provided, sofas to sink into, strategically placed lights to read by, wonderfully appointed beds with comfortable furnishings, inbuilt wardrobes for the storage of one's clothes and bags, and huge plate glass windows to watch the countryside roll past. Outside the bedrooms, each coach also has a seating lounge where passengers can get together, just sit and watch the cities as they glide past outside the windows, or enjoy a quiet cup of tea.

Tourism Rajasthan

Language and attitudes

Whenever we speak or write, we convey something of our own prejudices and beliefs. In recent years, much has been done to eliminate one of the most deeply embedded difficulties of the English language – its inherent bias towards a male-dominated view of the world, where the words used reflect a world where people who fight fires are by definition fire*men*, where people who run companies are always chair*men*. Nowadays, it's thought best to avoid sexist language.

Here are some real examples of messages that appeared on Twitter which were sent in to a website called www.everydaysexism.com.

- Playing *Football Manager 2013*, and there is no way to stop the game referring to me as a "he".
- Getting annoyed at programmes and speakers who use "man" instead of humankind, or humanity.
- Vax advert for vacuum cleaner "super power for super mums" – do dads never vacuum?
- People who send letters to my work addressed to "Dear Sir": You are aware that women work in offices now, right?

These examples demonstrate how the matter of framing, discussed above, shapes discourse. It may be unconscious on the part of the speaker or writer, but it's there all the same.

One of the key purposes of this rebalancing in terms of gender-based language is to eliminate causes for offence and to provide equality. This re-framing of language is sometimes called political correctness, although its true goal is to provide non-judgmental,

Activity 3.5

Write a similar advertisement for a local attraction near where you live.

Activity 3.6

How might you re-frame the following sentences in order to avoid gender bias?

1. Our group is going to need a new chairman.
2. I need to talk to the salesman next time he's in town.
3. The businessmen are meeting in New York next week.
4. The doorman always lets us in.
5. I want to be a policeman.

inclusive terminology. It has, at times, come in for much mockery, but that simply demonstrates that the labels we give things have enormous power over our perceptions of matters of gender, race, sexual orientation, and disability. The previous sentence, for example, creates a list which might be thought to imply a rank order. That is not my aim but I am bound by the conventions of linearity in prose.

The desire for inclusive language – think back to the discussion of the word "everyone" in the last chapter – can also lead to bizarre attempts not to say the wrong thing. Consider, for example, the rather odd briefing instruction to an interview panel: "the applicant does not have to tell us they are pregnant", using "they" to avoid "she". The interesting thing here, of course, is that gendered language exists on a grammatical level, whereas when in the cases of race, sexual orientation, or disability the re-framing is simply a matter of lexical concern.

In the following story, the writer takes a well-established genre and a well-known children's story in order to make fun of political correctness.

TIP

To eliminate sexism in your own writing:

- Avoid male words (chairman), preferring neutral alternatives
- Avoid traditional idioms (the man in the street)
- Use Ms as a neutral alternative to Mrs or Ms
- Rework sentences (see page 41) where male pronouns dominate unnecessarily
- Try not to use examples that only deal with one gender
- Avoid consistently putting reference to males before reference to females
- Choose words of equal status: if they are the men's toilets, then the ones for women are not the Ladies'
- Avoid modifications that suggest a normal state that is being deviated from: 'the lady doctor,' 'the male secretary'.

Text type: fairy story, USA

Little Red Riding Hood

There once was a young person named Red Riding Hood who lived with her mother on the edge of a large wood. One day her mother asked her to take a basket of fresh fruit and mineral water to her grandmother's house – not because this was women's work, mind you, but because the deed was generous and helped engender a feeling of community. Furthermore, her grandmother was not sick, but rather was in full physical and mental health and was fully capable of taking care of herself as a mature adult.

So Red Riding Hood set out with her basket of food through the woods. Many people she knew believed that the forest was a foreboding and dangerous place and never set foot in it. Red Riding Hood, however, was confident

enough in her own budding sexuality that such obvious Freudian imagery did not hinder her.

On her way to Grandma's house, Red Riding Hood was accosted by a Wolf, who asked her what was in her basket. She replied, "Some healthful snacks for my grandmother, who is certainly capable of taking care of herself as a mature adult."

The Wolf said, "You know, my dear, it isn't safe for a little girl to walk through these woods alone."

Red Riding Hood said, "I find your sexist remark offensive in the extreme, but I will ignore it because of your traditional status as an outcast from society, the stress of which has caused you to develop your own, entirely valid world view. Now, if you'll excuse me, I must be on my way."

Red Riding Hood walked on along the main path. But, because his status outside society had freed him from slavish adherence to linear, Western-style thought, the Wolf knew of a quicker route to Grandma's house. He burst into the house and ate Grandma, an entirely valid course of action for a carnivore such as himself. Then, unhampered by rigid, traditionalist notions of what was masculine or feminine, he put on Grandma's nightclothes and crawled into bed.

Red Riding Hood entered the cottage and said, "Grandma, I have brought you some fat-free sodium-free snacks to salute you in your role of a wise and nurturing matriarch."

From the bed, the Wolf said softly, "Come closer, child, so that I might see you."

Red Riding Hood said, "Oh, I forgot you are as optically challenged as a bat. Grandma, what big eyes you have!"

"They have seen much, and forgiven much, my dear."

"Grandma, what a big nose you have – only relatively, of course, and certainly attractive in its own way."

"It has smelled much, and forgiven much, my dear."

"Grandma, what big teeth you have!"

The Wolf said, "I am happy with who I am and what I am," and leaped out of bed. He grabbed Red Riding Hood in his claws, intent on devouring her. Red Riding Hood screamed, not out of alarm at the Wolf's apparent tendency toward cross-dressing, but because of his willful invasion of her personal space.

Her screams were heard by a passing woodchopper-person (or log-fuel technician, as he preferred to be called). When he burst into the cottage, he saw the melée and tried to intervene.

But as he raised his axe, Red Riding Hood and the Wolf both stopped.

"And what do you think you're doing?" asked Red Riding Hood.

The woodchopper-person blinked and tried to answer, but no words came to him.

"Bursting in here like a Neanderthal, trusting your weapon to do your thinking for you!" she said. "Sexist! Speciesist! How dare you assume that women and wolves can't solve their own problems without a man's help!"

When she heard Red Riding Hood's speech, Grandma jumped out of the Wolf's mouth, took the woodchopper-person's axe, and cut his head off. After this ordeal, Red Riding Hood, Grandma, and the Wolf felt a certain commonality of purpose. They decided to set up an alternative household based on mutual respect and cooperation, and they lived together in the woods happily ever after.

Little Red Riding Hood by
Jim Garner

Language change and variation

These days English is thought of as a global language – Globish, as it's sometimes called. If you are planning to continue your studies to A Level, then you will read a lot more about this in the second part of the course. For present purposes, it's enough to observe that British English is now a minority variant of a language that is spoken as a first language by more people outside the UK than within it. It's also the second language of choice across large sections of the world. In linguistic terms, this means that although the language is still called English, the British have very little to do with its current or its future developments, in the same way as Britain invented soccer and cricket and now finds that both sports are played with great facility elsewhere. Speakers elsewhere in the world are more creative with the language, and, indeed, they are the innovators.

The history of all this must wait until another time. The central point for you now is that you need to recognize that variations of the language across the world do not make one version more or less "correct". Instead, it means that the language exists in a number of different forms, although there is something called **standard English** which is the generally accepted currency for international communication in formal spoken and written situations.

One of the oldest variations is that which exists between British and American English. The Irish writer George Bernard Shaw took the view that "England and America are two countries separated by a common language". But it's actually more complicated than that nowadays because both British English and American English are sub-groups of the language as a whole.

One crucial distinction is, of course, that the two languages have a different lexicon. If people move to a new country, there are new things to name. A second point is that each culture chooses to name the same things differently. American readers may have been irritated, for example, to have cell phones described as mobile phones earlier on in this book. These are differences of vocabulary, most of which are easily translated.

American English has also tried to rationalize spelling (not always successfully or consistently): "doughnut" becomes "donut", for example.

The curious thing is, however, that the differences have tended to remain lexical or to do with pronunciation, rather than grammatical. Of course, there are preferences between the two – "a half an hour" (American), "half an hour" (British), "in the hospital" (American), "in hospital" (British) – but these are not deep features of the language.

Increasingly, American English influences British English (it hasn't happened the other way round for a long time), with words like "get" starting to replace the word 'have': "Can I get a coffee?" (American). To "fill out" a form is now more common in Britain than to fill one in.

One of the most interesting examples of significant difference of meaning is the American use of "gotten", a word that doesn't exist in British English. Americans use it to mean obtain – "She's gotten a new dress", which is rather different to the British phrase, "She's got a new dress". "Gotten" can also mean become: "he's gotten rather set in his ways". Oddly, "gotten" to mean simply "have" is unacceptable in American: "I've gotten the answer" is not acceptable. "Gotten" does allow some flexibility in expression that is not part of British English: "they've gotten to spend some time in Florida" does not mean that they have to spend some time there; it means that they have managed to do so.

The difference between British and American English is, of course, only one of thousands of possibilities, all of which could be usefully explored using the same methods.

English, the Internet, and electronic communication

Over the last few decades, English has established itself, for the time being at least, as the language of computing. This in turn has contributed greatly to the emergence of English as a global language. So it's worth considering some aspects of the pressures for change on the language that have been created through this new medium of communication.

Activity 3.8

Allocate each of the following word pairs to British or American usage:

diaper/nappy
boot/trunk
fall/autumn
windscreen/windshield
bumper/fender
CV/resumé
cookies/biscuits
closet/wardrobe
restroom/toilet
sidewalk/pavement

Obviously, we have needed some new words because of what computers and mobile phones can do: examples of new words are download, chat room, hyperlink, and hashtag. The majority of other words related to computing are simply borrowed or adapted from the current language already in existence: menu, options, font, track, mouse, avatar, troll, spam, and so on. Made-up words like "twitterati" and "twitterholic" won't last, so the actual contribution to the lexicon of the language consists of a few thousand words in relation to the million plus that already exist in English. There is little evidence that computer-specific words are passing into everyday life, or being used without any reference to computers, although a colleague of mine was once described as being in "energy-saving mode" when having a nap at lunchtime.

A more interesting area for study is the way that computers have created new possibilities for text production. David Crystal's book *Internet Linguistics: A Student Guide*[1], which was published in 2011, makes it clear that genre characteristics for electronic texts are not yet fully established or developed. Perhaps they never will be, as things change so quickly that new genres appear and disappear with great rapidity.

Email

Some forms are nevertheless now sufficiently established for linguists to be able to list the characteristics typical of the genre. Let's take email as an example. In one episode of *The Simpsons*, Homer asks his friends "What's an email?" He hopes for a nice clear answer. The response he gets from Lenny is, "It's a computer thing, like, er, a letter". Carl adds helpfully, "Or a quiet phone call". In fact it's both of those and more besides. As with many electronic media, an email sits awkwardly on the edge, uncertain if it is a spoken or a written text. This sort of meeting of old styles or forms of writing with new ones is called **convergence**, particularly where speech and writing come together into a **mixed medium**, where rules from both sorts of discourse coincide.

Emails can share some aspects of speech such as informality of tone, and few people these days would set one up as a letter. Nonetheless, there are instances where the written conventions of letters, such as politeness, have remained. In Japan, for example, it is thought very rude simply to start directly with the business of an email, so there will often be comments on the weather such as "Greetings! It's just becoming spring here in Tokyo".

However, an email is also a formal written record of things, as a number of large companies have discovered to their cost when they have been ordered to find emails as legal evidence, despite their protestations that they have been lost, deleted, or were not meant for wider public consumption.

Debrett's, a British guide to good manners, recently published a set of guidelines.

Text type: web page, UK

Email has replaced many traditional forms of communication, both verbal and written. The writer of an email must remember that their message may be stored permanently, and that there is no such thing as confidentiality in cyberspace.

- Delicate communications should therefore be sent by other means, and you must think carefully before hitting 'send' if the message is written in haste or when emotions are running high.

- Avoid sarcasm and subtle humour unless you know that the reader will 'get it'. If in doubt, err towards the polite and formal, particularly where you are not well acquainted with the recipient.

- Think carefully about using smiley faces, 'kisses', etc. Are these symbols really suitable for the recipient?

- Using capital letters looks like shouting and should be avoided. If you want to emphasise something, try underlining or using italics.

- Aim to stick as closely as possible to the conventions of traditional letter-writing. Close attention should be paid to spelling and grammar, and the habit of writing in lower case throughout should be avoided.

- A well thought-out subject line will ensure that the message gets the attention it deserves.

- Emails will often be printed and filed, and therefore close attention must be paid to layout. Again, treating the construction of an email just as you would a 'real' letter is the most effective approach.

- Where there is more than one recipient, list them alphabetically or, in the business environment, according to hierarchy. This applies also to the 'cc' line.

- Avoid blind copying ('bcc') where possible: instead, forward the original email on to the third party, with a short note explaining any confidentiality. Blind copying is, however, appropriate for distribution lists, for example, where all recipients must remain anonymous.

- If you send an email in error, contact the recipient immediately by telephone and ask them to ignore/delete the message.

- It is polite to reply to emails promptly – a simple acknowledgement with a promise that you will give the email your full attention at a given later point is preferable to 'sitting on' the message.

- Never use email to reply to correspondence or an invitation that was not sent by email or does not supply an email address as an RSVP option.

There is no replacement for paper and ink; in this day and age where propriety is so often sacrificed for the sake of immediacy, the truly sophisticated correspondent will put pen to paper rather than dashing off a quick email.

http://www.debretts.com

Blogs

Another example is that of blogs. Originally, they were a way for Internet users to share their journeying around the web, a track of sites visited that allowed the "blogger" to leave comments. In effect, early bloggers were creating a map of points of interest on the Internet: they were some of the first settlers. Nowadays, blogs have moved firmly into the area of mass communication, and there are professional bloggers who write for newspapers and magazines. This means that the rules and conventions have changed to be much more like those of magazines and newspapers. It's becoming clear, too, that blogs are no longer free from the intervention of the law, so the free-for-all of the early days of blogging is gradually becoming constrained by the rules of libel that would apply to remarks made in newspapers and magazines. Many blogs are also really advertisements, written to give you the impression that comments are being offered independently when they are, in fact, distinctly biased.

There are some obvious features that you would want to imitate if asked to write one. One of the most striking things is that, for all their sense of immediacy and spontaneity, blogs do not contain any of the typical characteristics of spoken language. Although the reader is often asked to engage in dialogue and leave a track, the blog itself is not interactive: the reader is not in a conversation with the writer, so there is no element of **turn-taking**, a crucial element of chat.

Typical characteristics of blogs seem to be:

- The topics appear chronologically, with the latest posting first.
- They are usually written in response to something that the blogger has read or seen, often on the Internet.
- They are simply laid out, with clear titles.
- Most blogs are brief.

- Millions of them are never read by anyone other than their creator and, perhaps, close friends or family.

- Many are not edited but are published directly by their creators.

- There is a button that allows you to subscribe and be sent updates.

- You can often access an archive of previous posts.

- If the blogger is selling something, this has to be kept in the background.

- There may be links to social media sites like Facebook or Twitter so that you can follow the writer in a number of different ways.

- Many blogs do not last very long – authors get bored with them when they realize that other people don't find their opinions fascinating.

Activity 3.11

Type "blog template" into a search engine. You will quickly discover that much of the formatting work can be pre-determined so that all a blogger has to do is to put in the content. This will help you to establish some of the genre rules.

Typing in the name of your hobby will produce thousands of examples of content. There is even one for people like me who work in garden huts, called Shedworking (www.shedworking.co.uk).

Netspeak

Perhaps the biggest language innovation has been that a hybrid version of English (it may be true of other languages too) called "Netspeak" is starting to emerge. If you go back to the table in Chapter 2 (see page 53) that describes the differences between spoken and written language, it will soon become apparent that many of those distinctions begin to blur once mobile phones and computers are involved.

We have seen some of this at work in our discussion of email. One of the most obvious difficulties is that if we write as if we are speaking, we can't often go back and correct ourselves, or adapt what we say to the audience as we gauge a reaction. This has led to the emergence of emoticons in some sorts of messaging in order to convey tone or mood.

Some messages also use angle brackets or asterisks (*...*) to provide a gloss on what is being said, for example, <smiles, hoping you understand>. Some of these features are trying to do exactly the same

thing that happens when a novel writer creates a passage of speech and then characterizes it with, for example, "he said, angrily". An example of this is the word "facepalm" which indicates ironic despair, as though the writer is dropping his head into his hands and is lost for words. The desire to write stage directions like this fits clearly into occasions where the pragmatics of the situation – almost spontaneous communication without the other person being present – call for signals to ensure that a writer's tone is not being misunderstood.

Moreover, many notionally spontaneous utterances over the Internet have elements of pre-planning that could more easily be associated with written texts. The most obvious elements of spontaneous speech (the ums, ers, you-know-what-I-means) are almost entirely absent, so it is clear that Netspeak is a very long way away from natural conversation. Even "instant" messaging has pauses and a sense of the other person taking a turn that would be slightly different if the conversation was being held face to face.

At the same time, Netspeak is also not nearly as bound up in the rules of writing, as there is a significant difference between a formally laid out web page and a text message. What we have is a hybrid that is still very much in the process of development. This has implications for your own writing. You may be asked to produce an article for a web page, and this is deeply problematic because you will have to think about issues of format as well as about the various ways in which issues of interactivity may be relevant to your text.

Text messaging

It's interesting that text messaging (SMS) has gained so much popularity. Although these are early days in terms of research, it seems that many people prefer to communicate by text rather than by speaking on the telephone because they feel that it is less intrusive to others and it means that they can plan what they want to say more carefully. Texting can, of course, be massively abused when one half of a couple dumps the other by text, or, as happened recently, 2,000 workers for a British insurance company were told they were being made redundant by text. Sometimes, face-to-face communication is simply more suitable.

Activity 3.12

- Find a range of different texts that illustrate your own use of electronic media. Discuss them in terms of genre, language choice, and register. Think about your status as producer, audience, or joint author of these texts.

- Now discuss these texts in terms of the characteristics they share with both spoken and written language. Make use of the table in Chapter 2 (page 53) to help you define the differences.

Diaries, autobiographies, and biographies

Think back to the work you did on first-person narrative in Chapter 2 (see pages 14–17). Although some diaries are written for publication, the vast majority are a record of events and private thoughts. As such, they will lack formality and may not have the coherence of something that is more fully planned.

Here's an example by a writer who tried to visit her London home from the country during the bombing of London in 1940.

Text type: diary, UK

Back from half a day in London – perhaps our strangest visit. When we got to Gower St. a barrier with Diversion on it. No sign of damage. But coming to Doughty St. a crowd. Then Miss Perkins at the window Meck S. [Mecklenburgh Square] roped off. Wardens there, not allowed in. The house about 30 yards from ours struck at one this morning by a bomb. Completely ruined. Another bomb in the square still unexploded. We walked round the back. Stood by Jane Harrison's house. The house was still smouldering. That is a great pile of bricks. Underneath all the people who had gone down to their shelter. Scraps of cloth hanging to the bare walls at the side still standing. A looking glass I think swinging. Like a tooth knocked out – a clean cut. Our house undamaged. No windows yet broken – perhaps the bomb has now broken them. We saw Sage Bernal with an arm band jumping on top of the bricks – who lived there? I suppose the casual young men & women I used to see, from my window; the flat dwellers who used to have flower pots & sit on the balcony. All blown to bits. The garage man

at the back – blear eyed & jerky told us he had been blown out of his bed by the explosion; made to take shelter in a church – a hard cold seat he said, & a small boy lying in my arms. "I cheered when the all clear sounded. I'm aching all over." He said that the Jerrys had been over for 3 nights trying to bomb Kings X [a London station]. They had destroyed half Argyll Street, also shops in Grays Inn Road. Then Mr Pritchard ambled up.

10 September 1940,
The Diary of Virginia Woolf by
Virginia Woolf

In an early diary entry (20 April 1919) Woolf articulated her aims for her diary.

> *What sort of diary should I like mine to be? Something loose knit and yet not slovenly, so elastic that it will embrace anything, solemn, slight or beautiful that comes into my mind. I should like it to resemble some deep old desk, or capacious hold-all, in which one flings a mass of odds and ends without looking them through.*

Activity 3.13

In what ways does the entry from 1940 confirm the view that Woolf's diary is:

- loose knit (that is, not formally structured)
- able to "embrace" a wide variety of experiences
- like "a deep old desk, or capacious hold-all"?

Activity 3.14

Write a diary entry – or a series of entries over a number of days – by someone who is confronting problems at school or in a new job.

An autobiography is different from a diary in that it is written to be read by other people.

Now look at a piece of autobiographical writing describing a writer's harsh upbringing by a religious mother in the north of England.

Text type: autobiography/memoir, UK

I got myself up for school every day. My mother left me a bowl of cornflakes and the milk in a flask. We had no fridge and most of the year we had no need of one – the house was cold, the North was cold, and when we bought food we ate it.

Mrs Winterson had terrible stories about fridges – they gave off gas and made you dizzy, mice got caught in the motor, rats would be attracted by the dead mice caught in the motor ... children got trapped inside and couldn't escape – she knew of a family whose youngest child had climbed into the fridge to play hide-and-seek, and frozen to death. They had to defrost the fridge to prise him out. After that the council took away the other children. I wondered why they didn't just take away the fridge.

Every morning when I came downstairs I blew on the fire to get it going and read my note – there was always a note. The note began with a general reminder about washing – HANDS, FACE, NECK AND EARS – and an exhortation from the Bible, such as *Seek Ye the Lord*. Or *Watch and pray*.

The exhortation was different every day. The body parts to be washed stayed the same.

When I was seven we got a dog, and my job before school was to walk the dog around the block and feed her. So then the list was arranged as WASH, WALK, FEED, READ.

At dinner time, as lunchtime was called in the North, I came home from school for the first few years, because junior school was only round the corner. By then my mother was up and about, and we ate pie and peas and had a Bible reading.

Later, when I was at the grammar school further away, I didn't come home at dinner time, and so I didn't have any dinner. My mother refused to be means-tested, and so I didn't qualify for free school meals, but we had no money to buy the meals either. I usually took a couple of slices of white bread and a bit of cheese, just like that, in my bag.

Nobody thought it unusual – and it wasn't. There were plenty of kids who didn't get fed properly.

Why be Happy When You Could be Normal by Jeanette Winterson

In the next passage, the New Zealand writer Janet Frame recounts an autobiographical childhood episode about her brother (Bruddie/Geordie). The second passage is the re-telling of the same incident by her biographer.

Text type: autobiography, New Zealand

It was not long after Grandad's death that we were awakened one night by a commotion in the house. I heard Mum crying out, 'Bruddie's having a convulsion; Bruddie's having a convulsion.' I ran with the others into the dining room. We sat together on the … sofa, watching and listening while Mum and Dad went back and forth from Bruddie's room to the bathroom. 'A convulsion, a convulsion,' Mum kept saying in her earthquake-and-tidal-wave voice. She fetched the doctor's book from where it was (unsuccessfully) hidden on top of the wardrobe in their bedroom and looked up *Convulsions*, talking it over with Dad, who was just as afraid.

In the meantime Bruddie had wakened, sobbing. 'A bath,' Mother cried. 'Put him in a bath.' Dad carried the crying Bruddie into the

bathroom. We four girls were sent back to our bedrooms, where we cuddled up to one another, talking in frightened whispers and shivering with the cold Oamaru night, and when I woke the next morning, my eyes were stinging with sleep and I felt burdened with the weight of a new awful knowledge that something terrible had happened in the night to Bruddie.

Our lives were changed suddenly. Our brother had epilepsy, the doctor said, prescribing large doses of bromide which, combined with Bruddie's now frequent attacks, or fits, as everyone called them, only increased his confusion and fear until each day at home there were episodes of violent rage when he attacked us or threw whatever was at hand to throw. There had usually been somewhere within the family to find a 'place' however cramped; now there seemed to be no place; a cloud of unreality and disbelief filled our home, and some of the resulting penetrating rain had the composition of real tears. Bruddie became stupefied by drugs and fits; he was either half asleep, recovering, crying from the last fit, or in a rage of confusion that no one could understand or help. He still went to school, where some of the bigger boys began to bully him, while we girls, perhaps prompted by the same feeling of fear, tried to avoid him, for although we knew what to do should he fall into a fit at school or outside at home, we could not cope with the horror of it. Mother, resisting fiercely the advice of the doctor to put Bruddie into an institution, nursed him while we girls tried to survive on our own with the occasional help of Dad, who now combed the tangles out of my frizzy hair each morning and supervised the cleaning of our bedroom.

To the Is-Land by Janet Frame

Activity 3.15

Compare the techniques used in this passage with those of Woolf in her diary. Pay particular attention to the voice that each writer constructs and also to the structure of each piece.

Now write a short section of your own autobiography where you try to amuse a reader about a specific episode from your life. You could choose a moment fondly recalled by your family from a holiday, or perhaps an account of your first day at a new school.

How might this have been different if you had been simply writing up the incident in a diary?

Text type, biography, New Zealand

Early in 1932 the family discovered a more traumatic and enduring source of tension and grief. One night, not long after Janet had thrown a lump of coal at her brother and hit him on the head, Geordie, now aged nine, suffered an epileptic seizure. Neither parent knew how to cope with this frightening visitation. "A convulsion, a convulsion," Mum kept saying in her earthquake-and-tidal-wave voice.' Later, as the fits recurred and the family knew what to do to make it less likely that Geordie would injure himself, the sense of horror and helplessness persisted. And for Janet, who feared that she may have caused this problem, the fits produced additional anxiety and guilt.

There were at this time no effective drugs to mitigate or control the condition. Large doses of bromide, the sole recourse of the family's doctor, only increased Geordie's confusion and fear. '[Each] day at home there were episodes of violent rage when he attacked us or threw whatever was at hand to throw. There had usually been somewhere within the family to find a "place" however cramped; now there seemed to be [none] ... Mother, resisting fiercely the advice to put [Geordie] in an institution, nursed him while we girls tried to survive on our own.' Epileptics were then defined as 'mental defectives' under mental health legislation. And what Lottie actually said as she rejected the doctor's advice was, 'No child of mine is going to Seacliff,' which was the Otago mental hospital. In the case of her son at least this ambition was realized. Geordie, deaf as well as epileptic, left school before he turned twelve and, in the recollection of his siblings, his mother 'devoted all her time to him'.

Wrestling with the Angel: A Life of Janet Frame
by Michael King

Activity 3.16

Compare the writers' different presentations of this moment in Janet Frame's life. Pay particular attention to:

- the difference between **subjective** (the writer is involved) and **objective** narration
- ways in which Michael King incorporates some of Frame's own narrative into his writing.
  Now go back to the Winterson passage (pages 76-77) and re-write it as though you were her biographer, using the King passage as a model.

Discuss with a partner the narrative choices that you made in order to present an objective view of Winterson's experiences.

Conclusion

All the examples in this chapter present us with examples of what linguists call "communicative competence". Language is not, as we now know, merely used because it is neutral and grammatically correct; rather, a speaker or writer has to know how, when, and where to use language appropriately, and with whom. A consequence of this is that analysis needs to take into account the social and cultural setting in which the text is produced, looking at the text producers' relationships with potential audiences and at a community's norms, values, and expectations for the type of text produced. Linguists therefore see grammatical competence as being only one aspect of a much wider range of pressures that are part of text production and consumption, namely:

- sociolinguistic competence, a knowledge of appropriate language use in specific situations.

- generic competence, an ability to respond to a text by showing awareness of how to construct, interpret, and exploit established conventions associated with the use of particular types of texts

- discourse competence, a knowledge of how to connect utterances in a text so that it is cohesive and coherent in its own terms

- strategic competence, an ability to examine breakdowns in communication, or to enhance a communication's effectiveness.

All of these factors joined together are sometimes described as "textual competence" or "discursive competence", which is achieved by a text producer or consumer being able to draw on textual, contextual, and pragmatic knowledge of what typically occurs in a particular text, how it is typically organized, and how it is usually interpreted, in order to create new texts or respond to texts that are unfamiliar.

In this chapter:

- you have looked at a range of text types and at issues that place textual detail into a wider context

- you have thought more deeply about genre and language use

- you have broadened your understanding of the term **discourse analysis** to enable you to talk about some of the social, political, practical, and ideological issues related to the production and reception of texts.

Reference

1. Crystal, David. 2011. *Internet Linguistics: A Student Guide.* London. Routledge. Chapter 2.

Your own writing

How will your writing be assessed?

For the purposes of assessment, what you have learned will be tested through written examinations. There are two types of writing that will be assessed:

- commentary on others' writing and then developing an imaginative response which imitates the style and concerns of the original.

- producing texts of your own based on a stimulus.

You will need to show an ability to shape texts for different purposes and audiences by writing both imaginatively in one piece, and by shaping an argument in another.

Commenting on others' writing and developing an imaginative response

Writing a commentary

As you read a text, start to underline important points: remember that it is the style and language of the piece, *not* the subject matter, that is of prime importance.

Let's just remind ourselves of something we covered earlier. When you deal with a text you need to ask yourself a range of questions:

- Why, when, and where am I reading this text? (Remember that readers of the original would not be in an examination situation.)

- What, basically, is this text about?

- What kind of text is it? (Genre, type of publication, purpose, register.)

  - Is it oral/written?

  - Is it formal/informal?

  - Does it have features of a particular text type that I recognize?

  - What is its function? (To inform, persuade, amuse, irritate, inspire further thought, answer questions, pose problems?)

- Who is talking and who are they talking to through, within, and around the text? What relationship are you, the reader/listener, being asked to develop with the text and the writer or speaker?

- What sorts of attitudes and values are being put forward? Are you being persuaded to share them with the text creator? If so, how?

These questions now need to be used along with the tools that you learned about earlier so that you can provide an overall view of the text and show an ability to analyse in detail. You will have to decide which are the most useful tools for the particular challenges that have been presented by a passage. Like a craftsman, you need to know when to use a hammer, when to use a screwdriver.

Often you will be given some background information about the author or the genre of the piece. Use it if you can relate it to points that emerge from the written text but don't simply re-write it in other words. Here, the writer is part of the British colonial administration in Burma in the 1930s.

Can you comment on the style and language of the passage?

Text type: prose essay, UK

But I did not want to shoot the elephant. I watched him beating his bunch of grass against his knees, with that preoccupied grandmotherly air that elephants have. It seemed to me that it would be murder to shoot him. At that age I was not squeamish about killing animals, but I had never shot an elephant and never wanted to. (Somehow it always seems worse to kill a large animal.) Besides, there was the beast's owner to be considered. Alive, the elephant was worth at least a hundred pounds; dead, he would only be worth the value of his tusks, five pounds, possibly. But I had got to act quickly. I turned to some experienced-looking Burmans who had been there when we arrived, and asked them how the elephant had been behaving. They all said the same thing: he took no notice of you if you left him alone, but he might charge if you went too close to him.

It was perfectly clear to me what I ought to do. I ought to walk up to within, say, twenty-five yards of the elephant and test his behaviour. If he charged, I could shoot; if he took no notice of me, it would be safe to leave him until the mahout came back. But also I knew that I was going to do no such thing. I was a poor shot with a rifle and the ground was soft mud into which one would sink at every step. If the elephant charged and I missed him, I should have about as much chance as a toad under a steam-roller. But even then I was not thinking particularly of my own skin, only of the watchful yellow faces behind. For at that moment, with the crowd watching me, I was not afraid in the ordinary sense, as I would have been if I had been alone. A white man mustn't be frightened in front of "natives"; and so, in general, he isn't frightened. The sole thought in my mind was that if anything went wrong those two thousand Burmans would see me pursued, caught, trampled on and reduced to a grinning corpse like that Indian up the hill. And if that happened it was quite probable that some of them would laugh. That would never do.

There was only one alternative. I shoved the cartridges into the magazine and lay down on the road to get a better aim. The crowd grew very still, and a deep, low, happy sigh, as of people who see the theatre curtain go up at last, breathed from innumerable throats. They were going to have their bit of fun after all. The rifle was a beautiful German thing with cross-hair sights. I did not then know that in shooting an elephant one would shoot to cut an imaginary bar running from ear-hole to ear-hole; I ought, therefore, as the elephant was sideways on, to have aimed straight at his ear-hole, actually I aimed several inches in front of this, thinking the brain would be further forward.

When I pulled the trigger I did not hear the bang or feel the kick – one never does when a shot goes home – but I heard the devilish roar of glee that went up from the crowd. In that instant, in too short a time, one would have thought, even for the bullet to get there, a mysterious, terrible change had come over the elephant. He neither stirred nor fell, but every line of his body had altered. He looked suddenly stricken, shrunken, immensely old, as though the frightful impact of the bullet had paralysed him without knocking him down. At last, after what seemed a long time – it might have been five seconds, I dare say – he sagged flabbily to his knees. His mouth slobbered. An enormous senility seemed to have settled upon him. One could have imagined him thousands of years old. I fired again into the same spot. At the second shot he did not collapse but climbed with desperate slowness to his feet and stood weakly upright, with legs sagging and head drooping. I fired a third time. That was the shot that did for him. You could see the agony of it jolt his whole body and knock the last remnant of strength from his legs. But in falling he seemed for a moment to rise, for as his hind

legs collapsed beneath him he seemed to tower upward like a huge rock toppling, his trunk reaching skyward like a tree. He trumpeted, for the first and only time. And then down he came, his belly towards me, with a crash that seemed to shake the ground even where I lay.

I got up. The Burmans were already racing past me across the mud. It was obvious that the elephant would never rise again, but he was not dead. He was breathing very rhythmically with long rattling gasps, his great mound of a side painfully rising and falling. His mouth was wide open – I could see far down into caverns of pale pink throat. I waited a long time for him to die, but his breathing did not weaken. Finally I fired my two remaining shots into the spot where I thought his heart must be. The thick blood welled out of him like red velvet, but still he did not die. His body did not even jerk when the shots hit him, the tortured breathing continued without a pause. He was dying, very slowly and in great agony, but in some world remote from me where not even a bullet could damage him further. I felt that I had got to put an end to that dreadful noise. It seemed dreadful to see the great beast lying there, powerless to move and yet powerless to die, and not even to be able to finish him. I sent back for my small rifle and poured shot after shot into his heart and down his throat. They seemed to make no impression. The tortured gasps continued as steadily as the ticking of a clock.

In the end I could not stand it any longer and went away.

Shooting an Elephant by George Orwell

Adapted from Cambridge AS & A Level English Language 8693
Paper 1 Q1 June 2009

One way to begin to look at the style and language used is to pick out one aspect and see how far you can get simply using that one idea. You might, for example, focus on figurative language in the Orwell passage. There's lots of it:

- grandmotherly air

- a toad under a steamroller

- as of people who see the theatre curtain go up at last

- an enormous senility seemed to have settled upon him

- like a huge rock toppling

- caverns of pale pink throat.

But simply picking out examples won't do. They have to be shaped into some sort of an order to demonstrate their function in the writing. For example, you could write the following.

> The image of the elephant as "grandmotherly" makes it seem unthreatening, as does the idea of "senility" later on; we are invited to feel sympathy for the helplessness of the elephant. This is contrasted with the images of size later on with the "huge rock toppling" and the "caverns of pale pink throat". The images demonstrate the narrator's uncertain attitude towards the creature. Similarly, he himself feels under threat but tries to deal with this by making a joke of what might happen: if squashed, he will be like a "toad under a steamroller". His feeling of being watched and judged by the Burmese is made explicit by him talking about them as "people who see the theatre curtain go up at last". The elephant itself could be seen as metaphor for the British Empire, which by the time Orwell was writing was lumbering out of control. Orwell clearly has in view an audience for his writing that would be sympathetic to the ambiguous emotions expressed about colonialism in the passage.

In other words, you are taking elements of the passage and starting to construct an argument. The features spotted are all contributing to your understanding of how the writer is conveying attitudes and values. An approach likes this encourages you to take an overall view of the passage, not simply to go through it line by line. In short, you are moving through a clear process, one that you need to practise until it is a matter of habit:

- locate

- describe

- analyse

- synthesize.

Activity 4.1

Using your understanding of discourse markers and sentence structure, discuss Orwell's presentation of the narrator's uncertain state of mind in this passage.

Start by collecting your examples ("but", "besides", for example) and then see if you can shape them into a paragraph. You could perhaps also talk about his choice of verbs ("shoved", for example) to make your points about him being unwilling and disconcerted by what happens.

What you will become aware of is that all of these different features work together to create an overall impression. So it doesn't really matter which ones you choose, as long as you are prepared to argue the case.

You could take other elements of the passage and develop them in similar ways.

You will see that you are building up a series of paragraphs, each with a very specific, language-based focus. During the course of an examination you will probably have time to create three or four paragraphs like this. You will want to ensure, too, that you have linked them, possibly using discourse markers, so that a reader can see that you are making logical progress through your points. Notice that you have not gone through the passage line by line. Nor have you been particularly concerned with the *content* of the passage. The focus has been on language and its effects throughout.

Under test conditions, you probably won't have time to do the very formal things that might normally be expected of essays such as an opening paragraph or a summarizing conclusion. Don't worry about this. It is vital that you get on with the task. Think of it as like making a sandwich: you want it to be stuffed with tasty ingredients, with the bread (the opening and the conclusion) merely holding it all together.

One crafty trick is to leave a space at the beginning and then write your opening once you have written the essay. This means that you know precisely what you are going to say, so you can introduce it briefly. It also means that you won't promise more than you can deliver. Never fall into the trap of an over-elaborate announcement of what you intend ("In this essay, there are fourteen important issues that will be considered.") because if you only get to number three in the time allowed, your reader will feel disappointed.

Writing an imaginative response

A second element of responding to a passage can be to write an imaginative response. You put yourself in the shoes of the original speaker but in a slightly different situation. It is important, therefore, to have a strong sense of the following four aspects of the original passage:

- register
- audience
- purpose
- point of view.

It might be a good idea to remember the acronym RAPP as a means of ensuring that you cover all these points in an examination.

As you move into this new area, you become the creator, not the consumer, of a text. This means that you have to ask yourself the questions about texts from a different point of view.

- Who am I writing this text for? Where will it be read?
- What is the text going to be about?
- What sort of a text is it going to be?
- What sort of relationship will I need to establish with an audience?
- What sort of attitudes and values will be conveyed through my text, both explicitly and implicitly?

Activity 4.2

Look at the question below with a sample answer and an analysis of that answer.

Later on the same day, the speaker arrives home to discover that his servant has been out watching the elephant being killed and has failed to prepare him something to eat. He writes about his encounter with the servant. Base your answer closely on the style and language of the original passage. Write 120–150 words.

Sample answer

Back in England, I never thought of myself as fussy – careful and precise, perhaps, but not over fussy. But here, being watched all the time, life is different. I don't want to order my man or supervise his every move, but he seems to have no sense of what is necessary and he has to be instructed in every aspect of laying out my kit for the following day. And now this. Like a kindly uncle, he watches and seems to indulge me, but as soon as my back's turned, he goes on his own sweet way. Looks like a row is in order. This is only the overture to an evening that has every chance of turning into yet another disaster.

Analysis

The writer has picked up on the fact that the narrator feels very uncomfortable in the role he has been given. As in the original passage, he feels constantly watched and judged by the people that he has been sent to govern. There is reference to his precision that links to the pleasure he feels with the gun in the passage. The imagery of the aged relative is also used, as is the idea of a theatre with the word "overture". The use of a sentence fragment ("And now this"), the dash in the first sentence, and the casual, colloquial "Looks like a row is in order" show that he is narrating his thoughts as he goes along, as does the original passage. A picture is being created where the speaker innocently ("I never thought of myself as fussy") is telling us more about himself than he perhaps realizes because we discover that he *is* very fussy. The reader is being asked to decide how much sympathy should be extended to the speaker, as the original does throughout.

Above all, have someone in mind that you are writing for!

TIP

You need to remember that you are being assessed on the quality of your writing and organization. There is often an upper limit of words on each assignment, but that does not mean you have to write that much to gain high marks. Benjamin Franklin apologised in 1750 for a report on his groundbreaking experiments with electricity saying: "I have already made this paper too long, for which I must crave pardon, not having now time to make it shorter." The more you write, the more you have an opportunity to make mistakes.

Producing texts of your own

Writing a story or opening

You could be asked to write a short story or the opening to a short story or novel. Here are a couple of examples for us to consider.

Text type: prose narrative, fiction, India

I was born in the city of Bombay… once upon a time. No, that won't do, there's no getting away from the date: I was born in Doctor Narlikar's Nursing Home on August 15th 1947. And the time? The time matters, too. Well then: at night. No, it's important to be more… On the stroke of midnight, as a matter of fact. Clock-hands joined palms in respectful greeting as I came. Oh, spell it out, spell it out: at the precise instant of India's arrival at independence, I tumbled forth into the world. There were gasps. And, outside the window, fireworks and crowds. A few seconds later, my father broke his big toe; but his accident was a mere trifle when set beside what had befallen me in that benighted moment, because thanks to the occult tyrannies of those blindly saluting clocks I had been mysteriously handcuffed to history, my destinies indissolubly chained to those of my country. For the next three decades, there was to be no escape. Soothsayers had prophesied me, newspapers celebrated my arrival, politicos ratified my authenticity. I was left entirely without a say in the matter. I, Saleem Sinai, later variously called Snotnose, Stainface, Baldy, Sniffer, Buddha and even Piece-of-the-Moon, had become heavily embroiled in Fate – at the best of times a dangerous sort of involvement. And I couldn't even wipe my own nose at the time.

Midnight's Children by Salman Rushdie

Text type: prose narrative, fiction, UK

One evening of late summer, before the nineteenth century had reached one-third of its span, a young man and woman, the latter carrying a child, were approaching the large village of Weydon-Priors, in Upper Wessex, on foot. They were plainly but not ill clad, though the thick hoar of dust which had accumulated on their shoes and garments from an obviously long journey lent a disadvantageous shabbiness to their appearance just now.

The man was of fine figure, swarthy, and stern in aspect; and he showed in profile a facial angle so slightly inclined as to be almost perpendicular. He wore a short jacket of brown corduroy, newer than the remainder of his suit, which was a fustian waistcoat with white horn buttons, breeches of the same, tanned leggings, and a straw hat overlaid with black glazed canvas. At his back he carried by a looped strap a rush basket, from which protruded at one end the crutch of a hay-knife, a wimble for hay-bonds being also visible in the aperture. His measured, springless walk was the walk of the skilled countryman as distinct from the desultory shamble of the general labourer; while in the turn and plant of each foot there was, further, a dogged and cynical indifference personal to himself, showing its presence even in the regularly interchanging fustian folds, now in the left leg, now in the right, as he paced along.

What was really peculiar, however, in this couple's progress, and would have attracted the attention of any casual observer otherwise disposed to overlook them, was the perfect silence they preserved.

The Mayor of Casterbridge by Thomas Hardy

In both pieces, the writers are in no great rush to give you a lot of action or to move the plot along. Instead, Rushdie is gently introducing you to a character; Hardy is setting up an atmosphere. If you are asked to write the opening of a novel, you have to bear in mind that the allowed number of words (600–900 words) is only the beginning of something that could be 100,000 words long. The implication here is that you must not be too impatient to move on to matters of plot and storytelling. Usually the question will give you a hint about the sort of story you are going to write and instruct you to create a strong sense of mood, sense of place, suspense, perhaps.

Therefore you need to focus on:

● building a character or a relationship that is going to be important later on

● creating atmosphere

● creating a relationship with the reader through voice and point of view.

It's important, too, that you think hard about a good opening paragraph and that even this early you draw a reader into the world of the novel.

Here are some more examples.

Once upon a time, many years ago – when our grandfathers were little children – there was a doctor; and his name was Dolittle – John Dolittle, M.D. "M.D." means that he was a proper doctor and knew a whole lot.

The Story of Doctor Dolittle by Hugh Lofting

Cannery Row in Monterey in California is a poem, a stink, a grating noise, a quality of light, a tone, a habit, a nostalgia, a dream. Cannery Row is the gathered and scattered, tin and iron and rust and splintered wood, chipped pavement and weedy lots and junk heaps, sardine canneries of corrugated iron, honky-tonks, restaurants […], and little crowded groceries, and laboratories and flop-houses.

Cannery Row by John Steinbeck

I was born in 1927, the only child of middle-class parents, both English, and themselves born in the grotesquely elongated shadow, which they never rose sufficiently above history to leave, of that monstrous dwarf Queen Victoria. I was sent to a public school, I wasted two years doing my national service, I went to Oxford; and there I began to discover I was not the person I wanted to be.

The Magus by John Fowles

Frenchman's Bend was a section of rich river-bottom country lying twenty miles southeast of Jefferson. Hill-cradled and remote, definite yet without boundaries, straddling into two counties and owning allegiance to neither, it had been the original grant and site of a tremendous pre-Civil War plantation, the ruins of which – the gutted shell of an enormous house with its fallen stables and slave quarters and overgrown gardens and brick terraces and promenades – were still known as the Old Frenchman's place, although the original boundaries now existed only on old faded records in the Chancery Clerk's office in the county courthouse in Jefferson, and even some of the once-fertile fields had long since reverted to the cane-and-cypress jungle from which their first master had hewed them.

The Hamlet by William Faulkner

There was a lark singing somewhere high above. Light fell dazzling against my closed eyelids, and with it the song, like a distant dance of water. I opened my eyes. Above me arched the sky, with its invisible singer lost somewhere in the light and floating blue of a spring day. Everywhere was a sweet, nutty smell which made me think of gold, and candle flames, and young lovers. Something, smelling not so sweet, stirred beside me, and a rough young voice said: "Sir?"

The Hollow Hills by Mary Stewart

Our coal-bunker is old, and it stands beneath an ivy hedge, so that when I go to it in wet weather, I catch the combined smells of damp earth and decaying vegetation. And I can close my eyes and be thousands of miles away, up to my middle in a monsoon ditch in India, with my face pressed against the tall slats of a bamboo fence, and Martin-Duggan standing on my shoulders, swearing at me while the rain pelts down and soaks us. And all around there is mud, and mud, and more mud, until I quit dreaming and come back to the mundane business of getting a shovelful of coal for the sitting-room fire.

The General Danced at Dawn by George Macdonald Fraser

The storm-force wind was blasting squalls of incredibly wet and heavy rain across the loch, blotting out the hills and the sky and flaying the rusty grass of the crofts until it cringed back into the ground from which it had sprung so ebulliently only a few short months earlier. All day there had been semi-dusk and when I had returned soaked and shivering from the moors that morning after a long hunt to give Bonny her morning hay, I had promised myself I would do nothing but change into dry clothes, put some food on a tray and then sit by the fire with a book. Nothing, that is, until it was time for me to don my sticky oilskins and my coldly damp sou'wester, strain on wet gumboots and go seeking Bonny again with her evening feed.

The Loud Halo by Lillian Beckwith

It was very still in the house. The sweet and solemn dusk was falling after one of the loveliest of September days, and high above the smoke of town and city the harvest moon was making for herself a silvered pathway through the stars.

The Better Part by Annie S. Swan

Ours is essentially a tragic age, so we refuse to take it tragically. The cataclysm has happened, we are among the ruins, we start to build up new little habitats, to have new little hopes. It is rather hard work: there is now no smooth road into the future: but we go round, or scramble over the obstacles. We've got to live, no matter how many skies have fallen.

Lady Chatterley's Lover by D.H. Lawrence

Call me Ishmael. Some years ago – never mind how long precisely – having little or no money in my purse, and nothing particular to interest me on shore, I thought I would sail about a little and see the watery part of the world. It is a way I have of driving off the spleen, and regulating the circulation. Whenever I find myself growing grim about the mouth; whenever it is a damp, drizzly November in my soul; whenever I find myself involuntarily pausing before coffin warehouses, and bringing up the rear of every funeral I meet; and especially whenever my hypos get such an upper hand of me, that it requires a strong moral principle to prevent me knocking peoples hats off – then I account it high time to get to sea as soon as I can. This is my substitute for pistol and ball. With a philosophical flourish Cato throws himself upon his sword; I quietly take to the ship. There is nothing surprising in this. If they but knew it, almost all men in their degree, some time or other, cherish very nearly the same feelings toward the ocean with me.

Moby Dick by Herman Melville

Call me Jonah. My parents did, or nearly did. They called me John.

Cat's Cradle by Kurt Vonnegurt

Yesterday I was fifty-nine, and in a year I shall be sixty – "getting on for seventy," as the unpleasant old phrase goes. I was born in November, 1865, and this is November, 1924. The average duration of life in England is fifty-one and a half, so I am already eight years and a half beyond the common lot. The percentage of people who live beyond sixty is forty-seven. Beyond seventy it is thirty. Only one in five thousand lives beyond one hundred, and of this small body of centenarians two-thirds are women. My expectation of life, says the table in the almanac, is fourteen years and four months. That table in the Almanac is not a mathematical marvel, but it is close enough to the truth to serve my purpose here.

The World of William Clissold by H.G. Wells

Through the fence, between the curling flower spaces, I could see them hitting. They were coming toward where the flag was and I went along the fence. Luster was hunting in the grass by the flower tree. They put the flag back and they went to the table, and he hit and the other hit. Then they went on, and I went along the fence. Luster came away from the flower tree and we went along the fence and they stopped and we stopped and I looked through the fence while Luster was hunting in the grass.

The Sound and the Fury by William Faulkner

Activity 4.3

Stage 1: Put yourself in the position of someone setting questions for the class. What focus could you give a question that might, as a result, produce the opening of each novel? For example, with the first extract, this might have come from the prompt: "Write the opening to a story for children. You should create a strong sense of the central character from the beginning."

Stage 2: Having established a question for each of the passages, now see if you can write an opening paragraph or two for each of the tasks you have devised. You do not need to imitate the original. Remember here that the focus is on drawing your reader into your piece of writing.

Stage 3: Choose one or two of the openings given here and write a continuation, picking up characters, point of view, themes, or atmosphere.

When asked to write a story, there's often a temptation to fill in all the details instead of letting a reader's imagination go to work on a situation. Many writers prefer to let their narratives work by implication, rather than explicit statement. In the following complete short story, Raymond Carver tells you a lot about the family and their relationships without having to describe each character in detail or fill in much background to the tale.

Text type: fiction, short story, USA

The baby lay in a basket beside the bed, dressed in a white bonnet and sleeper. The basket had been newly painted and tied with ice blue ribbons and padded with blue quilts. The three little sisters and the mother, who had just gotten out of bed and was still not herself, and the grandmother all stood around the baby, watching it stare and sometimes raise its fist to its mouth. He did not smile or laugh, but now and then he blinked his eyes and flicked his tongue back and forth through his lips when one of the girls rubbed his chin.

The father was in the kitchen and could hear them playing with the baby.

'Who do you love, baby?' Phyllis said and tickled his chin.

'He loves us all,' Phyllis said, 'but really he loves Daddy because Daddy's a boy too!'

The grandmother sat down on the edge of the bed and said, 'Look at its little arm! So fat. And those little fingers! Just like its mother.'

'Isn't he sweet?' the mother said. 'So healthy, my little baby.' And bending over, she kissed the baby on its forehead and touched the cover over its arm. 'We love him too.'

'But who does he look like, who does he look like?' Alice cried, and they all moved up closer around the basket to see who the baby looked like.

'He has pretty eyes,' Carol said.

'*All* babies have pretty eyes,' Phyllis said.

'He has his grandfather's lips,' the grandmother said. 'Look at those lips.'

'I don't know…' the mother said. 'I wouldn't say.'

'The nose! The nose!' Alice cried

'What about his nose?' the mother asked.

'It looks like somebody's nose,' the girl answered.

'No, I don't know,' the mother said. 'I don't think so.'

'Those lips…' the grandmother murmured. 'Those little fingers…' she said, uncovering the baby's hand and spreading out its fingers.

'Who does the baby look like?'

'He doesn't look like anybody,' Phyllis said. And they moved even closer.

'*I* know! *I* know!' Carol said. 'He looks like *Daddy*.' Then they looked closer at the baby.

'But who does Daddy *look* like?' Phyllis asked.

'Who does Daddy *look* like?' Alice repeated, and they all at once looked through to the kitchen where the father was sitting at the table with his back to them.

'Why, nobody!' Phyllis said and began to cry a little.

'Hush,' the grandmother said and looked away and then back at the baby.

'Daddy doesn't look like *anybody*!' Alice said.

'But he has to look like *somebody*.' Phyllis said, wiping her eyes with one of the ribbons. And all of them except the grandmother looked at the father, sitting at the table.

He had turned around in his chair and his face was white and without expression.

The Father by Raymond Carver

Activity 4.4   Discuss some of the ways in which Carver creates atmosphere and a sense of unease in this story.

Descriptive writing

Another task might get you to write a descriptive piece. You may also be given an instruction about a particular atmosphere that you should aim to create. Here is an example of this type of writing.

Text type: prose narrative, fiction, descriptive, USA

We went out at the French doors and along a smooth red-flagged path that skirted the far side of the lawn from the garage. The boyish-looking chauffeur had a big black and chromium sedan out now and was dusting that. The path took us along to the side of the greenhouse and the butler opened a door for me and stood aside. It opened into a sort of vestibule that was about as warm as a slow oven. He came in after me, shut the outer door, opened an inner door and we went through that. Then it was really hot. The air was thick, wet, steamy and larded with the cloying smell of tropical orchids in bloom. The glass walls and roof were heavily misted and big drops of moisture splashed down on the plants.

The light had an unreal greenish color, like light filtered through an aquarium tank. The plants filled the place, a forest of them, with nasty meaty leaves and stalks like the newly washed fingers of dead men. They smelled as overpowering as boiling alcohol under a blanket.

The Big Sleep by Raymond Chandler

You will notice that Chandler has made strong use of descriptive words (adjectives and adverbs) and that he aims to give you a very visual picture to establish the **setting** (time and place) of his story. The orderly set-up of the garden is strongly contrasted with the murk of the greenhouse. Note too that he plays particular tricks with imagery. Many of the words – "larded" and "cloying" – give a strong sense of excess and discomfort and suggest that the speaker has a negative view of the situation he finds himself in. These words are associated with decaying food. There is also the distasteful image of the stalks, "like the newly washed fingers of dead men", combined with something slightly sinister too – "the light had an unreal, greenish colour". The writing is setting up a strong sense of anticipation. You will also have started to have some view of the sort of man telling the tale. He has told you nothing explicitly about himself, but you have a strong view of his world view, which seems rather obsessed with death and corruption. It will be no surprise to learn that we are at the beginning of a murder mystery.

> **Activity 4.5**
>
> Read the extract from *The Big Sleep* and comment on Chandler's methods for creating a scene.

What you will also have noticed is that the writing here is setting up a series of possibilities but is in no great rush to get on with telling you a story. For the time being, plot and character are less important than the setting up of the scene.

Text type: prose narrative, description, travel writing, UK

Lahore, 1997

It is barely dawn, and the sky is as pink as Turkish delight. Yet already, at 5.45 a.m., Lahore Central Station is buzzing like a kicked hive.

Bleary-eyed, you look around in bewilderment. At home the milkmen are abroad at this time, but no one else. Here the shops are already open, the fruit and vegetables on display, and the shopkeepers on the prowl for attention.

'Hello my dear,' says a man holding up a cauliflower.

'Sahib – what is your good name?'

'*Subzi! Subzi! Subzi!*'

'Your mother country?'

A Punjabi runs up behind the rickshaw, waving something horrible: a wig perhaps, or some monstrous vegetable. 'Sahib, come looking! Special shop OK! Buying no problem!'

Lahore station rears out of the surrounding anarchy like a liner out of the ocean. It is a strange, hybrid building: The Victorian red-brick is imitation St Pancras [an elaborate Victorian station in central London], the loopholes, battlements and machicolations are stolen from some Renaissance *palazzo* – Milan, perhaps, or Pavia – while the towers are vaguely German, and resemble a particularly Wagnerian stage set. Only the chaos is authentically Pakistani.

As a tape of the Carpenters' greatest hits plays incessantly on the tannoy, you fight your way through the surge of jammed rickshaws and tottering red-jacketed coolies, through the sleeping villages splayed out on the concrete, past the tap with the men doing their ablutions, over the bridge, down the stairs and onto the platform. In the early-morning glimmer, Platform 7 seethes with life like a hundred Piccadilly Circuses [a major traffic interchange in central London] at rush hour. Porters stagger towards the first-class carriages under a mountain of smart packing cases and trunks. Further down the platform, near third class, solitary peasant women sit stranded amid seas of more ungainly luggage cases and boxes, ambiguous parcels done up with rope, sacks with lumpy projections – bits of porcelain, the arm of a chair, the leg of a chicken. Vendors trawl the platform selling trays of brightly coloured sweetmeats, hot tea in red clay cups, or the latest film magazine. Soldiers wander past, handlebar moustaches wobbling in the slipstream.

The Age of Kali by William Dalrymple

In writing about this piece you could focus on the use of the following:

- the second-person pronoun "you"
- European references
- metaphorical language
- the present tense
- senses of sight, sound, taste, smell, touch
- attitudes and values, both implied and explicit.

Comparative pieces

You could also be asked to write two separate pieces which ask you to see the same scene or events from different points of view or at different moments in time.

You will have to make a number of decisions about:

- the continuity of theme and technique in the two pieces
- a structure for each piece: what sorts of parallels of content or style you might create
- using a narrative voice or two voices contrasted
- tone
- how much story to include, if any.

In the next extract, a character in a novel contributes contrasting blogs to a website as a response to government demolition of roadside, illegal food shops in Lagos, Nigeria.

> **Activity 4.6**
>
> Write a short piece describing a busy place that you know well. Try to see it as an outsider, from the point of view of someone for whom it is a new experience.

Text type: blog, prose fiction, Nigeria

It is morning. A truck, a government truck, stops near the tall office building, beside the hawkers' shacks, and men spill out, men hitting and destroying and levelling and trampling. They destroy the shacks, reduce them to flat pieces of wood. They are doing their job, wearing "demolish" like crisp business suits. They themselves eat in shacks like these, and if all the shacks like these disappeared in Lagos, they will go lunchless, unable to afford anything else. But they are smashing, trampling, hitting. One of them slaps a woman, because she does not grab her pot and her wares and run. She stands there and tries to talk to them. Later, her face is burning from the slap as she watches her biscuits buried in dust. Her eyes trace a line towards the bleak sky. She does not know yet what she will do but she will do something, she will regroup and recoup and go somewhere else and sell her beans and rice and spaghetti cooked to a near mush, her Coke and sweets and biscuits.

It is evening. Outside the tall office building, daylight is fading and the staff buses are waiting. Women walk up to them, wearing flat slippers and telling slow stories of no consequence. Their high-heeled shoes are in their bags. From one woman's unzipped bag, a heel sticks out like a dull dagger. The men walk more quickly to the buses. They walk under a cluster of trees which, only hours ago, housed the livelihoods of food hawkers. There,

drivers and messengers bought their lunch. But now the shacks are gone. They are erased, and nothing is left, not a stray biscuit wrapper, not a bottle that once held water, nothing to suggest that they were once there.

Americanah by Chimamanda Adichie

In analysing these two contrasting paragraphs, we can see the following.

- Continuity is created by the use of the simple present tense in both paragraphs. This creates a sense of immediacy, as does the use of the present continuous tense, which is used for rather different purposes in each paragraph, with verbs like "smashing, trampling, hitting" making the violence of the first paragraph more aggressive, whereas in the second the tense is used to create tranquillity because it is the daylight that is fading, the buses that are waiting.

- References to the time of day and the fact that both the demolition crew and the office workers might use these hawkers' stalls create parallels. The plight of the female hawker ("a woman") with her business reduced to nothing and the female office workers ("the women") with their "high-heeled shoes" demonstrates disparities of wealth and opportunity, and the connection is made absolutely clear as the demolition workers wear their overalls "like crisp business suits".

- Links are also provided through the use of the word "they" to open sentences in both paragraphs. Even the reference to biscuits in paragraph one, followed by the littered biscuit wrapper in paragraph two, creates a connection.

- In both paragraphs the voice is objective and distant, but a clear sense of the narrator's attitude to these events can be inferred through the writer's decisions about tone and register.

- A story is not being directly told, but an audience is being invited to piece one together from the contrasts and comparisons.

Activity 4.7

Look again at the writing that you did for Activity 4.6. Write a contrasting piece, describing the same place from the point of view of someone who has lived there since childhood.

> **Descriptive writing** **TIP**
>
> In descriptive writing you will need to plan out what you want to say. Remember that you will be seeking to create atmosphere. You want your readers to feel that they are with you and sharing the experience. This will certainly have implications for the writing in terms of point of view and voice.
>
> When creating an atmosphere in your writing, it's always good to try to appeal to a reader's sense of touch, smell, hearing, vision, and taste.

Activity 4.8

Choose one of the sample prompts below and write a response.

- Describe your school or college as it might be seen during the day and in the middle of the night.
- Describe your school or college as it might be seen by the youngest pupil and by the oldest pupil.
- Describe your school or college as being like a prison. Write another piece in which it is seen as being like a holiday camp.
- Describe your school or college as it might be seen by the head or principal as compared to one of the pupils.

Writing discursive or argumentative text

Structure

Your writing will benefit from a strong sense of organization. This means that it is worthwhile creating a plan. Some people like to do this as a mind map, with the central idea in the middle and then a series of links to minor ideas.

For example, you could be asked if home schooling is a good or bad thing for children and come up with a diagram such as Figure 1:

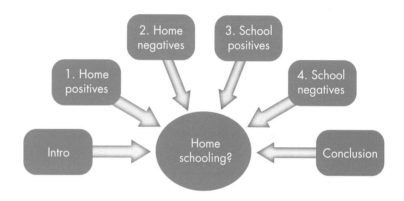

Figure 1

The trouble here is that you haven't really thought about the different relationships between the points that you want to make or ranked them by importance.

It might be better to see your planning as being like a tree (or your wrist and hand). You have a big idea, and then each of the paragraphs is a branch (or a finger) as in Figure 2:

Everything grows out of the big idea, and the sentences all feed back through the paragraphs to the "trunk" of the tree. This model encourages you to see which ideas are central and to treat them equally. It

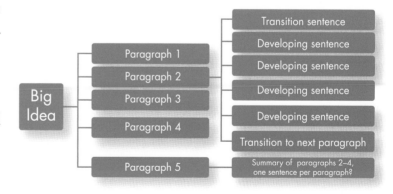

Figure 2

also gives you the possibility of shaping a case by contrast ("on the one hand", "on the other hand") within a paragraph, a sophisticated approach to dealing with a topic. Notice, too, that your plan is limited to a few words – just enough to keep you on track as you write.

TIP

If you are writing under timed conditions
Keep an eye on the time to ensure that you are moving through your plan and won't get left with half of what you wanted to say unwritten because you went into too much detail early on.

TIP

Remember page 85!
In writing where you are trying to develop an argument, it may be useful to leave a space and only write the opening paragraph at the end, so that you will not promise more than you can deliver in the time allocated.

In an essay of only 600–900 words you have limited space to develop ideas, so five or six paragraphs is probably about right: it gives you space to go into some detail on each of the points that you want to make. If you are writing a speech you may want to write more and shorter paragraphs because you will want more pauses for an audience to reflect on what you have said.

In commentaries and argumentative essays you will probably want to make use of words that help to move your discussion forwards. These are called discourse markers. You saw some of them at work in Lincoln's Gettysburg Address in Chapter 2 (page 22): "now", "but". They are vital if you are to give a sense of logical forward movement to your writing, and can often get you over the rather difficult issue of how to move from one paragraph to the next.

Furthermore (see exactly such a transition there!), you can use them to demonstrate that you have a variety of strategies for developing a discussion, something that will improve your writing (see table below).

Discourse markers					
Ordering	*Consequence*	*Continuation*	*Simultaneity*	*Concession*	*Conclusion*
Firstly	Because of this	Furthermore	Meanwhile	However	Finally
Secondly	Therefore	Moreover	At the same time	On the one hand … On the other hand	In conclusion
Thirdly		Another aspect to consider	While	Admittedly	To sum up
Next		In addition	In the meantime	Yet	Overall
Ultimately		Another		Notwithstanding	
Lastly		Then		Nevertheless, nonetheless	
		Similarly		In spite of this	

You need to anchor some of these words into your everyday writing and get used to them as the "oil" that allows you to move from one thing to another. This can be useful when you are writing commentaries too.

Activity 4.9

Tell a story (it will need to be nonsense), in which the first word of each sentence moves the tale on in one of the ways described in the headings of the discourse markers table above.

For example: The other day I went to the zoo with my brother and his pet crocodile. Meanwhile my mother went shopping. Because of this ….

Review the table of discourse markers and see if you can add some other words or short phrases that serve the same purpose.

Activity 4.10

For the time being, leave aside matters of audience. Here are three essay topics. Write a plan for each one. Get someone else to evaluate their effectiveness.

- Is it better to support local shops rather than large supermarkets?
- "There is too much money in sport." Do you agree?
- "A woman's place is in the boardroom." Discuss this statement.

The important thing is that the structure should be solid – think of it as being like building a table that doesn't wobble. It may not be the best table ever built but it should do the job it was designed to do and be serviceable.

Style

Now that we have established how to build a structure, it's time to work on matters of audience, form, and style. You must bear in mind that you are writing *for* someone, so you need to put yourself in their position and ask yourself if you would want to read or listen to the material that you are preparing. This takes us back to earlier discussions about genre in Chapter 2. Look again at the table on page 11 and use it in your planning from now until the end of this section.

Questions may also ask you to include strong elements of persuasion or argument. Fundamentally, there are three possible lines of attack:

- you can argue strongly *for* a given discussion topic
- you can argue strongly *against* a given discussion topic
- you can argue about a given discussion topic in a *balanced* way, as you might do in a history essay if asked the question "To what extent …?"

You are perfectly entitled to put in examples from your own reading and personal experience, and this will often make your work stand out as original or highly individual, something that will be well regarded.

Getting started

It can be difficult to get going, so you may want to adopt one of the following methods. Let's imagine that we have been given the theme "Team sports should be compulsory in schools". The topic is usually quite generally framed, so the skill of this assignment is to make something interesting of the prompt you are given. You will not be required to have any specific knowledge about the topic. You will be rewarded for your ability to shape a case and hold an audience's attention, not for gathering lots of evidence.

You need to draw the audience in from the start. You can choose from a wide variety of strategies for this. You can be:

- provocative – "No one in their right mind would subject themselves to the ritual humiliation at school that disguises itself as 'team sports'."

- balanced – "Although many children dislike being forced to participate in school sports, there are strong reasons why they should be considered a compulsory part of the school day."

- illustrative – "There is nothing better than the sight of a game of school cricket, with all it implies about the values of sportsmanship and good health."

- anecdotal, telling a story – "The thought of soccer practice makes me sick. It's not that I'm really sick. It's just that I have to spend time faking illnesses in order to avoid it."

You could also try using a quotation, or a misquotation: "'If at first you don't succeed, try and try again.' Or in my case, on the school sports field, 'If at first you don't succeed, give up.'"

One of the best things that you can do to grab hold of a reader's attention is to present your points in relation to personal experience, as the anecdotal approach demonstrates. You are trying to hook your audience into your writing, to make them carry on reading. Don't be afraid of using your own stories and history to make your points. The best pieces of writing are praised for their originality, in terms of either voice or content, and this is most easily achieved by making some of what you say personal.

Activity 4.11

Write five different openings for an article on compulsory team sports by using each of the strategies outlined here.

Activity 4.12

Read the article by Farrukh Dhondy and then try to analyse how he advances his arguments by using personal examples. Discuss, too, the ways in which he creates a personal voice that aims to persuade you of the validity of his arguments. Dhondy was writing in 2012, just after Britain had hosted the Olympic Games and there was much debate about the role of sports in school, both in the UK and elsewhere in the world. The British Prime Minister, David Cameron, caused considerable offence by suggesting that only team sports were valid forms of exercise.

Text type: prose narrative, India/UK

"Kya Bholey?
Bhej dey soney or
chandi key goley —
Khush rahey guru
or cheyley!"
From *Charasnama* by Bachchoo

The Paralympics have followed the Olympics and are bringing incredible feats to Channel 4's screens every day. The side industry to the grand international summer display, which has overtaken London and indeed the whole of Britain, is the political enthusiasm for sport and the scramble of politicians and worthies to endorse the physical health of the nation. This takes the form not of banning the purveyors of fatty foods or putting extra taxes on hamburgers and chips, but on a feigned concern for the next generation's sporting health.

Politicians are riding the wave of Olympic popularity, so much so that Jeremy Hunt, the British secretary for sport, media and culture has been immediately promoted in a ministerial shuffle to the very heavyweight and responsible post of secretary for health. It is as though a minister for broadcasting in India was suddenly elevated to the post of Prime Minister. Unthinkable!

In Britain the debate rages about the role of sports in the curriculum of schools. British Prime Minister David Cameron and Boris Johnson, the mayor of London, have both made pious statements about the two hours of sport they thoroughly enjoyed during their time at Eton. Their remarks seemed to amount to a demand that all schools should set this as a target.

Mr Cameron went on to say that there was an allocation for compulsory physical education and sport but that some schools were passing off activities such as "Indian dancing" as contributory to this quota. He seemed to disapprove.

I don't suppose that Mr Cameron spends much time watching the likes of Shah Rukh Khan or any of our glamorous actors of both sexes shaking and wobbling their every muscle in the vigorously choreographed and exhausting "item numbers" of contemporary popular Indian cinema and stage. A respectable BBC programme, in a light-hearted but targeted report of Mr Cameron's remarks, made the point, presenting viewers with a troupe performing the most strenuous "Bollywood" routine. Seeing that, one would rather run the marathon. The score? Indian dance and the BBC — 1: David Cameron — 0 and a minus point for being a bit out of touch with multicultural UK.

The other debate on this theme that followed the Olympics was a political dispute over the selling off of sports facilities of schools under the present coalition government and its Tory education secretary Michael Gove.

Mr Gove has, it seems, allowed or encouraged individual schools to sell off their land assets and put the money to alternative use. His defenders argue that schools don't need to own sports facilities, they simply need to have access to them. It reminds me of a quote from the late businessman and fraudster Robert Maxwell who said, "the really rich don't have money, they have access to money."

I hate to agree with fraudsters (or any complacent capitalists for that matter) but my own schooldays in Pune confirm this approach to playing fields — if not to money and richness.

My school in those decades made sport compulsory. We had terms of football, hockey, athletics and seasonal cricket. The hockey and football were played on pitches in the centre of Poona (as it then was) Racecourse. The boarders at the school were marched off from the school gates down one hill and up the other to the plateau where the white staked fences of the racecourse formed an uneven oval.

The players would cross the different racing tracks paved with bark, grass and sand to the enclosed central space and then break into teams. Those of us who were day-scholars and lived at home had to dash off after school, get our "gear" and return at the appropriate time, mostly by bicycle to this racecourse arena.

In the athletics term, our sports training consisted of running around the periphery of this area, probably a good mile and a half distance, a few times in a pseudo-military squad formation with our PE (physical education) teacher riding a bicycle behind us.

The teacher was a Mr Thomas Sewell, a strict but compassionate Welshman who had been an NCO (non-commissioned officer) in the Army of the Raj and had stayed in India after Partition. He was the principal games teacher and when he pursued us on bicycle he carried with him a length of banyan-tree root. He used this flex as a whip to encourage those laggards who fell back to make a greater effort. I carry the marks on my back to this day! (Surely that's a lie! — Ed. Okay yaar, just a bit of currying sympathy — fd)

Sports were the respected dimension of excellence in our school. A 100 per cent score in a trigonometry exam or a perfect performance of a violin sonata was considered nothing compared to being the hockey team's vice-captain. The Captains and the Kings of our school were the boxers and cross-country runners, the young men who were almost always totally indifferent to the achievements or exercise of the intellect or the acquisition of such skills as would contribute to the construction of rockets.

It inspired some in the school, and I have to count myself amongst them, to make a contrary assessment of the real world and come to the conclusion that there was something inherently distorted in the school's value systems. After all Jawaharlal Nehru, Mahatma Gandhi, Albert Einstein or William Shakespeare had probably never been hockey captain of their schools or knocked someone senseless in the boxing ring. Yes, one had to admire Milkha Singh, the Indian Olympian, but even he suffered the derogatory joke: When asked whether he was relaxing he answered, "No, I am Milkha Singh." For me, it was not an anti-Sikh joke, but one that placed athletic achievement in the larger framework of human achievement. Of course, had I known then how much Manchester United footballers or Indian Premier League cricketers earn a week, I may have changed my mind, run faster and not been scarred by banyan roots.

Run and Dance your way to health, The Asian Age,
September 08, 2012, by Farrukh Dhondy

Writing headlines

If you are writing a newspaper or magazine article, comment column, or blog, remember that you should also write a headline to get a reader interested in what you have to say. There are many ways of doing this, but you might like to consider some of the following tried and tested methods.

- Include a number: 10 ways to gain promotion at work.

- Provide an offer: The secrets of promotion at work revealed.

- Make someone want to find out more: How I gained four promotions in three months.

- Be useful and make a promise: How you can win the promotion race at work.

- Be controversial and cheeky: They all hate me, but now I'm the boss.

- Ask a question: Are you stuck in a rut at work?

It could even be seen as a formula (use with care): trigger word or number + adjective + keyword + promise.

For example: Six surefire tricks to achieve promotion in a week.

Above all *be brief*.

Writing a letter

Another task you might be asked to do is to write a letter, most often to a newspaper. The task is usually to outline an issue of concern. You need to remember that this is a formal communication and that it will therefore need to be written using a formal register and tone. This is a specific genre, with very particular conventions.

You are writing as a member of the public in order to argue a point, and you will be addressing both the editor of the newspaper and the wider public.

Make sure that you do the following:

- open the letter formally

- use the first person, either singular (I) or plural (we)

- state clearly the problem or issue that concerns you

- expand on your point by explaining how this problem affects you or others, and give some examples

- try to suggest some possible resolutions to the problem

- review any positive steps that have already been taken to deal with the issue

TIP

Again, you may want to leave a space at the top of your writing and then come back to the headline at the end once you are clear about the shape and general direction of your writing.

Activity 4.13

Collect a range of newspaper or magazine articles and discuss the methods they use to make a reader want to read on, such as layout, sub-headings, different print fonts, illustrations, and so on.

Activity 4.14

Discuss the structure and effectiveness of the letter on page 103 to *Newsweek* magazine.

- be clear about what needs to be done, when, and by whom

- sign off formally.

Here's an example.

Text type: letter to magazine, USA

August 15, 2011

Newsweek
395 Hudson Street
New York,
NY 10014

Re: "The Queen of Rage" (August 15)

To The Editor:

On behalf of the Women's Campaign Forum Foundation (WCF Foundation) and the Women's Media Center, we are writing to express our disappointment with the sexist nature of your August 15th coverage of presidential candidate and Congresswoman Michele Bachmann (MN-06). As organizations committed to eliminating political gender bias in the media, we found the cover photograph, title, and accompanying article to be demeaning and degrading. It is ironic that you also featured Gloria Steinem [an American feminist write and activist] in this issue. As the creator of the name of our joint initiative, *Name It. Change It*, she stresses that media coverage of candidates must pass the test of reversibility – if it wouldn't be directed at a man, it shouldn't be directed at a woman. *Newsweek* failed that test.

Women make up 51% of the United States population, yet occupy only 17% of the seats in Congress and a mere 23% of state legislatures. Only six out of fifty state governors are women. The United States ranks 86th in the world in the number of women elected to public office. Having a greater female presence in government would be exceedingly beneficial to our national discourse, and yet the media continues their disturbing trend of judging women based on their gender rather than their professional merits.

The media's unfair portrayal of women is one of the leading reasons cited by potential female candidates for declining to seek public office[1]. Choosing an unflattering picture of Congresswoman Bachmann and representing her as "The Queen of Rage" is precisely the type of subversive sexism that depresses female involvement and deprives our nation of a much-needed balance in perspective. Our research shows that this type of mild sexism can be just as electorally damaging to female candidates as out-and-out misogyny[2]. In order to combat this, WCF Foundation, Women's Media Center, and Political Parity have joined forces to create our national *Name It. Change It.* initiative. *Name It. Change It.* is a non-partisan project devoted to erasing the pervasiveness of sexism against women candidates across all media platforms. With the U.S. economy in crisis, wars being fought overseas, and attacks on women's health running rampant, it is time to choose our politicians based on their resumes instead of their wardrobes.

Neither WCF Foundation nor Women's Media Center take any position on Congresswoman Bachmann's political views. However, a sexist attack on one woman is an attack on all women, regardless of party. We challenge the editors of *Newsweek* to stop engaging in the same tired, sexist portrayal of women that has become the unfortunate norm in our media. This type of coverage moves our national discourse backward at a time when we need to push ahead. For more information on sexism in the media, we encourage your readers to visit *www.nameitchangeit.org*.

Sincerely,

Siobhan "Sam" Bennett   Julia Burton

President/CEO   President

WCF Foundation   Women's Media Center

[1] Lawless, Jennifer L., and Richard Logan Fox. *It Takes A Candidate: Why Women Don't Run for Office.* Cambridge University Press, 2005.

[2] Lake Research Partners, (September 2010). *Name It. Change It: Sexism & Equality Don't Mix.* http://www.lakeresearch.com/news/NameItChangeIt/NameItChangeIt.pres.pdf

You may be asked to write two contrasting letters, each taking a different point of view about the same issue. In this case, it will be worthwhile trying to establish a different voice for each letter – think back to your work on tone and register to help you with this.

Activity 4.15

Find an article in a paper or magazine that you disagree with the writer's point of view and then write a letter to the editor.

You could also be asked to write an informal letter where, for example, you are writing to a younger relative about how to cope with the transition to a new school. In this case, anything goes in terms of colloquial language and register, but you still need to plan carefully so that you are making logical progress through a range of points. The key here is to keep the audience for your writing clearly in view throughout. If you are writing for an 11-year old, for example, you need to ensure that you use words that are not likely to puzzle them and sentence structures that are easy to follow. Remember, too, that an 11-year old's preoccupations and concerns might be different from yours, with questions about lunch and making friends looming far larger than those about how the college admissions programme is organized.

Activity 4.16

Find some further examples of letters to newspapers or magazines that conform to this genre of letter writing. You could contrast them, perhaps, with the sort of letters that appear on the "problems page" of a magazine.

Activity 4.17

Write a letter to a friend in which you explain your ambitions in life.

Writing a review or report

Writing a review of a cultural or sporting event – a television show, a music festival, a film, a concert, a baseball game – offers a means of showing that you have a strong sense of genre requirements. It also means that you can use your own experience, which tends to give writing a stronger sense of voice and personal involvement.

Text type: movie review, India

Mere Dad Ki Maruti   Review

Mere Dad Ki Maruti

Renuka Vyavahare, TNN, Mar 15, 2013, 06.29 IST

Critic's Rating:	★★★☆☆
Cast:	Saqib Saleem, Ram Kapoor, Prabal Panjabi, Rhea Chakraborty
Direction:	Ashima Chibber
Genre:	Comedy
Duration:	1 hour 41 minutes

Story: *A comedy of errors, the film revolves around a brand new Maruti car which goes missing, days before it is to be presented as a wedding gift!*

Movie Review: Everyone's dancing and making merry in the Khullar household, especially Tej (Ram Kapoor) who is all set to gift would-be son-in-law Raj and daughter Tanvi a brand new Maruti Ertigagaddi on their wedding day. While the wedding preparations are in full swing, Tej's son Sameer (Saqib Saleem) is the daft guy who aspires to woo the hot 'Shakira of Chandigarh' Jazzleen (Rhea Chakraborty). She calls him 'psychic' (thinking it's the same as 'psycho') and he tells her, 'I am love you'.

In order to *patau the pataka*, Sameer uses the new car and ends up losing it! The car goes missing, thus forcing Sameer and his best friend Gattu (Prabal Panjabi) to form a complex web of lies to save Sameer from the wrath of his father.

The film sticks to a YRF's (Yash Raj Films) staple brand of entertainment; it revolves around a Punjabi family, the backdrop a lavish Punjabi wedding. Since the 'Punjabi' card has been used in films for years, it makes the film look a tad conventional.

However, in spite of certain clichés, the film manages to entertain you with its effortless performances, simple story and situational humour. Scenes where Sameer and his friends are being chased by cops, Gattu referring to Sameer's poor English as 'tatti English', are hilarious. The bride's outrageous dance number on her wedding day and the *Kabhi Haan Kabhi Naa-esque* climax are few of the high points of the movie.

Rhea Chakraborty as Jazzleen is easy on the eyes, Prabal Panjabi as Gattu is adorable. He evokes maximum laughter. Saqib Saleem is pleasant but lacks the charisma of a lead actor. Ram Kapoor acts over-the-top as required, Ravi Kissen is wasted.

Don't expect an out-and-out comedy, the film is a light-hearted family entertainer with a message for the youth. Do take your dad along for it, in his gaddi!

Times of India, 15 March 2013, by Renuka Vyavahare
(© 2014, Bennett, Coleman & Co. Ltd)

Text type: movie review, UK

Skyfall, James Bond, review

Daniel Craig remains Bond incarnate in the new James Bond film Skyfall which is often dazzling and always audacious, writes Robbie Collin.

★★★★☆   **By Robbie Collin**

12A cert, 142 min; dir: Sam Mendes; Starring: Daniel Craig, Javier Bardem, Judi Dench, Naomie Harris, Ralph Fiennes, Ben Whishaw, Bérénice Marlohe, Albert Finney

"JAMES BOND WILL RETURN" promise the closing credits of almost every film in the 007 franchise. Yes, but in what form? Set aside the series's pulpy orthodoxies – the cars, the guns, the dames – and Ian Fleming's secret agent is something of a chameleon, either blending in with or cashing in on the movie craze du jour. Think of Moonraker, rushed into production after Star Wars took popular cinema into orbit, or Live and Let Die, exploiting blaxploitation, or the twitchy, unsmiling Quantum of Solace, Bond's latter-day Bournefication.

Skyfall, the often dazzling, always audacious new entry directed by Sam Mendes, is no different. For better or worse we live in the age of the superhero, and so Mendes's film is less hardboiled spy saga than blistering comic-book escapade. The template here is Christopher Nolan's The Dark Knight, a film that has almost singlehandedly reconfigured the modern blockbuster since its 2008 release, when it left Quantum of Solace bobbing in its wake.

We join Bond in Istanbul, chasing a stolen computer disk that contains the secret identities of embedded Nato agents. After a hair-raising chase across marketplaces, rooftops and a thundering train, the disk is lost, and for a moment so is 007. But after a gothic title sequence he rematerialises in London, older, unshaven and off his game. Nevertheless, M (Judi Dench) puts him back on the case, which takes him to some of the world's most exotic corners: Shanghai, Macau, Glencoe...

Daniel Craig remains Bond incarnate, although six years on from Casino Royale he has become something more than a brawny cipher. There's a warmth to his banter with pretty field agent Eve (Naomie Harris), the one-liners make a tentative return, and we even learn about the loss of Bond's parents: the must-have back story for this season's conflicted superhero.

Neal Purvis, Robert Wade and John Logan's script constantly reminds us Bond's physical prowess is on the wane, but his verbal sparring, both with M and new foe Raoul Silva (Javier Bardem), a former agent turned vengeful computer hacker, is nimbler than ever.

Silva is almost as inscrutable as The Dark Knight's Joker himself: Bardem's lip-lickingly camp turn makes him the oddest Bond villain since the Roger Moore era, and his nicotine hair flops queasily over his forehead in a way that calls to mind Julian Assange. By acknowledging the rise of cyberterrorism in the same way Nolan played on the West's new vulnerability in the wake of 9/11, Skyfall is a Bond film for the Anonymous generation.

Mendes, whose American Beauty and Revolutionary Road were light on explosions, lets the quieter moments breathe, and a conversation between Bond and Silva that's simply buttered with innuendo drew cheers at an early preview screening. But Mendes is rather good at being loud, too, and his nine times Oscar-nominated cinematographer Roger Deakins makes the wildly ambitious action sequences the most beautiful in Bond's 50-year career. (The release of Skyfall marks the series' half-centenary.) The sensational Istanbul prologue is soon bettered by the Shanghai segment, where Bond pursues an assassin through a soaring glass skyscraper lit up like a neon Aurora Borealis.

It's pearls like these, not to mention the deliriously arch fight scene involving two komodo dragons, that give Mendes's film enough momentum to power through its scrappy third act, when Silva's diabolical plans start to feel a tad scattershot, even for a Bond villain.

"We don't go in for exploding pens any more," quips a fashionably tousled Q (Ben Whishaw). Nor do audiences, and I suspect Skyfall will be a stratospheric hit.

The Daily Telegraph, 24 October 2012, by Robbie Collin

Activity 4.18

Thinking about the genre table from Chapter 2 and paying particular attention to register, write a review of a film or a TV show that you have seen recently.

Activity 4.19

Go back to your work on genre and register in Chapter 2. Try to establish the rules that apply to the writing of reviews. Look too at differences and variations that are obviously acceptable within the genre. You will recognize the table below from Chapter 2. Complete it for each of the reviews above.

	Mere Dad Ki Maruti	Skyfall
Author		
Audience		
Purpose		
Situation		
Physical form		
Constraints/rules		
Content		
Level of formality/register		
Style		
Written language		
Structure		

Writing a voiceover or a speech

The first thing to understand is that writing a voiceover or speech is very different from writing for the printed page. When you're reading a book, magazine, or web page you can go at your own pace, and even skip back and re-read bits that aren't clear. Audio is different. When you write a script, you need to remember that your listeners have to understand your words the first (and maybe only) time they hear them.

So your number-one priority is to write English that is clear and simple. That sounds easy, but it isn't. If you aim for simplicity, the big danger is that your voiceover ends up sounding like a teacher talking to a class of five-year-olds. That's patronizing, and the last thing you want to do is alienate your listeners, especially if you're trying to persuade them or to sell them something.

The trick is to aim for a conversational effect, a suitable register. That doesn't mean you have to be chatty or informal. It means using the style and tone of voice you would use if you were having a direct, honest, face-to-face conversation.

The best way to do this is to be as specific and direct as possible, starting with the words you use. The difference between a good voice-over script or speech and a bad one often comes down to word choice. Keep your words simple, preferring short ones to long ones. Avoid business and marketing jargon. Above all, use concrete words rather than abstract ones. Try to create pictures with your words.

That means steering clear of words like cost-effective, efficient, impact, focused, competent, and cutting-edge. They are difficult for listeners to grasp right away, and you'll be making life hard for the speaker who has to get his or her mouth round them. Choose words that are easy to listen to, and easy to say: fast, low-cost, free, now, great.

You also need to limit the length of your sentences. In general, short is good, but if every sentence in your voice-over script is short, you'll find that the whole thing sounds stilted and a bit awkward. Aim for variation: one good technique is to use a relatively long sentence followed by a very short one or a long sentence followed by a phrase (no main verb), possibly repeating a key idea, as here:

> Come to Dave's Garage for Miami's best prices on tires. Best prices guaranteed!

Any sentences longer than 20–25 words may need to be split into two, and you should aim for an average length somewhere in the region of 8–15 words.

When you're writing your script, the best tool available to you is reading aloud (but not in an examination situation). Write a draft, then read it out. Don't whisper or mumble – blast it out in a good, strong, clear voice. When you're doing dry runs like these, take care to **enunciate** clearly, just like a speaker would. That means making all the syllables of a word stand out crisply and clearly, while still maintaining a relatively natural tone of voice. If you're doing it properly, you should find that you're using your teeth and the muscles in the lower part of your face and jaw more than you would in normal conversation.

You could even record yourself. Ask yourself how does this sound? Are there any parts of the script that seem jumbled or untidy, even if they make perfect grammatical sense on the page?

More importantly, did you find yourself tripping up or struggling to say particular words or phrases clearly? Those are the danger points in your script that you need to revisit and perhaps rewrite. If you have to work hard to say something clearly, the audience for your speech – whether it's part of a radio advertisement, an e-learning tutorial, or a podcast – might have a hard time understanding it.

Remember that reading aloud is your most valuable tool. Write an initial draft, read it aloud, spot the problems, and re-write accordingly. Keep going through this process. If possible, get other people to read it.

Now have a look at a speech by a student who has been asked to address a conference of teachers about the power and influence of the media:

Text type: planned speech, India

The model on the glossy magazine cover page captivates its readers, as she wears a gorgeous Versace outfit revealing her paper-thin, fragile body. Her soft-cushioned flawless white skin attracts and mesmerizes the reader's eyes, but there is something disturbing about that model's lean, sleek, malnourished body structure, almost mocking the reader for an unattainable body just like hers.

The readers fantasize about this "size 0" cult and develop an obsession about this "utopia" world of fashion.

The media, thus, definitely has a major impact on the masses, overshadowing the "realistic" world. The growth of the impact is so rapid that without media's influence, businesses slack out and brand ambassadors may not survive and influence the people. Admittedly, the "visual media" brings about this obsessive state of mind and changes the patterns of brain chemistry in most young teenage women.

Children also are desensitized at a very early age as they believe that the "violent" animated shows are not so different from reality.

The first global impact of the media is to imitate the super glamorized images of paper-thin models. Women who view such models further feel worse about themselves and that leads to extremely low self-esteem and, ultimately, depression.

According to statistics, 80% of the teenage girls mimic their favourite celebrities on screen and feel insecure about their own self-image.

Has the media any right to destroy an individual's identity?

The media has immense power to drive the society in a stereotypical way. Consequently, media betrays its own purpose of projecting "the truth" to the society, as it is controlled by influential people. Instead of making people aware of various scams and scandals of the political or social world, it successfully hides and reverses the picture. It promotes the wrongful acts of the political leaders and allows hooliganism and vandalism.

Furthermore, media has developed the power to mislead the masses while portraying deceitful images of famous people. Market gimmicks are practised in the name of charity and noble causes. These could be utilized in better developmental areas of health and education.

In conclusion, though media has immense power to influence its readers, it also uses its power to contradict its own purpose. Nevertheless, it can utilize its power in a more positive way and build a bond of trust with its readers.

Thank you.

Student, India

Activity 4.20

How effective do you find this speech?

You should think about:

- structure
- audience
- content
- creation of voice
- fluency in terms of a text that is to be spoken, not read.

If there are any parts that you find slightly difficult to follow, re-write them.

Now, using the original, see if you can expand some of the ideas so that the speaker could give a rather more detailed talk. You should stay with the original's structure.

Another speaker, a representative of the media industry, has been invited to speak next. Write his or her response. Read it aloud to your classmates – they might spot problems you miss.

Activity 4.21

In Chapter 2 there are a number of examples of speeches. Go back to them now and consider their effectiveness as examples of scripted spoken language in the light of what you have just read.

When writing a voice-over, you may also want to indicate to your reader the images that will accompany the voice (imagine that this is being vetted before going into production). Remember that the words are only part of the ultimate product.

Consider the following voice-over by David Attenborough in the introduction to his series of nature films about Africa. Remember that Africa, not Attenborough, is the star of the show.

Text type: voice-over, UK

Various shots of Africa – dung beetles, mountain ranges, elephants, flamingos, wildlife footage.

Voice-over (Attenborough): **"Africa. The world's greatest wilderness. The only place on earth to see the full majesty of nature. There's so much more here than we ever imagined."**

Cut to picture of Attenborough talking to camera on top of a hill:

"I'm standing where the equator cuts right across the middle of the continent. To the north of me there's an immense desert the size of the United States of America. To the west, a vast rainforest the size of India. And behind me, for thousands of miles, the most fertile savannahs in the world."

Cut to other pictures of Africa – waterfalls, mountains, jungle, gorillas, lions.

Voice-over (Attenborough): **"From the roof of Africa, to the deepest jungle. Rarely seen places and untold stories."**

Cut to Attenborough: **"There's nowhere in the world where wildlife puts on a greater show."**

Voice-over (Attenborough): **"This is the last place on earth** (cut to Attenborough) **where you can come eye to eye with the greatest animals that walk our planet."**

Cut to more pictures.

Voice-over (Attenborough): **"This is Africa."**

Activity 4.22

Write the opening to a voice-over for a video prospectus for your school or college, with a view to making it attractive to both new students and their parents.

Orwell's checklist of good practice

This a checklist of good practice that can be used no matter what sort of text you are trying to produce. It was written by George Orwell.

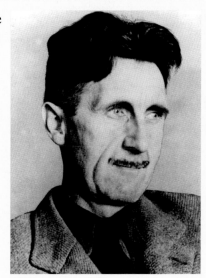

George Orwell

- Never use a metaphor, simile, or other figure of speech that you are used to seeing in print.

- Never use a long word where a short one will do.

- If it is possible to cut a word out, always cut it out.

- Never use the passive when you can use the active.

- Never use a foreign phrase, a scientific word, or a jargon word if you can think of an everyday English equivalent.

- Break any of these rules sooner than say anything outright barbarous.

Activity 4.23

Discuss Orwell's rules for effective writing. Do you agree that these are sound principles? Are there any further points that you would add?

Conclusion

In this chapter you have:

- reviewed different types of question that you might be asked to respond to in order to demonstrate your understanding of others' writing

- thought in detail about your own writing strategies for producing a wide variety of texts for a range of audiences.

Assessment

How to use this chapter

All of the samples in this chapter have been written under timed conditions (one hour per answer) by real students who are studying for a qualification in English language at this level. They have been reproduced as written, including errors in spelling and grammar. You might want to write a response to each question for yourself before comparing it to the work of others.

Writing a commentary and imaginative response

Your assessor will be asked to work with a mark scheme. Unlike a mathematics exam, this subject is not content-led, so the marks will be based on you demonstrating a variety of skills, not on notionally "right" or "wrong" answers. In other words, the assessor will read what you offer and then try to fit your response to a series of criteria. The assessor will take an overall view of what you have done (a "holistic" approach) and will try to balance the strengths and weaknesses of your response.

> **TIP**
> There are more marks for the commentaries (15) than for the directed writing (10), so you must allocate your time proportionally.

Question A: commentaries

You will need to show that you have understood the passage given and that you are aware of matters of structure, form, audience, and purpose. Discussions of genre and style will be central. Without being comprehensive and covering every aspect of the passage, you will need to demonstrate how language creates effects. To do this, you will need to move easily between matters of detail and of general significance. Your work should be presented in a logical form, with your points supported by direct reference to the text.

We can simplify all of this out into a series of prompts that you could use each time you tackle an analysis. Ask yourself if you have:

- communicated a secure knowledge of the text and its context (if given)
- given relevant responses to key themes and ideas in the text
- produced coherent, accurate, and well-structured writing

- used suitable terminology
- analysed and shown an understanding of the form (shape) of the text
- looked at the structure of the text
- analysed aspects of the text's language
- supported your ideas with relevant, brief quotations
- checked for errors in expression and punctuation.

Question B: directed writing

Here you should demonstrate a willingness to shape a piece of writing in imitation of the original. You will need to show that you understand the requirements of the exercise in terms of form, style, content, and audience, and your response will need to be fluent and accurate.

As you write you could usefully have the following prompts in mind to keep you on track, as noted on page 85:

- register
- audience
- purpose
- point of view.

Sample question 1

The following passage is an extract from the speech given by Nelson Mandela at his inauguration as the first President of the Democratic Republic of South Africa on 10 May 1994. Before this, during the time of apartheid (white rule with different laws for the black population), Mandela spent many years as a political prisoner.

- **Question A:** Comment on the style and language of the speech.
- **Question B:** The same speaker delivers another speech to the United Nations. In it, he suggests that South Africa can be a model for other countries that need to heal wounds after periods of political disturbance. Write the opening of the speech (120–150 words).

Base your answer closely on the style and language of the original extract.

Text type: scripted speech, South Africa

We, the people of South Africa, feel fulfilled that humanity has taken us back into its bosom, that we, who were outlaws not so long ago, have today been given the rare privilege to be host to the nations of the world on our own soil.

We thank all our distinguished international guests for having come to take possession with the people of our country of what is, after all, a common victory for justice, for peace, for human dignity.

We trust that you will continue to stand by us as we tackle the challenges of building peace, prosperity, non-sexism, non-racialism and democracy.

We deeply appreciate the role that the masses of our people and their political mass democratic, religious, women, youth, business, traditional and other leaders have played to bring about this conclusion. Not least amongst them is my Second Deputy President, the Honourable F.W. de Klerk.

We would also like to pay tribute to our security forces, in all their ranks, for the distinguished role they have played in securing our first democratic elections and the transition to democracy, from blood-thirsty forces which still refuse to see the light.

The time for the healing of the wounds has come.

The moment to bridge the chasms that divide us has come.

The time to build is upon us.

We have, at last, achieved our political emancipation. We pledge ourselves to liberate all our people from the continuing bondage of poverty, deprivation, suffering, gender and other discrimination.

We succeeded to take our last steps to freedom in conditions of relative peace. We commit ourselves to the construction of a complete, just and lasting peace.

We have triumphed in the effort to implant hope in the breasts of the millions of our people. We enter into a covenant that we shall build the society in which all South Africans, both black and white, will be able to walk tall, without any fear in their hearts, assured of their inalienable right to human dignity - a rainbow nation at peace with itself and the world.

As a token of its commitment to the renewal of our country, the new Interim Government of National Unity will, as a matter of urgency, address the issue of amnesty for various categories of our people who are currently serving terms of imprisonment.

We dedicate this day to all the heroes and heroines in this country and the rest of the world who sacrificed in many ways and surrendered their lives so that we could be free.

Their dreams have become reality. Freedom is their reward.

We are both humbled and elevated by the honour and privilege that you, the people of South Africa, have bestowed on us, as the first President of a united, democratic, non-racial and non-sexist South Africa, to lead our country out of the valley of darkness.

We understand it still that there is no easy road to freedom.

We know it well that none of us acting alone can achieve success.

We must therefore act together as a united people, for national reconciliation, for nation building, for the birth of a new world.

Let there be justice for all.

Let there be peace for all.

Let there be work, bread, water and salt for all.

Let each know that for each the body, the mind and the soul have been freed to fulfil themselves.

Never, never and never again shall it be that this beautiful land will again experience the oppression of one by another and suffer the indignity of being the skunk of the world.

The sun shall never set on so glorious a human achievement!

Let freedom reign.

God bless Africa!

Nelson Mandela's inaugural speech

Scripted speech – response 1
Question A

Mandela's lexis is primarily positive, wholey reflecting on the mood and atmosphere of not only himself, but the nation of South Africa.

Firstly Mandela's use of a tripartite structure, 'Let there be justice for all. Let there be peace for all. Let there be work, bread, water and salt for all', illustrates how Mandela is attempting to raise spirits of South African people, through his use of emphatic linguistic features. The use of the abstract nouns shows how Mandela will attempt to bring such things as 'justice' and 'peace a true sense of meaning during his time in power, whereas previously these things may have seemed abstract and unreachable. For him to then mention basic necessities and simple human wants such as 'bread', 'water' and 'salt shows how Mandela believes that the abstract nouns spoken of above, should be and will be as simple to obtain or see as bread and water. Finally, Mandela assures this to his people through the imperative 'let.' The imperatives makes it seem as if this plan of his is certain to be acheived but through the use of the dynamic verb 'let', it has a sense that he is asking the inhabitants of South Africa to not stop these changes and allow him to change their country for the better.

Secondly, throughout his speech, Mandela uses the personal pronoun of 'we' on a number of occasions. In using this Mandela makes the speech personal to every person listening, giving them a sense of accomplishment in helping towards his release. Also, by making the speech so personal, it makes the listeners feel more involved in what he's saying, therefore listening closer to every word.

Finally, Mandela tries to reflect himself in a manner of high interlect, trustworthiness and reliability all through his use of polysyllabic, high register, low frequency lexis. This is illustrated though lexis such as 'emancipation', 'reconciliation' and 'discrimination' with the effect being that he appears to the audience of a man who they feel comfortable in giving the power of their country to. Consequentially, as Mandela refers to the 'distinguished international guests' present at his inauguration, this sophisticated lexis reflects well on South Africa, with countries leaders possibly thinking of starting a trade partnership with Mandela's South Africa as a result of how Mandela has presented himself and his country.

In conclusion, Mandela's style is sophisticated and flamboyant and his language reflects this as well. He is aiming on making a good impression on his voters and it is clear that he achieives it thusly.

Question B

I sat in that prison cell, day after day, wondering how the country I loved was coping under the regime I fought against so strong. However, as I sat there, I did not weep, I did not pity in my sorrows, I kept faith. Faith that in the end has brought me to where I am at at this very moment. And Ladies and Gentleman, if you want to replicate the astonishing show of courage and love for a flag that we have all seen in my great nation of South Africa, you need just one thing, faith.

Faith is a powerful thing. It can be felt, seen, used by many, and when the opposition try to tarnish your faith, it only grows stronger. They will try to bring you down to their level with violence but do not be foolish enough to sink to their level, stay strong, remain as an enmity. If you have faith and show strength as a movement you will be given opportunities and that is when you must put your faith to use. All the emotions you feel within must be translated to your public, and if you can achieve all of this, you too will be able to see the prosperity that I do.

Comments on response to Question A

The response deals carefully with a range of linguistic points that are linked to matters of content. Points are usually clearly made, although there is a slight lack of fluency in the paragraph about inclusive pronouns. There is a logical structure. However, there is not much overview, and this leads to the points appearing to be slightly randomly presented. The discussion about lexis makes clear, interesting points about Mandela's emerging status as a world leader and how he tries to engineer this. More could be made of the speech as an example of scripted spoken language. The final paragraph adds little to the discussion. The writer has avoided the temptation to go through the passage line by line. This is competent work that demonstrates ability, though its lack of depth would prevent it from receiving a top-level mark.

Comments on response to Question B

The writing picks up some aspects of Mandela's tone and makes good use of "tripartite structures". However, having identified inclusive pronouns and formal, at times ultra-formal register in section A, the writer does not make clear use of them in this section. There is a clear sense of audience throughout. A high-level sense of the original speaker's voice would make this a better response. Again, the work is competent.

Scripted speech – response 2

Question A

The prepared speech by Nelson Mandela has many linguistic features. There is a huge repetition of 'we' and 'us' which presents the idea that Mandela has wanted to make sure the people of South Africa know that they are united and the use of the pronouns 'we' and 'us' creates a sense that the country is whole, as well as engages all of the audience together, which is reinforced when he says 'we must therefore act together as a united people', the use of the word 'must,' emphasising the force of his words which also highlights the idea that he is sure of what he is saying, so the audience has no doubt to his words and may also have been used to persuade the audience that they must act in this way or the country will fall again, and there will be different laws for the black population again. Therefore 'must' could have been used as a scare tactic, as it is a command which is reinforced by use of another strong modal verb 'will' which is also repeated throughout the text. By using the modal 'will', Mandela has again managed to create a sense of certainty to his words, whilst reinforcing the idea to himself and persuading the audience that everything he is saying – 'will be able to walk tall,' 'you will continue to stand by us' is true, and it will happen, managing to gain the trust of the audience.

The text also contains imagery. The use of the imagery 'humanity has taken us back into its bosom,' 'implant hope into the breasts of the millions of our people,' 'out of the valley of darkness,' helps the audience to visualise the consequences, and emphasises the severity of the situation. In the first piece of imagery, the use of the phrase 'taken us back into its bosom,' gives the imagery of being cared for and safe, which is reinforced by when he says 'implant hope into the breasts.' This imagery of breasts, highlights back to when people were cared for when they were babies by their mothers, which creates a sense of purity and innocence, whilst being cared for and looked after in this new South Africa. This contrasts when he says 'out of the valley of darkness,' which presents the imagery that pre Nelson Mandela being freed was a very dark, sinister place, with the use of the common noun 'valley' emphasising the idea that it was a deep area, giving the imagery that it was a hard place to come out of, and that the depth of the darkness was hard to be freed from and perhaps they were trapped. This contrast reminds the audience of how horrible the old South Africa was, which gives a greater sense of freedom and happiness to Mandela's speech. This is also reinforced by his use of the phrase 'rainbow nation,' creating a sense of being a happy, bright future, as the black population and white population can live together peacefully.

In this speech separate lines start with 'let,' 'let there be work, bread, water and salt for all.' This highlights the gravity and forcefulness of his words again, as each line holds more importance than the next. In this, Mandela is building up the tension, which would help to encourage the crowd to believe in his words and pull together and highlight what he is stating to achieve while being president and what he considers is best for the country and its people. By using tripartite structure and lists, Mandela has created the sense that the country and its people can achieve more than what he has just stated 'for justice, for peace, for human dignity.' He has also left 'human dignity' until the end of the line, and thus he is emphasising human dignity, possibly implying that without it, justice and peace can't and will not follow. By leaving this till last, he is stating that it is the most important quality people can have.

Finally, Mandela uses polysyllabic lexis 'humbled and elevated,' 'honour and privilege,' 'bestowed,' because as it is a prepared speech and he is educated, he will need to sound sophisticated. It also helps to persuade the audience of the certainty of his words, especially with the juxtaposition of 'humbled and elevated' implying his overall mood is elevated, and he considers this to be most important and possibly what he wants the people of the country to feel also.

Question B

We all know what our countries in the United Nations need. Equality, justice, peace.

I come to you today with hope in my heart and certainty in my mind that we can all come together, will come together, to support, protect and care for each other.

South Africa, a country that was deemed hopeless, that we thought would never be united, never see the light, never survive the darkness, has done just that.

The impossible.

My friends, Nelson Mandela has been freed. To bring hope, justice, peace and equality to the country once again and end the divide between the white and black population. End the endless gap between right and poor. End the poverty, despair, hunger for freedom in everyone.

We my friends can learn from these actions. We too can unite and prosper.

Comments on response to Question A

This is sophisticated and perceptive work, worthy of a high mark even though there are some moments where the writing is not completely fluent. The writer has a clear list of linguistically based points to discuss, and they are reviewed one by one in paragraphs that analyse in order to develop an overall view of the methods, strategies, and context of the original. Points about the language of the passage are discussed first, and then the writer moves on to matters of syntax. This gives the response a clear line of argument because the writer has dealt with things serially, rather than with the slightly random approach taken in response 1. Quotation from the speech is used selectively and with discrimination to substantiate the points made.

Comments on response to Question B

Again, this piece shows high level of skill in the subject. The writer picks up on a full range of Mandela's techniques, both lexical and syntactic, and incorporates them. Lists of three and repetitions are clearly used, as are inclusive pronouns and imperatives. The register is appropriate to a formal occasion, with abstract nouns ("justice" and so on) echoing Mandela's use of polysyllabic diction. The image pattern of light and dark creates the same sort of vividness that Mandela gains from his line about the sun never setting and South Africa's emergence from the "valley of darkness". Ideas here are original but the techniques used to express them can all be traced to aspects of Mandela's speech.

Sample question 2

The extract below is a newspaper article about raising children.

- **Question A:** Comment on the style and language of the extract.
- **Question B:** The same author is asked to write an article about the difficulties of supermarket shopping for the following week's paper. Write the opening (120–150) words of his column. Base your answer closely on the style and language of the original extract.

Text type: opinion column, journalism, New Zealand

Relax and enjoy kids

How did raising kids ever get so bloody complicated? Our parents had it far easier than us. Oh sure, they had little things to worry about - like the Cold War, Rogernomics[1] and carless days - but generally speaking, parenting was a doddle back then.

For one thing, self-esteem hadn't been invented, which made their job much easier. Instead of worrying about whether or not we had enough of it, they just got on with things.

Conveniently, they weren't burdened with guilt if they smacked our bottoms. Politicians left children's bottoms alone in those days, which seemed to work quite well.

Another reason our parents had it easier is that they had to look after only their own social life. It wasn't their responsibility to make sure that we had one as well. They didn't have to arrange "play dates", because we simply walked to our friends' houses.

What's more, after-school activities were much easier to schedule, because there were none. After-school activities consisted of whatever you wanted to do, as long as you didn't get into trouble.

Parents did not have to organise ballet, art classes, after-school maths tuition, Pippins[2], athletics, soccer, drama, advanced drama, hip-hop classes, swimming lessons and karate.

Most of all, they did not have to suffer the long darkness of the soul that is Tee-ball season.

Those were also the days before punishment became extinct. Instead of giving little Tarquin time to reflect on his poor choices, they just punished him, which took a lot less time. We have cunningly replaced the p-word with the c-word: "consequences". Why? Because after they invented self-esteem, we had to get rid of punishment, which makes children feel bad. We don't want children to feel bad. Oh no, we want them to "make better choices". We want them to feel good all the time.

I cannot wait until the children raised under this new regime graduate to adulthood, because then I will finally start reaping the benefits. Once these kids are running the IRD[3], I won't be fined for not paying my taxes on time, I will simply be asked politely but firmly to "make better choices". If I don't pay up, they won't take my house, they will simply utilise "planned ignoring" and look for more positive behaviours to reinforce.

Education was much easier in those days, too. For instance, our parents did not have to attend endless meetings about our behaviour because the teachers were still allowed to discipline children. If I was bad, I was strapped, and then, as I grew older and my buttocks grew more robust, I was caned. Incredibly, neither of these experiences led to my choosing a life of crime and violence. Instead, I came to the stellar conclusion that being good and following the rules meant that life was less painful.

Most of all, our parents were lucky because Google had not been invented. If they didn't know something, they just had to muddle on. When I googled "parenting advice", I got 7,340,000 hits. Similarly, toilet training got me 1,430,000 hits. Even "children's self-esteem" got me 1,630,000 hits. Pick one - any one. Hell, pick two, because there's a ton of advice to go round.

One can't help but wonder if this is all getting just a bit out of hand.

From Nigel Latta, *The New Zealand Herald*, 3 June 2007

1. The economic policies of Roger Douglas, New Zealand's Minister of Finance in 1984.
2. The most junior section of the girl guide movement for 5 to 7 year olds.
3. The New Zealand tax office.

Journalism – response 1

Question A

The purpose of this text is to express the vast number of changes in parenting that have occurred between his childhood and his children's childhood. The journalist has expressed this through the use of the verbs 'invented' and 'extinct'. These contrast and help show that anything in his children's life is new and was not existent before and anything from his childhood is extinct. There is no overlap between the two generations, and this helps to show his view on the divide between the generations. He explains his school activities 'were much easier' the use of the pre-modifying auxiliary verb 'were' suggests that this ease of living is for the past and is no longer accurate for today's standards. It emphasises that when he was younger there was no need to scheudal making a direct comparison to how it is today. The comparative verb 'easier' also shows that he finds that he fit into the old way of living much less difficult.

As well the writer showing a clear divide between the two generations with the activities that they share and things they have he didn't. The people's views are also shown to be presented differently. 'I will simply be asked politely but firmly to "make better choices".' If I don't pay up they won't take my house, they will simply utilise "planned ignoring."' The writer's use of inverted commas, show that these are someone else's words, not his own. And show that either he doesn't agree with what they would say to him, or that he believes now that all they would say to him because 'nowadays' everyone seems to have the same view on this and punishment is 'extinct' as well as the idea of people having new ideas and ways of viewing a situation there have also been an introduction to new activities in this generation. 'Ballet, art classes, after-school maths tuition, Pippins, Keas, athletics, soccer, drama, advanced drama, hip-hop classes, swimming lessons and karate.' The use of this list helps to show the sheer quantity of the activities available compared to his activities 'because there were none.' This again helps to explain why he sees this generation as having over active over planned lives. Getting a better idea of his view by looking at the adverbs he chooses to use such as 'burdened,' 'responsibility,' to show how unwilling and opposed he is to these changes of life style.

The writer chooses to use a contrast between the childhood he knows and understands to that of the childhood he has witnessed.

Question B

If it weren't for childrens TV the weekly shop would become so much easier. I find myself having to drag my screaming child away from the Cocopops, while he sings the theme tune through his tears. I can't explain to him that things cost money, because all he cares about is THAT monkey cartoon on the front and having chocolate milk in his breakfast bowl in the morning.

Conveniently, I now know all the songs and words to the advert, for at least one item on every aisle, which seems to keep shopping time a fairly interesting experience for the song competition amongst my family.

Although this is interesting, the brands cost far more, making my weekly shop cost extaushionate prices. Gone are the days when you went to the individual small town shops for those special items, and got a fair price. I now find myself having to check the price of everything I buy or I have to come back with half the food for the same amount.

Comments on Question A

The opening paragraph here contains many ideas and some support. However, there is no clear line of discussion, and in trying to deal with both content and style at the same time, the response becomes rather unfocused. As the writer moves on, there is some engagement with lexis and grammar, although technical terms are not securely used. Some of them are not fully understood, perhaps. There is a tendency to narrate what is going on in the passage rather than to offer strategic points about the writer's techniques. Points are made but not developed, and at times the piece lacks coherence.

Comments on Question B

Like Latta, the writer here makes a strong and personal opening point. There is an engaging tone, and what is said seems to come from direct experience. The response to the content of Latta's original is strong, but the parallels in terms of linguistic imitation are more limited. Sentences are short, as with Latta, and the lexis is straightforward and informal. Contrasts of past and present are not developed. There is no headline to show understanding of genre, although the purpose of the piece is clear. There are some technical errors too: childrens not children's, extaushionate, not extortionate.

Journalism – response 2

Question A

This extract from a newspaper article referencing raising children and parenting techniques adopts a causal and friendly tone from the start. It opens with a rhetorical question which can be seen as setting up an informal, chatty style. The use of the phrase 'Oh, sure' emphasises the lighthearted tone the author of the article has adopted, which is added to further by the use of the colloquialism 'doddle.'

The first paragraph introduces the use of collectives, which continue throughout the article. 'Our parents,' creates a sense of unity between both the author and the reader, but also the generation as a whole, who during their childhood had experienced the way of life the author refers to. Nigel Latta, the journalist responsible for this article appears to view his generations childhood as far preferable to today's, as the parenting skills recquired were minimal. He portrays parenting today as a difficult, incredibly time consuming task, emphasised by the use of the long list of activities that parents are expected to organise.

There is a clear semantic field of hardship and struggling which parents face by the use of the verb 'worrying' and 'burdened with guilt.' Also the description of the 'Tee-ball season' as the 'long darkness of the soul' although this is clear use of exaggeration for dramatic effect it portrays parenthood as a difficult, labourious task. The article also contains a great sense of nostalgia, how everything appeared to be so much easier and preferable in the past. However, in recent times 'punishment became extinct.' The use of the lexical choice 'extinct' suggests that the author and readers parents methods of parenting are dead and gone, with such attitudes towards firm simple discipline being practically prehistoric in comparison to the present day.

Furthermore, there is a synical tone when referencing how these children who have been subjected to no real punishment or instillment of boundaries will grow up. There is a hint of sarcasm as these children who have been indulged with 'ballet, art classes.... drama, advanced drama' but have lacked any punishment will fail in later life to implement rules, and in the instance mentioned, the law. As instead of punishing someone who doesn't pay their taxes, they will merely politely request that they 'make better choices.'

The fact that Latta uses the adjective 'kids' in 'once these kids are running the IRD' suggests that these children will not mature and learn due to the lack of good, solid parenting that Latta and his generation are an outcome of.

Question B

Since when did supermarket shopping become so difficult? The moment you step foot in the door, you are bombarded by bargains and special offers, 'Buy one get one free,' 'Three for the price of two' is all you can see plastered across the aisles.

Years ago if you needed the basic items such as bread, milk and eggs, you would be in and out within ten minutes, leaving with exactly what you came for, and satisfied with your purchases.

Nowadays, however, it is a different story, you pop up to the supermarket for the essentials and emerge an hour and a half later, feeling stressed, and significantly worse off financially, returning home with bags upon bags of goods you know you don't need.

I'm not saying it's our fault, oh no, the supermarkets have just identified our weakness and exploited it....

Comments on Question A

The writer covers a range of points. The piece is clearly identified as an opinion column. Several of Latta's techniques are located and analysed, and there is clear awareness that Latta is writing humorously while at the same time making some serious points. Discussions are detailed and are continuously supported by evidence from the text. There is a strong structure, based on linguistic issues, rather than discussing the content of the passage. Towards the end, the points become slightly disjointed: each is relevant, but they are not linked into an overall argument. Small technical errors do not spoil the overall flow of the writing, and work of this quality would score high (though not the highest) marks.

Comments on Question B

The writer reproduces the first-person narrative viewpoint and slightly humorous yet grumpy, ironic, tone of the original with skill. Both open with a question and there is a specific audience in view throughout. A headline might have contributed too in order to emphasize that this is an opinion column from a newspaper or magazine. Sentences and paragraphs are brief, echoing the structure of Latta's piece. The informal, colloquial expression "doddle" is echoed by "pop up" here. Contrasts between past and present are managed in the same way as in the original. The writer has only a limited space, so has decided to focus on techniques used in the opening of Latta's article. This is a sensible, strategic choice. This is strong work that should be highly rewarded.

Imaginative writing

Ideally you will take an original, imaginative approach to the task. This means that you must be careful to avoid the sort of responses that all other candidates will give. Your originality might be expressed through an unusual point of view, the creation of an interesting voice or through structural devices, if not through originality of subject matter. You will be aiming to create a tight structure and to create effects through your use of language. Your writing will be fluent and relevant, with few mechanical errors. Above all, you will want to create a piece of writing that sustains a reader's interest throughout.

As you write therefore you need to ensure that you are paying attention to the following:

- voice and point of view

> **TIP**
>
> Get a friend to read all of your work with the bullet points from the beginning of the chapter in view and then offer some comments on what you have written. This doesn't have to be an expert; you just need someone to check that what you have done is clear and relevant.

> **TIP**
>
> Often it is useful to write down four or five ideas for a piece and then pause and ask yourself which of them is the most obvious. The chances are that hundreds of other candidates will choose the same one, so if you want top marks you have to choose something slightly more unusual.

- originality, either of content or technique
- imaginative and controlled use of language and syntax
- clear expression.

Sample question 1

Write the opening to a novel called *The Visitor*. In your writing, create a mood of anxiety and uncertainty.

Novel opening – response 1

I woke. Sounds filled the space around me, but I heard them distorted, indirectly, as one might hear a voice when submerged in a pool of water. I decided best to keep my eyes closed for the time being, for as long as it took me to regain my hearing properly, allowing each sense to return individually lest I should be overwhelmed by my new surroundings. How I had come to be here was not entirely absent from my memory, but rather came through in short flashes of the mind: an image here, a half-remembered sentence there. Contrary to my plan to allow each sense its own time to adjust and return to me, my sense of tough acted of its own accord altogether, bringing with it the sensation of metal – yes, some form of cold metal against which my hands and feet were pressed. Touching about the place, I found my location to be cylindrical, scarcely more than three feet in diameter and extending a mere inch or two above my head in its height. It was I that moment too that my olfactory senses jumped the gun: smoke, seeming almost viscous as it poured into my lungs with my next breath, causing a hacking cough. I knew I had to escape from it before I choked on the heavy fumes. Upon opening, it was of course unsurprising that my eyes were stung by the self-same smog I sought to free myself from; though they watered,

I could make out a thin, luminous outline in the dark. I reached out my hands, pushed against it with all I could muster in my recently-returned conscious state, and it gave way. This panel of metal toppled outwards, and I with it.

Face-down atop the fallen panel, I felt the area round the metal, touching out at my surroundings in order to establish some sense of location. My left hand tapped along the panel slowly and steadily, much as a robin redbreast might hop along the ground tentatively in its search for worms. It met with the feeling of something smooth, cold, porous and unyielding to the touch. I reasoned that I must have stones around me. My right hand moved then with a greater ease, more secure in the knowledge that there was some solid ground beneath me. Its journey took it along much the same sensation to the other side of me, of rock, before finally reaching something different: coarse strands, dry and somewhat prickly, reaching some five-and-a-half inches or so in height. Some sort of plant life, a long grass or thistle, perhaps? Beyond the immediate sensations of my active hands, my body as a whole felt warm, as though bathed subtly in heat – not uncomfortably so, but perhaps a little more than I was used to. The air here was a faintly sweet smell, that of plants in bloom on a warm day, although tainted somewhat by the smoke from within the cylinder spilling out, polluting the breeze.

I decided to properly open my eyes now so as to better inspect the strange land I now found myself resident in. My first mistake, in hindsight, came from looking upwards as my eyelids lifted, straight into the blistering orb of a sun which scuppered my vision almost entirely. The bright light laid waste to my vision in an instant, rendering me effectively sightless. The difference between one's eyes being voluntarily closed and one's vision being made useless lies in the distinction of consent: whereas before my hands and nose had been explorers, forward parties to assist in my discovery of this landscape, they were now fallen back on as a last line of defence in desperation; I was no longer a man seeking knowledge, now little more than a blind, groping child grasping aimlessly into a white void to try and find help. This lasted for perhaps two minutes, but to me it seemed an eternity, being robbed of my window into the world; after that, my vision slowly returned, although very much blurred. I saw naught but desert, endless expanses of rock punctuated only by the occasional sparse thistle or desert bush, as though placed as a token gesture to Mother Nature. Alone, a foreigner in some alien land with little recollection of what brought me here, and with severely hampered eyesight for the time being, I would have to survive.

Comments

Narrative voice is clearly established here. From the rather arresting beginning onwards, a reader shares the speaker's puzzlement about what is going on. The use of the senses acts effectively to help build the atmosphere of anxiety and uncertainty as the narrator starts to explore a strange world. The relationship between the title given and the writing is not entirely clear, though it is implied throughout. Some of the imagery and metaphorical language ("like a blind groping child") is effective; the image of the robin perhaps less appropriate. At times the language register is slightly mixed, with words like "naught" used; there may, however, be an attempt to characterize a narrator here because he or she often uses complex words ("viscous", "punctuated") or makes unusual lexical choices. The feeling that the writing is not fully controlled means it is not quite top quality; assessors would hope to see work that is better than this.

Novel opening – response 2

I don't quite know what happened or what went wrong... Was it a mistake on my behalf? Or was it all just destined to turn out how it did? If only I had known the consequences of answering the door that fateful day, I would never have.... I suppose I should start at the beginning.

It had been another typical day for me. I got up, brushed my teeth, ate breakfast and went to work. I felt no relief when I returned that afternoon, no comfort. You see, living in a dying city never seems to have a bright side. I'd appreciate any weather these days rather than the dull, cloudy skies that hang over our heads. Whenever I cross the threshold into my 'humble abode,' I am welcomed by that damp, stale air that is always happy to see me apparently.

I turned on the TV and collapsed on the couch, and by the looks of it, I wouldn't be surprised if the couch collapses too one of these days. I looked round the living room. Peeling wallpaper, almost antique furniture and a distinct lack of heat. The heater works just fine but the living room seemed as though no living actually ocured there.

Why am I telling you all this? It's simple. What I'm trying to get at is that I lived a solitary life. I don't want to talk about my parents – too painful. My only friends are the sights and sounds of my home. I have plenty of partners in crime but that's just business. Even three cockroaches seem to be walking out on me. So you can only imagine how I felt when the doorbell rang. What am I saying? It wasn't the sound of cheerful bells as you'd expect – no. Just a short electronic inhuman buzz. It sounded so foreign. The sky was beginning to form and ugly mauve colour as I glared towards the window. I hesitated. Who could it be? I wasn't expecting anyone, nor was there any doubt that there is definitely something strange about a visitor at this time of day. What should I do? If it's the men in blue then I may have to use force but that won't do me any good. No it can't be. They promised to keep me safe if I did as they said. Would they go back on their word?

I sluggishly rose from my chair and approached the door. My mind was racing but my body was in the lead. All sorts of questions flooded my mind but I had to keep calm. It seemed so quiet. The TV was on showing a programme about renovations but all that seemed to slowly fade away; another world, distant from mine. I was sweating. Globs of perspiration formed on my forehead. Darn it! Why couldn't I get a hold of myself? All I had to do was see who it is! Who was it?

I forced the key into the lock and twisted it with much force. I yanked open the door and prepared for the worst.

A boy.

A boy and a young woman.

He was dressed in a plain white hoodie with faded jeans and yet she was wearing an expensive high quality suit that you would wear only to the most formal of occasions. So this was the visitor? Should I have been scared? Certainly I should have, as now the events had been set in motion. Right now, I was intrigued.

'Greetings,' the boy whispered. 'May we come in?'

Comments

This is imaginative and original work. The reader is plunged straight into the situation and is immediately engaged with the first-person narrator's voice and wonders what sort of a person is talking. There is a clear sense of the narrator wanting to engage the reader's sympathy, particularly when remarks are explicitly addressed to the notional listener ("Why am I telling you all this?"). The narrator's feelings of gloom are vividly caught, with even the sofa, the personified damp air, and the unyielding key in the lock seeming to contribute to his negative feelings. There is a strong feeling of events unfolding in a rather uncomfortable way. There is complexity of narrative method because we have a present time introduction which then takes us back in time. The reference to "the men in blue" suggests he might be expecting a visit from the police, and this helps build up the reader's enthusiasm to find out what happens next. Much is implied without being explicitly stated, and this means that a reader has to try to decode the smallest of signs – a clear indication that he or she will be fully engaged. The last line builds suspense and makes us want to read on.

Sample question 2

Write two contrasting pieces (300–450 words each), the first about a place before a natural disaster, the second about the same place after the disaster has taken place. You should aim to create a sense of the impact that the place has on the narrator or narrators.

Adapted from Cambridge AS & A Level English Language 8693
Paper 2 Q4 June 2003

Contrasting pieces

A pair of bright red Converses stroll along the busy pavement, jumping from paving stone to paving stone to playfully avoid the cracks. Anywhere else, the bold shoes would have made a statement, but here in the buzz of city life, they fit perfectly. They seem to dance down the street to the sound of car horns beeping in frustration and the hum of human voices as they pass by, all completely oblivious of one another. There is something uniting every person in that city – the fact that each is focused on living their own life in this shiny playground. Looking up, there is something wonderful about the skyscrapers that tower over the people reaching into the heavens. These giants are perhaps the only solid thing about this city. They observe the chaos of change below, witnessing each individual moment of joy or disaster which go unnoticed by passers by. The colour and the noise and the continuous motion of the city gives it a life of its own. Its energy is overpowering.

Then the Converses descend to the Underground, perhaps seeking refuge from the intense experience above. But here is not the place. They weave between the lawyers, the bankers, the teachers and the artists whose faces are never registered. They wander past the beggar as the song of his guitar fills the space but ignore him. They jump into the carriage just as the doors begin to close, and they are, for a little while, trapped inside the intense atmosphere of the train. The people inside are thrown about like children's toys in a fast-paced game. Not soon enough the train stops, the doors open, and the Converses burst out onto the platform. Fighting upwards though the swarms of people, being pulled in every direction as though caught in an undercurrent, they reach the street once more. And in a strange and surprising way, the exhilarating experience only makes the city sweeter.

A pair of ripped shoes pick their way through the rubble, carefully treading where pavements used to be. The city is eerily silent. The noise of cabs' horns would be a welcome surprise – anything to bring back to life the city so many love. Men, women and children struggle through the streets they used to strut down, any sense of purpose destroyed by the earthquake. Dust and dirt mar their faces, the faces that used to go unacknowledged. Not any more. Strangers comfort one another in an uncharacteristically friendly way. Who knew that one day could change a city so completely? The big shot bankers who used to unapologetically barge their way to work now sit, head in hands, in front of what used to be home. The shining towers that once dominated the skyline now lie on the floor, crumbled in shame. The initial confusion of sirens and shouting has given way to a numbness that fills every corner of the city. There is no escape from it. Like a burst balloon, the shape of the city has been destroyed in an instance and the idea of getting back to that exciting place that was once here seems impossible. The confident swagger of the city has been replaced by a lame limp as its people wander around in a dazed state of shock. All its power has been crushed, falling along with its buildings. The entrance to the Underground still stands, inviting the red shoes in once more. But it no longer promises the excitement it did as the trains that charged through the tunnels have been brought to a standstill.

Comments

These two pieces offer complex contrasts as a response to the question. There is an oddly disembodied but engaging feeling about the writing because the focus is on two pairs of shoes (Converses are a type of trainers), an original way to tackle the topic. Images used in the first part are re-used (the personification of the towers, for example) to different effect in the second. The use of the present tense gives the writing immediacy. The idea of the shoes is picked up as a vivid personification as the city's forward striding of the first part is reduced to a "lame limp" in the second. The writing is complex, fluid, and highly controlled in order to create specific effects. Throughout, the reader wants to know how this writing will resolve, and this level of engagement with the writing suggests that the writer will do very well in this assignment.

Writing for an audience (discursive/argumentative)

In these assignments, what you say is, in some senses, less important than your ability to imitate a genre and to develop a strong voice that develops ideas in a logical, engaging manner. You have the opportunity here to show off a wide range of language devices, possibly even using some of the rhetorical techniques discussed earlier. You will need to show that you have a clear grasp of whether you are being asked to explain, argue, or persuade. At the top end, you would be expected to offer complexity of discussion (which could, of course, be quite simply written), and to show that you can write fluently and correctly.

In summary, you should keep in mind:

- audience
- purpose (to explain, argue or persuade)
- voice
- genre (particularly spoken/written conventions)
- fluency.

Sample question

Write an article for a teenage magazine directed at young adults who are about to live away from home for the first time. You should aim to give both practical advice and reassurance.

Magazine article – response 1

5 Problems You May Not Have Considered Before Leaving Home

Congratulations: you're successfully leaving the nest! Whether it's to university or your own house or flat, there are some things you probably won't be prepared for. Even if you're totally confident about leaving home, it's best you give this a read. Y'know, just to check. So, in reverse order of importance:

5 SHARING

It's no longer family, so you choose your mates to live with. Great. But you need to be careful that everyone understands the deal. Housework isn't done by elves. Other people's worn socks lying round may not be your idea of fun. Try to work things out before you reach boiling point.

4 BILLS

This is the big one that everyone harps on about, but just before you roll your eyes and abandon this article, just think: are you absolutely certain you know how much utilities in your area cost? Or how about balancing a check book? Or even how to budget properly? If you feel even a hint of doubt about any one of those subjects, you need to learn fast.

Luckily there's a readily available source of information from people who have to do that sort of thing every day. Yes, we are talking about your parents. Your parents would much prefer to spend half an hour teaching you how to budget your student loan/wages than have to bail you out in a couple of months when you don't have enough money to eat. Really – just ask them.

3 CLEANING

Whilst this may sound like a strange one, all homes get dirty fast, and at some point you will have to start cleaning. The difference is between starting on a slightly dirty place, or something that looks like it belongs on a TV show about hoarders.

This is a problem relatively easily solved: just clean constantly. Cleaning constantly doesn't mean being obsessive or even particularly neat. It just means washing up every other day instead of once a week, and vacuuming every other week, instead of once every three months. After a while, cleaning will just become routine, and you'll never be faced with a two-foot pile of plates in your sink, or having literally nothing to wear!

2   DIY

No. Don't even attempt Do-It-Yourself. It is inevitable that something in your new accommodation, sooner or later will break. This is not a chance to break out your toolbox with tools still in their wrappings. The absolute minimum you do in that situation is call your parents. We cannot emphasise enough the need for you not to attempt to fix a blocked drain or blown fuse if you do not know what you are doing. It's far better to be embarrassed in front of a professional that to get yourself injured. Of course, if you are practical and experienced at such things go right ahead, but don't try and fix something if you don't understand completely how it works.

1   FOOD

For the first time in your life you'll be completely in control of your eating habits, but don't break out the ice cream and chips just yet, and remember that the same rules still apply – bread still makes you fat, you have to eat your greens and living on noodles and crisps will kill you. We're not saying stop eating what you like. Just rein it in a bit so you don't end up with scurvy.

So there you have it: 5 Problems You May Not Have Considered Before Leaving Home. Remember these and you won't screw up completely. Good luck!

Comments

This piece is very clearly laid out, with a strong structure and a clear, summative conclusion. There is awareness of the form and genre characteristics of a piece of journalism, through the strong title and the subheadings. It is just short of the required 600–900 words and this keeps it out of the top level. However, this is a useful reminder too that the word limit is precisely that – a limit not a target. You can do well by writing a minimal amount. Lexical choices are carefully made and colloquial expressions used to maintain an informal, friendly tone throughout ("Y'know, just to check", "harps on about"). Different grammatical structures, including fragments such as "No", give variety and create a voice that is helpful, although slightly bossy.

Magazine article – response 2
Taking the big step: Moving Out

Moving out from home can seem daunting to many teenagers, but once you've settled in it really is the best time of your life. Here are just a few simple steps to take that allow you to get the most out of your time at university and become a fully independent young adult.

Firstly, once you have chosen the universities which you are going to apply to, you should go on Open Days and make the most out of the opportunity to look around the accommodation on offer, to get a feel for how the students function and live. Having done this, you will feel much more comfortable when you actually move in.

So, secondly, have a look online at the accommodation and decide what suits you personally. Think –'Do I want catered or non-catered, en-suite or shared facilities. Really look into each choice of accommodation to decide which suits you personally. Making sure you've picked the right choice for you will make getting into the regime much easier.

When you are happy with your choice of accommodation and you have applied through the university website you can relax; all the hard work is done.

On the big day, when you arrive at the university and settle into your room, make it as personal as you can to make it seem like your own space. Then head out to the main university building or wherever you have been told, to start making friends. Remember that everyone here is in exactly the same situation as you. So however nervous you feel, they are no different. This is a fresh new start and an exciting time, so start chatting to people and introducing yourself. After this there really is nothing to worry about! Try to find people in the same accommodation as you as you'll be seeing a lot more of them over the next few years.

The university knows that the first few days can be tough, but induction week is designed for you to get to know people you life near, as well as those who share your interests or are studying the same subjects. Although it is your first time living away from home, it is also a chance to meet new people who think like you, share the same interests as you, and are jumping into this new experience alongside you.

Don't panic. Don't fear it. Just go and have fun.

Comments

This is a short piece of work, and there would be a small penalty for not fulfilling the task requirement. However, there is evidence of engagement with the topic, and the writer demonstrates one of the genre conventions of magazine journalism by providing a headline. A friendly tone is maintained throughout, and the question requirement for reassurance is well met through the last paragraph. The piece has a clear structure, but there is quite a lot of repetition over the issue of accommodation, which suggests that the writer has not quite fully thought through the structure of the piece before beginning to write. Addressing the reader directly is an effective way of engaging interest.

To move up to the next level, the writer would need to develop ideas more and have a wider variety of points to make.

Conclusion

In this chapter you have:

- read work from a number of candidates
- thought about assessing this work and seen examples of a range of techniques for answering questions on examination papers
- reflected on what you need to do to maximize your score when you are assessed.

6

Conclusion

We've come a long way, so let's summarize what you have achieved.

- You have worked on a suitable vocabulary and strategies for the analysis of texts, both written and, to an extent, spoken.

- You have responded to a wide variety of extracts in order to demonstrate your understanding of how texts create meaning.

- You have also developed your own writing skills in terms of writing in a variety of genres and for a number of different purposes.

- You have looked at other students' work in order to establish how you might be assessed and to analyse your own strengths and weaknesses.

At the same time, you have gained an understanding of some of the central debates that confront linguists when they try to study a language in use. These discussions will form the basis of much of what you do in an A Level course. However, if you are leaving us now, let's just summarize those issues.

- In any language, change is natural and unstoppable.

- Both spoken and written texts are legitimate territory for analysis, though the methods of analysis are slightly different.

- There will be variations of English within cultural and social groups, even though the broad outlines of the language are shared.

- Standard English enables diverse groups to communicate both within a country and internationally.

- The varieties of English and points of contrast with standard English are worthy of study and analysis.

- Non-standard varieties of English are not inferior – they allow people to express their regional, cultural, and national identities.

- Standard and non-standard English are both subject to change, and there is natural variation between the written and spoken forms.

- Standard and non-standard English are differentiated by variations in both grammar and lexis.

- Non-standard versions of the language may influence and change the standard form over time (the incorporation of "loan words" into the standard form is an example of this).

- There are already "regional" standard Englishes (the difference between American and British English, for example), and other regional standards are emerging as English becomes a global language. Examples are Chinglish, Singlish, Spanglish, Australian, and New Zealand English.

Good luck for your exams.

Introduction to Part 2

Helping yourself

At the start of Part 1, you were introduced to this book as a companion, a friend to help you along the way. Your companion is not going to abandon you as you start the second year of your studies; but, having completed your AS Level course, you now have the skills and knowledge to help yourself a bit more.

Students who are well prepared generally do well in English Language examinations. (It should be obvious that students who are well prepared generally do well in all examinations!) But the students who do the best are the ones who are able to demonstrate a genuine interest in language and how language works.

I hope you have such an interest. Even if you started your AS Level a bit uncertain about your own motivation and ability, your study of English Language over the last year will have helped you develop and cultivate your interest.

You'll have noticed I used a metaphor there. By using the verb "cultivate", I compared the way you can develop your interest in language to the way you might encourage a plant to grow. I also paid you the compliment that every writer pays to every reader when using a metaphor: I assumed you would understand that I was making a comparison, and that my choice of verb was not literal but figurative.

From a linguistic point of view, I was using lexis from the field of vegetation and growing. (No pun or joke intended there, but, as a sophisticated reader, you would understand that there is one.)

Activity 7.1

Cultivating an interest

The extract that follows is part of an article from the *Hindustan Times* (February 2012). It describes how a young man returned to his home village after graduating from university and began a scheme to make money from vermiculture.

As you can see, vermiculture involves using worms in addition to microbes and bacteria to turn organic waste into a nutrient-rich fertilizer.

As you read the article:

- think about how the writer has combined literal and figurative language
- try to find signs of how the reader is being included in the text (or not)
- make a note of any prominent lexical fields other than those of cultivation and agriculture
- look for any metaphorical expressions which come from outside the field suggested by the headline.

CULTIVATING AN INTEREST

He returned home … to discover people living on the edge. He convinced them to sign up for a club whose members would be engaged in the production of vermi-compost and start organic farming.

Kumar's initiative has clearly begun to energise the local economy. As one winds one's way through his village, hundreds of green makeshift vessels assembled out of synthetic sheets come into view. There is one almost outside every house. Each of those containers, filled to the brim with cow-dung, rotting banana trunks and earthworms, is sealed tight at the mouth. Three months later, they yield six quintals of organic manure worth Rs.3000. More than 150 women and 300 men of the village are producing this in their bid for self-reliance, and so that their children have a chance at education. Before 2006, the 3000-strong village had only five graduates and two post-graduates. Today, there are 15 post-graduates, including four women, in Mustafaganj.

Initially, Kumar had a tough time convincing farmers to follow his example. With time, he was able to persuade them that organic farming and production of vermi-compost involved no extra expenditure. "They started taking interest because the banks and agricultural scientists backed us," he said.

His persistence paid off. Nearly 350 farmers are at present organised into a green brigade that has branches in 10 neighbouring villages. But Kumar hasn't hung up his boots. He continues to move around educating farmers about the latest agricultural techniques and encouraging women to cultivate and become self-reliant.

What did your critical and analytical skills detect?

I hope you noticed some of the following, starting with two points about the title.

- The writer *did not* continue with the metaphorical use of cultivation-of-interest.

- There was just one use of the abstract noun "interest" (*They started taking interest because the banks …*) in a literal sense.

Other significant linguistic points:

- There was a prominent lexical field of numbering and measuring: amounts of money, numbers of participants, proportion of villagers going to university, for example.

- There's no direct address to the reader – no use of first-person pronouns (to include the reader with the writer) or second-person pronouns (to "speak" to the reader). But there is the use of the impersonal/formal third-person pronoun "one" to indicate the writer's presence in the text and in the location (*As one winds one's way through his village …*).

- There were two noteworthy examples of figurative language: in line 1, Kumar's fellow villagers are described as "people living on the edge"; and near the end, the writer tells us that "Kumar hasn't hung up his boots. He continues to move around educating farmers …". It's likely that you were able to understand the first of these as a metaphor for "in danger" or "at risk", of isolation or even starvation. With the second, you could probably work out from the following sentence that Kumar hasn't stopped. But you may be puzzled about the idiom "hung up his boots" so we'll come back to that later.

Why do you think the writer didn't exploit the cultivation-of-interest metaphor? Journalists often structure an entire article according to the clever wordplay they have invented for the headline.

Where should we expect to find an answer to the question "Why does the writer make (or avoid) particular choices of language?" This is a basic question about any text, so it's not surprising that we encountered it at the very start of the course, in the section of Chapter 1 called "The big picture".

The article on "Cultivating an interest" has a fairly serious purpose and a potentially wide audience: the English-language newspaper in which it was published has a circulation of nearly 4 million readers. The writer needed to consider whether to take a straightforward factual approach or a more light-hearted line, and has evidently chosen the former.

Thinking about the **purpose** and **audience** also helps to explain the other features of language that I hoped you would pick out.

- The article has an informative purpose – to tell us about Kumar's initiative and to support this account with some facts and figures, so we have vocabulary to do with numbers and amounts, the lexis of measuring.

- The formal third-person pronoun "one" allows the writer and the reader to imagine what it might be like for a third party to walk through the village and observe what the writer describes. But it doesn't create a close relationship between writer and reader.

To sum up, we've managed to explore a number of significant language choices in a text and to account for and explain most of them on the basis of what you learned at AS Level.

That just leaves the curious idiom "hang up his boots". The immediate context of the expression suggests that it usually means the opposite of "continue". So "to hang up one's boots" means "to stop doing something which one had been doing habitually".

But where does the expression come from? What are the **semantics** and the **etymology?** You could just look it up online. Or you could exercise your capacity for independent thought.

Time to get out the linguistic toolbox, and perhaps add to it.

Meaning

Linguists use the word **semantics** to refer to the study of meaning in language and logic. What is there in your toolbox to help with understanding meaning?

Well, we've already decided that some expressions, like most idioms, make use of the figurative (metaphorical) properties of language.

Denotation and connotation may, however, be a new distinction for some of you. **Denotation** refers to the literal meaning of a word, the "dictionary definition". For example, if you look up the word "apple" in a dictionary, you will discover that its primary denotative meaning is "the round fruit of a tree of the rose family, which typically has thin green or red skin and crisp flesh". **Connotation** refers to the associations that are connected to a certain word or the emotions suggested by that word. The connotations for the word "apple" could include innocence, wholesomeness, or purity.

The astute independent reader – that's you! – will have noticed that connotation is a two-way linguistic process. The word "apple" occurs in various idioms such as "the apple of my eye" (meaning something or someone valued and cherished above all others) with a connotative meaning of "perfection", and this reinforces the likelihood that the word will in future connote such ideas.

Let's see how this works with a couple of apparently simple concrete nouns and one apparently simple adjective. You may add your own.

Activity 7.2

Exploring meanings

Simple word	Usage, e.g. idiomatic	Denotative meaning	Connotative meaning
apple		(*noun*) 1. edible fruit of the apple tree	symbol of temptation: Adam and Eve in the Garden of Eden
	"an apple for the teacher"		a gift offered in the hope of gaining favour
	"a rotten apple"		an immoral person who may corrupt others
	"the apple of his father's eye"		child favoured above her/his siblings
Apple		2. an internationally known brand of computers and other consumer electronics	

Simple word	Usage, e.g. idiomatic	Denotative meaning	Connotative meaning
boot		(*noun*) 1. a sturdy item of footwear covering the foot and ankle, and sometimes also the lower leg 2. footwear especially designed for a sport (e.g. football boots, cricket boots)	
	"to hang up one's boots"		to decide to retire from an activity – usually because it's too physically demanding
		(*verb*) to give a hard kick	
	"booted out"		forcibly ejected from a place or an organization
		(*noun*) 3. (in British English) an enclosed space at the back of a car for carrying luggage or other goods. (In American English this space is called the trunk.)	
green		(*adjective*) 1. colour between blue and yellow in the spectrum	a green light suggests it's safe to proceed
		2. covered with grass or other vegetation	concerned with protection of the environment
		3. (of a plant or fruit) young or unripe	innocent and naive
	"the green-eyed monster"		jealousy personified (from Shakespeare's *Othello*)
	"green with envy"		

Simple word	Usage, e.g. idiomatic	Denotative meaning	Connotative meaning
zone		(*noun*) 1. area or stretch of land having a particular purpose or use, or subject to particular restrictions (e.g. a pedestrian zone) 2. (archaic use) a belt or girdle worn round a person's body	
	"in the zone"		(especially in sport) a state of such concentration that one is able to perform at the peak of one's physical or mental capabilities

See if you can add some more examples from your own experience. If in your culture the dominant "variety" of English is not British-English – it may be American English or Asian English or Caribbean English – you may be able to add a number of more "local" idiomatic uses in the second column.

Semantic change

You can see in the example of "zone" in the table above how the meaning of a word can change over time. Some meanings are lost altogether: no-one nowadays uses "zone" to denote (or connote) a belt or girdle, although you may come cross this usage in 16th or 17th century poetry.

Semantic change may refer to narrowing, broadening, amelioration, pejoration or indeed a combination of these.

Narrowing and broadening involve shifts in denotative meaning, while amelioration and pejoration also involve shifts in connotative meaning.

Semantic narrowing

This is the process by which a word's meaning becomes less general over time. For example, the word "accident" nowadays means an event that is at least unfortunate and possibly disastrous, and which was not foreseen. In previous times, it could mean any event that was not foreseen, so a 19th century writer could innocently refer to a chance meeting with a long-lost friend as a "happy accident", whereas now this meaning would only be employed in a joking or ironic way.

Semantic broadening

Not surprisingly, this is the opposite process, where a word gains broader or additional meanings over time. Some people would argue that this is happening at a faster rate now than at other times in history because of information technology: not only do words spread around the globe, changing meaning as they go, but additional words are needed for new technology and new processes. The obvious example is "mouse", which no longer denotes only a small furry rodent.

Some words shift word class as well, for example, from noun to verb. The word "friend" was for a long time only a noun; now people use it as a verb and talk of being "friended" (or "unfriended") in social media.

Semantic amelioration

This is the process by which meaning undergoes an improvement over time, coming to represent something more favourable than it originally referred to. A simple example is the word "nice", which nowadays is a vague or empty adjective meaning "pleasant" or "agreeable", but which originally (when it entered the English language from French) meant "stupid", then "precise".

Semantic pejoration

Pejoration involves a word acquiring negative connotations that it didn't have previously. For example, the word "attitude" has begun to have the connotation of "disagreement" or even "aggression". Formerly, it had a more neutral meaning of a person's mental state or way of thinking, without any suggestion that this was a positive or a negative state in a particular situation. Now – especially in American English – to say that someone "has attitude" is to suggest that he/she is uncooperative. The word "issue" is undergoing a similar shift.

An old British-English joke involving pronunciation as well as semantics goes as follows.

A man is walking in the park on a windy day. The wind blows his hat off, and another man's dog runs off with it and starts chewing it.

The dog owner does nothing.

The hatless man strides up to him: "What are you going to do? Your dog's eating my hat!"

The dog-owner shrugs his shoulders.

The hatless man takes hold of the dog-owner by the lapels and shouts, "I don't like your attitude!"

The dog owner calmly replies, "It wasn't *my* att-it-ude. It was *your* hat-he-chewed."

Activity 7.3

How meaning changes

Look back at the four categories of semantic change – narrowing, broadening, amelioration, and pejoration – and make sure you've understood each one.

Now you're going to do some independent research.

For each of the different kinds of semantic change, choose and research one example. From your findings, you're eventually going to write a page about how the process of meaning change has taken place for each of those particular words.

Choosing examples

You will often hear people complaining that they've heard or seen a word being misused, that someone else has employed it without understanding its "proper" meaning. Are there any words whose usage irritates members of your family?

Alternatively, look in recent newspapers and magazines, print or online editions: the supposed misuse of words is always cropping up.

Researching the change process

A survey among classmates, friends, and family should produce plenty of data. Older family members might offer more examples of broadening and pejoration.

As I was writing this, I came across another usage of "showcase" in the sense of "display". "Showcase" was originally a compound word – in this instance, a noun made up of a verb and a noun – and has been in use for some time as an unhyphenated noun. More recently, it has shifted word class from noun to verb, while retaining its earlier meaning.

Use the table below if you think it would help; you might prefer to adapt it, or create your own.

word	"original" meaning	contemporary meaning(s)
showcase	(*noun*) 1. (literal): a case (usually glass) for displaying objects (usually valuable or delicate) in a shop or museum 2. (figurative): an opportunity or a place to display something to advantage, e.g. "today's recital provided a showcase for this young violinist's talent"	Both of the original meanings Plus (*verb*) to show off or display an object or skill, e.g. "a platform to showcase top creative talent, putting the future of design in your hands"

Hint: Look at words whose uses are controversial, for example, some people object to the word "gay" being used to denote "homosexual", although this has been its dominant meaning for the last couple of generations.

Attitudes to language change

If you hadn't previously come across the debate between descriptivists and prescriptivists, then you probably have now! We will come back to this in Chapter 11.

Activity 7.4

Humpty Dumpty

In *Through the Looking Glass*, by Lewis Carroll, Alice meets Humpty Dumpty and has a long conversation with him, in the course of which they discuss the meanings of words.

Read the following extract from that conversation, then make a list of words used by you, your family and your friends which follow Humpty Dumpty's rule: that words can mean what you choose them to mean.

"I don't know what you mean by 'glory'," Alice said.

Humpty Dumpty smiled contemptuously. "Of course you don't – till I tell you. I meant 'there's a nice knock-down argument for you!'"

"But 'glory' doesn't mean 'a nice knock-down argument'," Alice objected.

"When *I* use a word," Humpty Dumpty said, in rather a scornful tone, "it means just what I choose it to mean – neither more nor less."

"The question is," said Alice, "whether you *can* make words mean so many different things."

"The question is," said Humpty Dumpty, "which is to be master – that's all."

Alice was too much puzzled to say anything; so after a minute Humpty Dumpty began again. "They've a temper some of them – particularly verbs: they're the proudest – adjectives you can do anything with, but not verbs – however, *I* can manage the whole lot of them! Impenetrability! That's what *I* say!"

Through the Looking Glass by Lewis Carroll

Back "in the zone" again

So far, the intention of this chapter has been to encourage you to think more widely about ways in which language works and develops, and to remind you of your own critical and analytical skills.

As you become more aware of the remarkable extent of these skills, it's just a short step to the most important way in which you can help yourself. Get yourself into the habit of thinking about your own language environment, and how much of your everyday experience of the world depends on words and the way they are used.

Thinking skills are like any physical skills you have – running, yoga, martial arts, cycling, playing a musical instrument – in that they improve amazingly when you practise them. The knowledge and skills you acquired through studying AS Level English Language are now part of your repertoire. Your critical faculties should be switched on automatically every time you look at (or listen to) a text, and we are surrounded all the time by a huge range of texts.

Are you in the zone?

Activity 7.5

Looking at transcriptions of spoken language

Top athletes sometimes talk about the way they function automatically in some high-pressure situations as being "in the zone".

You're going to read two extracts based on transcriptions of athletes talking to a television sports presenter. As you read, make a note of ways in which each speaker uses language to describe what it felt like to be "in the zone".

If you're not familiar with transcriptions of spoken language, you may be surprised to find no conventional punctuation. These are very simple transcriptions, keeping to a minimum any information about how the speakers sounded.

Transcription key:	(1) = pause in seconds	(.) = micro-pause
	underlined = stress/emphasis	

Extract 1

Sally Gunnell (SG) was a champion British athlete. The following extract is a transcription of her being interviewed about the final of the 400-metre hurdles event at the 1993 World Championship. As a result of winning this race, she was the reigning Olympic, World, and Commonwealth champion.

Before the extract begins, the interviewer Brian Moore (BM) had been asking SG about how she went into the race suffering from a cold, but covered up her illness and acted as if she felt normal.

SG: it's weird really but um (.) you (1) you totally forget everything (.) I (.) I can't really (.) recall why I mean it's probably

only ever happened to me probably twice in my whole (1) career

BM: mm hmm

SG: but I don't (1) ever remember (1) coming off (.) the last (1) hurdle and and knowing that she was there (.) and this is what happened she was actually right ahead of me and she was ahead of me all the way in but I don't (1) remember this and it was only me sort of like fighting and going over the line and (1) y'know I stood over the line and it was like (1) my life was almost starting again (.) it had almost been on hold for that last (1) y'know fifty-two (.) seven seconds

BM: yes

SG: and it was like "well what's happened" (.) y'know (.) I didn't know that I'd actually won (.) and that I'd actually broken the world record (1) everyone thought "oh she's very calm" y'know (.) "she's just walking around" (1) but I was looking to see you know what actually happened in that race (.) I had no idea it was as though I'd just run my own (.) y'know (.) tunnel vision all the way round I don't remember any of it

BM: and it's almost like a religious experience

Extract 2

Derek Redmond (DR) was a 400-metre sprinter. His career was marked by a number of serious injuries, including his most famous failure, the 1992 Olympic semi-final 400-metre race in Barcelona. Here the presenter Brian Moore (BM) introduces DR's account of the race.

BM: despite a career plagued by injury (.) Derek Redmond began the semi-final of the four hundred metres in Barcelona in nineteen ninety two (.) as a strong favourite (.) not only for a final place (.) but for a medal

DR: I was in the zone (.) heh heh heh heh (.) I was (.) everything had gone right (.) yeah at the start I said (.) "on your marks" (1) and I knew I'd won it (2) and I was just (.) floating down the back straight I felt like I was running on air (.) I look at the film now (.) just the way I was running was absolutely brilliant (2) and all of a sudden I heard a (.) what I thought was a gun shot from the crowd (.) um (.) I carried on running (1) next thing you know (.) that (.) I thought

SG: yeah you feel as though someone's almost (.) helping you (1) I must admit just because it (.) it does feel so alien (.) at times (.) y'know as I said before it doesn't actually (.) particularly feel like (.) me out there and you almost get into its like a trance (.) and uh you feel as though someone (1) y'know I always said (.) someone's watching you and just sort of like you know (.) pulling you round (.) the track and and and (.) and letting you flow around that track yeah it's a yeah (.) it is (.) an amazing feeling

somebody had shot me and I thought I'd been shot in the back of the leg and (.) that was it (.) y'know (.) your hamstring goes there's nothing you can do you go up and you come straight back down again (.) game over

BM: you really believed

DR: I remember (.) getting up (.) and thinking (.) "if you get up now you can still qualify" (.) and they've got fifty metres to go and they're all flying (.) I've got two hundred and fifty metres to go and three hamstrings (.) and I'm still thinking that I can qualify

BM: you really believed that you could still get through

DR: if you had come up to me then and said I'd bet you anything you won't (.) you (.) you can't qualify I would have said (.) you're on (.) I honestly felt (.) I could still qualify (.)

BM: (speaking to the audience) Redmond was so deeply in the zone (.) that his mind simply refused to accept what his body was telling him

How will I be assessed?

It's all very well taking an excursion through a number of ideas about language and a range of texts, as we've just done. And you may feel encouraged when you think about the skills you've acquired through your AS Level course, and how far you've come in a year.

But you need to be aware of how you're going to be assessed this year.

The examinations will cover some ground similar to what you encountered last year. You will be expected to:

- deal with a wider range of texts, including transcripts of spoken language

- re-cast original texts for a different purpose or audience

- compare your re-cast text with the original

- analyse texts in terms of their linguistic features: vocabulary, word order and the structure of sentences/utterances, figurative language, formality/informality of tone, communication of attitudes, bias, or prejudice

- compare the language and style of different texts – including your own – and to take into account their function and context.

In addition, you will be expected to demonstrate an informed knowledge of topics central to more advanced study of language, including:

- how language is acquired by children, and how it develops as they get older

- aspects of spoken as well as written language: for example, how particular social or occupational groups use language

- issues and debates in linguistic theory, such as:

  ○ the status of English as a global language

  ○ standard and non-standard English; local varieties of English

  ○ language change over time, and especially the effects of information technology

  ○ descriptivist and prescriptivist attitudes to language

  ○ the interrelationship of language with culture and society.

Questions on exam papers on language topics are likely to offer two kinds of linguistic data for you to make use of.

1. Transcriptions of spoken language or other "live" data: for example, extracts from blogs, websites, advertisements, special-interest articles.

2. More formal academic writing about linguistic theories and issues, for example, extracts from published research or textbooks.

You will also be expected to have a range of ideas and examples from your own reading. For example, if you were asked to discuss some of the recent effects on language use of information technology, you would need to be able to refer to some specific examples of your own.

Some of these will need genuinely to be your own. As you can imagine, many students would be able to refer to how the word "mouse" has been appropriated to refer to a peripheral computer device; while this does not make it a useless example, it would be to your advantage if you had thought about some other examples beyond the most obvious ones.

Similarly, you need to be able to refer to linguistic theories and research. But it is not enough just to mention Leech's Politeness Principle or Giles's Accommodation Theory: you need to show that you understand these ideas and (most importantly) that you can apply them.

In the next few chapters, you will be introduced to some new ideas and given opportunities to practise how to apply them. You will also revisit some old friends, like aspects of formality, colloquial and vague language, lexical fields, non-standard grammar, and contextual variations.

Advanced textual analysis: media texts

8

Introduction

Your A Level course is intended to develop in you "a critical and informed response to texts in a range of forms, styles and contexts".

Most of the texts you encounter every day – songs, posters, advertisements, notices, signs, news broadcasts – can be classed as "media texts". They are transmitted to you through at least one particular "medium", which might be print but might also include sound and images.

Where more than one medium is involved, the text might be referred to as "multi-modal" – as many on-line texts will be, with pages of text giving access to moving images and sound.

Read the text below, and ask yourself: What sort of text is this?

Voice-over:	Persil asked kids what they think are the toughest stains.
Kid 1:	Oh ... that's a hard one.
Kid 2:	Yeah, isn't it? It's hard.
Kid 3:	Blackcurrant. It's black and purple so you can see it more.
Kid 4:	Mud!
Kid 5:	Mud!
Kid 6:	Brown sauce.
Kid 7:	And all sorts of, like, runny food.
Kid 8:	You need to wash it really, really hard.
Kid 9:	Felt tip pen.
Kid 10:	That's the hardest one.
Kid 11:	Chocolate ice cream!
All:	(*Laughter*)
Voiceover:	New Persil "Small & Mighty" is now better than ever with unbeatable results on tough kids' stains.

Activity 8.1

Re-read those 15 lines of text.

- Jot down any features of *form*, *structure*, or *language* which you think are significant.

- Look at your list – see if the features you've selected fall into any particular categories, for example, adjectives of colour.

- Think about the *purpose* of this text, and its likely *audience*.

There's a detailed analysis at the end of this chapter, but for now, you'll have deduced a number of things about this text.

1. It's an advertisement – it's trying to *sell* you something by *persuading* you it's good.

2. It assumes you're familiar with the brand and/or product by referring to the brand name.

3. It's probably a transcript of the words used for a television or radio advertisement.

4. It's informal in structure – it introduces a variety of voices and just leaves them to "speak" to the listener/viewer.

5. It's informal in language – it refers to the children as *kids*.

We could have reached some of the judgments above by thinking from the opposite direction about what the text is not.

It's not:

- detailed
- formal or technical
- explicit.

And in fact we deduce much of our everyday understanding of the world by thinking about what's not.

- It's not dark any longer, so it must be morning and time to get up.

- People outside in the street haven't got their umbrellas up any longer, so it must have stopped raining.

- This notice is giving me information but it's not ordering or requiring me to do anything.

This idea of understanding the world by opposites is a very old one. It's a simple version of Aristotle's logic, and it leads on to a Big Idea.

In Part 1 of this book, examples were introduced with some information about their text type. Use that information to think about what text type you have just read.

TIP

Binary opposition – a Big Idea

One way of organizing the way we see the world is to think in **contrasting pairs**: when we consider an idea or a feeling, we generally understand it in terms of its opposite.

Activity 8.2

When we see someone driving a new car, we perhaps think of our own (not new) car in terms of how *different* it is. We set up in our minds a binary opposition, which we can represent in two columns.

a new car	*my old car*
clean/shiny	dirty/dull
(likely to be) reliable	(likely to be) unreliable
symbol of higher status	symbol of lower status
smart	scruffy

Take 10 minutes to think up (and write down in two columns) some contrasting ideas of your own about the two cars.

Now look at your two columns. It's likely that the words you've written are mostly of two types:

- adjectives in semantic fields of appearance and performance, differentiating between the new and the old

- abstract nouns or noun phrases with contrasting connotations or associations.

Binary opposition can be very useful when studying the English language. For example, perhaps you already use a binary method to generate ideas for your own writing? You can automatically produce twice your original number of ideas by considering the opposite for each one.

However, a word of caution: this is a Big Idea that has to be handled with care. It's often helpful to think of differences and even opposites, but there's a danger you might see only the extremes at opposite ends of the spectrum.

For example, one of the first things you notice about a text is likely to be the level of formality – the register. It's important not to jump to the conclusion that a particular text (or text type) is completely formal or informal. Formality, like many concepts in language study, is a *continuum*: many texts and text types vary from line to line or sentence to sentence in their levels of formality.

One of the more advanced skills at A Level is the ability to *compare* texts without distorting them. Students who insist on seeing texts as polar opposites – when really they're not so unlike each other – are in danger of tripping up.

You also need to be careful not to make assumptions about texts based on what you believe the text type to be, even when that text type seems simple and obvious.

Activity 8.3

The following extracts (a question and a reply) are from an online technical forum for owners of a particular model of four-wheel-drive vehicle.

Before you read them, take a few minutes to jot down what you would expect to find in posts to this kind of forum:

lexis	technical jargon to refer to car components
syntax	simple and/or minor and/or incomplete sentences
grammar	non-standard with casual attitude to accuracy
register	…………………………………..
address to reader	…………………..

> **TIP**
>
> Look back at Chapter 2, especially the section on style, register and tone. This should remind you of the formality continuum, and how tone and register shift in even short texts.

(Question) Post 1: Wed 9 Apr 2008 21:58

I have a 1988 EFI 3.5 Range Rover, which has developed the sort of fault that drives one to drink (well, I can't drive the car so I might as well.) It starts well from cold, and runs fine. When hot tho' it doesn't want to know. Leave it 15 minutes and it will start again instantly. I've changed the ECU for a spare and the symptoms are unchanged.

I suspect the answer is quite simple – once one knows what it is. My suspicion is a sensor related to temperature is telling fibs to the electronics. The question is, is this a fault that is familiar to anyone, and can someone suggest which component(s) to change first (and where they are)?

Oh, one other point! There is a cold start injector on the plenum chamber. When I had starting problems a couple of years ago (finally traced to unclean connector on the ECU) someone on here told me to disconnect it. I did so, and the thing has started perfectly ever since – until now. I've also taken the obvious step of cleaning the ECU connector again. Any ideas, anyone????

(Reply) Post 2: Thu 10 Apr 2008 21:05

On a 3.5 EFi, the commonest causes of hot starting faults are that coolant sensor, the tank pump and a lack of heat-sink compound under the ignition amplifier on the side of the dizzy. Although, as you always have a spark; then we can rule out the amplifier.

By no means can the fuel pump be eliminated by assumptions like that. They are perfectly capable of refusing to spin when hot. Not hard to check; you can hear the fuel returning through the pressure reg on the end of the fuel-rail.

The ECU's coolant sensor should have a 2-pin square plug with a silly wire clip. As a rough rule of thumb; they should be around 2800 Ohms cold and 280 hot. I've never seen one stuck at 65 before. The thermo time-switch runs the cold-start injector for a few seconds at start-up – very rare to see one.

Other than that: the little rev info resistor on the coil needs to be tightly connected and the engine control and fuel-pump relays can't be ruled out either. They are unique types, although they look normal.

Commentary

Both contributors use technical lexis or jargon. This can typically be used to *include* or *exclude* other readers: here, both contributors clearly have shared knowledge, so each of them can refer to "fuel-pump relays" and "coolant sensors" without confusing the other.

There are some minor sentences and elliptical constructions in both posts: "Leave it 15 minutes and it will start again instantly" would in Standard English be a complex sentence starting with the conditional: "If you leave it …"

However, pronoun use is quite varied, and includes the usually formal third-person "one", used by the first writer to refer to himself in a joking way: "the sort of fault that drives one to drink …"

And writers use a wide variety of sentence constructions. (Some of them are casual and conversational, breaking "rules" of correct English grammar, rather like the first sentence of this paragraph.) The second post begins with a complex declarative sentence written in a formal style which would not be out of place in a textbook until the final word "dizzy". You may not know what the "dizzy" is, but you can work out that it must be a concrete noun, so it's probably a joking, slang or colloquial term for some engine component.

The most surprising thing is the construction of the first sentence in the second paragraph of the second post. Such syntax – it could be called inverted syntax, since the auxiliary modal verb "can" is placed before the subject (the fuel pump) – would be expected in 18th or 19th century writing, but is very rare nowadays. Why has the writer done this? (Hint: think about *fronting* – and if you don't know what that is, look it up!)

In fact, both writers here are using a mode (online posts to a forum) which is usually characterized by extreme informality to interact in a rather formal way.

Activity 8.4

Although you have been warned recently not to make assumptions, it might be interesting to work with a fellow student on further features of language in the two posts above. Each take one of the posts and consider the following points.

1. How does each writer refer to the vehicle and to its component parts?

2. What do you notice about use of adjectives?

3. Look at phrasal verbs and idioms.

4. Look also at the next post (on the next page) in the sequence. What differences do you notice between this post and the first one?

    Consider:

    – tone

    – sentence structure

    – syntax.

Formal or informal?

An overheard chat from reveals the real special relationship between Tony Blair, prime minister of the UK at the time, and George Bush, President of the USA at the same time.

During a quiet moment at the G8 summit yesterday, Tony Blair and George Bush swapped candid views on the Middle East. Only after several minutes did Mr Blair realise that a microphone had been left on.

Bush: Yo, Blair. How are you doing?

Blair: I'm just...

Bush: You're leaving?

Blair: No, no, no not yet. On this trade thingy ...[inaudible]

Bush: Yeah, I told that to the man.

Blair: Are you planning to say that here or not?

Bush: If you want me to.

Blair: Well, it's just that if the discussion arises ...

Bush: I just want some movement.

Blair: Yeah.

The Guardian, July 2006

Post 3: Sat 12 Apr 2008 13:52

If I had any hair left, I'd be tearing it out!!!

The symptoms are unchanged. When cold, it starts almost instantly. When hot (15 minutes ticking over in drive) if ignition turned off and then immediately key turned it will probably start again. Wait 5 seconds and it won't start for about 10 minutes. If left for 10 mins or longer starts almost immediately again.

ECU has been changed. Coolant temp sensor changed. Engine speed reference relay checked. There is pressure in the fuel lines when it won't start. When being cranked over there is a spark of at least 1/4?

Oh, and it's probably a red herring? but the rev counter has just stopped working.

Anyone got any further suggestions? or a match!!!

By the way, after a further fortnight, and many more exchanges on the forum, the vehicle was still not going!

Comparison

You've just made a brief comparison of two short written texts by the same writer. From your toolkit of analytical strategies, I directed you to tone and sentence construction/syntax.

As you were told in Chapter 4: "You will have to decide which are the most useful tools for the particular challenges that have been presented by a passage. Like a craftsman, you need to know when to use a hammer, and when to use a screwdriver."

Students who do well in English Language develop real discrimination. They learn to focus on what is genuinely significant. That means choosing the right analytical tools for the job. And you can only develop this through practice.

So we'll have some more now.

Activity 8.5

Here are two texts concerned with business and profits.

The first is from an Australian website which claims to provide a daily round-up of business trends and ideas from around the world.

The second is from an interview with the President of the USA, Barack Obama.

Business looking up despite economic gloom: Economy round-up

Most small business owners are looking forward to business picking up in the year ahead, but remain pessimistic about the broader economic outlook.

According to a survey of more than 1600 Australian small business owners, 56% believe their business performance will improve over the next 12 months.

Improved marketing and better customer relationships was the chief reason for optimism given by businesses owners with a positive outlook for next year, while 97% said they also expect cheaper petrol to help their business.

Almost 75% of business owners also said their business is currently performing very or quite well, broadly consistent with results over the past year.

But while they are feeling good about their own chances, business owners see storm clouds looming over the economy as a whole, with 58% saying they expect economic conditions to worsen over the next 12 months, way up from 6% this time last year.

Interviewer: "Do you think that you might have the unemployment rate down to 8 percent by the time the election rolls around?"

President Obama: "I think it's possible. But…I'm not in the job of prognosticating on the economy. I'm in the job of putting in place the tools that allow the economy to thrive and Americans to succeed. Sometimes when I'm talking to my team, I describe us as: I'm the captain and they're the crew on a ship, going through really bad storms. And no matter how well we're steering the ship, if the boat's rocking back and forth and people are getting sick and they're being buffeted by the winds and the rain, … at a certain point, if you're asking, 'Are you enjoying the ride right now?,' folks are going to say, 'No.' And are they going to say, 'Do you think the captain's … doing a good job?'? People are going to say, 'You know what? A good captain would have had us in some smooth waters and sunny skies, at this point.' And I don't control the weather. What I can control are the policies we're putting in place to make a difference in people's lives."

Have you read and thought about both texts?

From your linguistic analysis toolkit, take out the box labelled "literal and figurative language". Open it carefully, because it may contain volatile substances such as images and metaphors.

Now write a paragraph about each text, explaining how the writer in each case uses language, facts and images to communicate a particular purpose.

Hold on to what you have written until you reach the end of this chapter.

> **TIP**
>
> Remember to keep in mind how the context and the likely audience affects a writer's choices of language.

Reminder: how your work is assessed

At AS Level you were used to a sequence of thinking which usually went like this:

Reading (a) passage(s) ➔ Writing a commentary/analysis ➔ Doing a directed writing task based on the passage(s)

So far in this chapter, we've concentrated on the commentary/analysis stage.

You've practised your skills of :

* critical reading

* note-making

* (brief) comparison.

And, so far, your analyses and comparisons have shown direct or *explicit* understanding: you have been looking directly at texts and commenting on how they work.

But it's also possible to show understanding in an indirect or *implicit* way. We do this all the time in everyday interaction.

I've just had an email from a friend who ended by saying that she was "waiting for the postman". The implied meaning that I deduced from this was that she was expecting something particular in today's post, so in my reply I asked what she was expecting. I didn't think I needed to make explicit my assumption that she was expecting something important in the post. (I might be wrong – she might be waiting for the postman because yesterday he mistakenly delivered something which was not intended for her, and she wants him to take it away.)

In writing about the theory of conversation, linguists call this process in which a speaker *implies* and a listener *infers* **conversational implicature**.

We'll come back to this in Chapter 10. It's part of what linguists call **pragmatics**: you may also remember this from Chapter 1.

(By the way, my friend emailed back to say the reason she was waiting for the postman was that she was expecting a parcel for her son's birthday.)

Topic shifts and side sequences

We've just been through the equivalent of what in conversational theory is called a *side sequence*: I started explaining how implicit as well as explicit understanding was important for assessment, and made a slight *topic shift* into a personal example.

Now we'll make a *topic loop* back into our original subject.

Reminder: how your work is assessed

At A Level, the sequence of what you will be expected to do in an examination is different from what it was at AS Level:

Reading a text ➜ Doing a directed writing "re-cast" task based on that text ➜ Writing a comparative commentary

A comparative commentary is one that compares the style and language of your re-cast with the style and language of the original.

There are two main reasons for this different sequence:

1. Writing a "re-cast" response to a previously unseen text has been found to be a very good way of assessing a student's understanding of that text. In order to make the linguistic choices necessary to shift a text from one genre or purpose to another, you need to have a good (implicit) understanding of the construction of that text and of questions to do with purpose/audience and genre.

2. The second stage – writing a comparative commentary – then follows naturally, and you can make implicit understanding explicit by making specific comments on choices of form, structure, and language.

You're now going to try the entire sequence.

Activity 8.6

A medical advice website describes itself in the following terms:

" ... one of the most trusted medical resources in the UK, supplying evidence-based information on a wide range of medical and health topics to patients and health professionals ..."

As you can see, the target audience for this website is very broad. One of its articles or blogs might be read (at one extreme) by a confident expert in a particular field of medicine or (at the opposite extreme) by an anxious individual with very little medical knowledge.

Imagine you had to compose an article for this website, suitable for the non-expert, explaining some of the possible dangers and side effects of taking medication.

For the moment, don't worry about the content of your article. Think about the style, tone, and register: in other words, how to match the message to the audience.

Let's start by making a basic list of choices about language you might expect to make. Examples are given here but you can add your own ideas and examples.

Tone/register	• friendly • modified formal
Mode of address	• direct second person, "you" • inclusive – writer invites reader to join in and agree so first person plural, "we"
Lexis	• simple/colloquial • non-specialist • concrete nouns where possible • avoiding complex nominalisations
Syntax	• simple (and minor) sentences • non-standard grammar, with some function words missed out • active verb constructions • some abbreviations or contractions ("you'll", "I've") • conversational/colloquial

Now look back at the list of features above, and your additions.

Think again of the *purpose*: you are explaining some of the possible dangers and side effects of some medicines.

Think again of the *audience*: you are explaining some possible risks to a general audience, the non-expert reader.

The material you are going to use appears below. It consists of the expert reactions of four senior health professionals to research into the side effects of commonly prescribed drugs. Read the material, and select up to eight points to include.

TIP

Don't expect to understand all of the content of the material that you're offered for directed writing-type tasks in the course of your studies or in examination questions.

You're not being assessed in this task on your understanding of medical side effects. What you have to show is that you can make helpful linguistic choices to match the context of your writing. And before you can focus on *how* to express yourself, you need to decide *what* you want to communicate.

Expert 1:

The negative effects of anticholinergic drugs on brain and cardiac function have been known for decades and this study reinforces their dangers. The wide use of amitriptyline and related tricyclic antidepressant drugs in primary care for depression, and also unproven indications such as insomnia, is therefore a significant concern. For these reasons most experts have recommended that antidepressants such as amitriptyline should be replaced by the SSRIs which are much safer.

Expert 2:

All drugs have possible side effects, but the results of this study should not lead anyone to stop current medications without discussing this with their doctor first. Before starting any drug, it is important for the doctor and patient to discuss the possible benefits of the treatment, compared with the potential downsides, so that the patient can make an informed decision. As a cardiologist, many of the drugs I use (such as beta-blockers) have been definitely proven to make people with heart disease live longer, so it's important to balance these proven benefits against the risk of side effects

Expert 3:

This comprehensive study could have some far-reaching effects. The results underline the critical importance of calculated drug prescription. Further investigation needs to establish exactly how and why drugs with an anticholinergic effect are increasing mortality, which might offer clues to influence safer drug design. It's important for people prescribed medicines with an anticholinergic effect not to panic, but to discuss with their doctor the best possible personal treatment plan.

Large cohort research is essential to understanding what might influence the prevalence of dementia in a population. These broad studies can be invaluable in shaping public health policy, yet funding for such research remains shamefully low. With the 820,000 people currently living with dementia set to increase drastically, research is the only answer and we must invest more now.

Expert 4:

Older people are prescribed many drugs, as this study shows. Yet again some of these drugs have been shown to have adverse effects, including an association with cognitive decline. This is an important and very large study and although we cannot assume that the drugs are actually causing the increased decline, there is good reason to think they may be. This study has important clinical lessons for all doctors looking after older people.

Ready? Here's a reminder of the task.

Write about 150 words of an article for a medical website, suitable for the non-expert, explaining some of the possible dangers and side effects of taking medication. Base your writing on the information in the four extracts above.

Think about communicating simply and clearly and matching your language to your audience.

Give yourself 15 minutes to re-read the material and make some notes, then 30 minutes to do the writing, and finally 5 minutes to check carefully what you've written. Now put it aside and go and do something else.

Comparative commentary

This chapter has been full of warnings and advice about what you should not do. One of the greatest dangers for students of A Level English Language is that they go into an examination with a checklist in their heads of features they expect to find in a text and a determination to write about those features even if they're not there.

You can protect yourself against this by remembering these anti-jokes:

> **TIP**
> There's no point in trying to write, for example, about pronoun use in texts where pronoun use is not significant.

Q. What's not red?	Q. What's red and fluffy?
A. No tomatoes.	A. A blue rock, if blue were red and rocks were fluffy.

Look back at your re-cast of the medical side effects material and make some notes about your own uses of language. It may be that you ended up using some features that you weren't expecting to and/or missing out some features you had intended to include. That's fine: it can be useful to discuss both in the comparative commentary.

Do the same with the original material. Pick out what you think are the most significant aspects of language use, not worrying about whether they match the features you've highlighted in your own writing. Keep the notes you've made. You'll be using them after you've read the next section.

Comparing

Command words in examination questions – imperative verbs like "discuss", "explore", "analyse" – are obviously important, and you ignore them at your peril! However, there are many acceptable ways of fulfilling the instruction to "compare", and you don't have to do the comparative commentary task in the same way every time. You might find that one particular way suits you and leads to better results, but it's good to be flexible. Different passages might lend themselves to different approaches.

You might:

- examine your own re-cast first, commenting on what you see as genuinely significant choices of form, structure, and language
- refer to the original text whenever there's a genuine overlap
- examine any aspects of the original text which you haven't already covered.

You might do these in the opposite order – there's no great virtue in concentrating on either text before the other.

Alternatively, you might try to write a fully integrated comparison which moves constantly between your re-cast and the original.

> **TIP**
>
> Many students neglect to analyse the *language* of their own writing, and only comment on the *content*. The best answers are the ones that apply a genuinely linguistic focus.

Activity 8.7

You're now going to write your comparative commentary. Use the notes you made earlier to carry out the following instruction:

Compare the style and language of your re-cast with the style and language of the original four passages.

Give yourself 40 minutes to do this.

There will be further chances in the next two chapters to practise the sequence of directed writing then comparative commentary. Although having a mental checklist of features every time is not recommended, over the course of a number of attempts at this kind of task you should find that you cover a range of features of written and spoken language, including:

- vocabulary
- word order and the structure of sentences/utterances
- figurative language (for example, use of metaphor and simile)
- formality/informality of tone
- the communication of attitudes, bias, or prejudice.

The last of these can be tricky, especially when a writer is using irony. More of this in the next chapter.

Conclusion

We've looked in this chapter at a number of texts that can be classed as media texts. Sometimes these texts might be referred to as "non-literary" texts; but, as we've seen, we can't assume that any particular text type will have a defined set of features or a single position on the formality/informality continuum.

Short texts which are apparently quite simple and which have no obvious literary purpose can still have literary features. The radio advertisement which opened this chapter involved a product whose name "Small & Mighty" is a playful reversal of at least one well-known **collocation**. (You might be familiar with Susan Hill's 1983 novel *The Woman in Black*, whose title is a similar reversal of the title of Wilkie Collins's 1859 novel *The Woman in White*.)

"High and mighty" was for centuries a **pejorative** expression whose dictionary definition is "behaving as though one is more important than others". Although the individual adjectives "high" and "mighty" have mostly positive connotations when used separately, the combination has always suggested a misuse of higher power and status. (Mini activity: Try to think of some situations in which the adjective "high" is not used positively.)

More recently, the collocation had undergone a certain amount of **semantic amelioration** through its use as a trading name by a company which describes itself in the following (rather formal) way: "High & Mighty always has been and continues to be the market leader in UK big and tall clothing for men delivering fashion that fits for men of above average stature."

That last noun phrase – "men of above average stature" – is perhaps a **euphemism**, itself a literary feature …

Follow-up to activities

1. Look back at Activity 8.5. I'm hoping that in looking at the two texts on the economic outlook you noticed how the first one made extensive use of facts and percentages, while the second sets up an image of the nation as a ship and the President as the Captain.

2. In addition to Activity 8.6, below is an article written with a similar purpose to the directed writing re-cast you did. The author is an expert – a doctor – but is explaining things for a non-expert audience. Read the article carefully, paying attention to how the writer imagines a reader.

How do you know the medicine you're taking is safe? Well, you can trust your doctor (I would say that, wouldn't I!) to use all the information they have to weigh up the risks and benefits for you. But what if your doctor doesn't know either?

For a medicine to be licensed (approved for prescribing by doctors) in the UK, it has to jump through hundreds of hoops. In the UK, the Medicines and Healthcare Products Regulatory Agency (MHRA) is responsible for weighing up all the evidence for all medicines and medical devices in the UK and deciding whether they work and are acceptably safe. Before the MHRA licenses a medicine, it looks at all the scientific studies a new medicine has been put through, the dose which offers the best ratio of effectiveness and safety, the condition it's trying to treat, the length of treatment and a host of other factors.

High-quality scientific trials compare the medicine being studied either with another medicine which is already licensed or with a placebo. A placebo is a 'pretend' medicine with no active ingredient. But importantly in placebo-controlled trials, neither the doctor nor the patient knows if they're taking 'the real thing'. If one in three patients gets a nasty rash or chest pain while taking the medicine being studied, it would probably never get licensed – unless exactly the same proportion of patients gets the same symptoms when they're taking the placebo but don't know which of the two they've been given.

This system is good, but it isn't totally foolproof. Some side effects are rare, and may not be picked up by trials even on thousands of people. Others are really common, but happen often in people who aren't on the medicine either. For instance, just in the last few weeks a major review has linked high doses of the common anti-inflammatory tablets ibuprofen and diclofenac with an increased risk of heart disease. They've both been around for years, but it's only when many millions of doses of some medicines have been given that the true size of the problem comes to light.

Advanced textual analysis: literary texts

Introduction

We saw in the previous chapter that "non-literary" texts can have literary features. Similarly, written texts can have features of spoken texts.

On the next page, we'll explore ways in which knowledge of spoken language can help us to reach a deeper understanding of a short written text. First, we'll have an initial look at that text.

> Pleasure is everything
>
> Give in to happiness
>
> Reject propriety; embrace variety
>
> Prudence is sooo 1658
>
> Life is fleeting; clasp it hard with both hands
>
> Seek delight
>
> Trust your impulses
>
> Ordinary is pointless
>
> Break free
>
> All hail the Gü decadents

What sort of text have you just read?

It could be an example of a "found poem" – a collection of words which seem to have come together by accident in a form which encourages the reader to see them as "poetic".

In fact, it's far from accidental. It's a very deliberate construction. The lines above are a kind of manifesto – a declaration of aims – made by a company which manufactures desserts and markets them as a luxury item and a symbol of personal indulgence.

When this advertisement became widely known, some readers found it intensely irritating. As students of how the English language works, we ought to be able to understand why that should be.

Activity 9.1

Look at each of the 10 lines of the text. Work out and write down what each line is in terms of sentence or utterance type, for example, an interrogative or a modulated declarative.

If you don't know what these are, look in the Glossary.

What did you discover?

Using knowledge of spoken language

Although that advertisement was not designed as a text with an obviously literary purpose, it certainly arouses emotions in readers.

And although it's a written text, a knowledge of spoken utterance types is very helpful in understanding how it works.

- The first, fourth, and eighth lines are *declaratives*, as is the first clause in the fifth line.

- The remaining clauses in lines 1 to 9 are *imperatives*.
- The final line is an *exclamative*, although it doesn't end with an exclamation mark.

We could go into further detail. Declarative sentences/utterances can be divided into several types.

Declarative sentence/utterance types

Using the theory of *speech acts*, we can think about three types of declaratives:

1. **Constative** utterances, which transmit information or make assertions. We might need to be careful here to make sure we notice whether what's being asserted is a fact ("the temperature is five degrees higher than it was yesterday") or just an opinion ("it's too hot to work today!").

2. **Directive** utterances, which are designed to get the listener to *do* something ("I want you to listen very carefully …")

3. **Commissive** utterances, in which speakers or writers commit themselves to a course of action ("I promise never to do that again.")

You will have realized that the effect of a directive utterance on you as a listener/reader is similar to that of an imperative: you feel you have been told to do (or not do) something.

Activity 9.2

Let's go back to our 10-line text.

Using the speech act categories above – and any other suitable ideas from your analytical toolkit – write a page about how that text works to affect you as a reader. You might be amused, delighted, moved, infuriated, or left completely cold by it. As a student of language, your task is to use your growing knowledge to explore how it works.

Many of the declarative utterances in our 10-line text could be understood as slogans, and you could probably think of a number of groups who would adopt "Seek delight!" or "Trust your impulses!" as a motto.

However, it's human nature to question what we're being told to do or believe. And I think that's why this text annoys some readers intensely.

TIP

It's better to use the term "utterances" than the word "sentences" when discussing spoken language because people seldom speak in grammatically perfect sentences. And it's always a bad idea to consider spoken language as an inferior version of written language, full of "mistakes".

Slogans

A dictionary offers the following definitions of the word "slogan":

1. (*historical – from Scottish Gaelic*) a Scottish Highland war cry

2. a motto associated with a political party or movement or other group

3. a short and striking or memorable phrase used in advertising.

Short declaratives often have great force, especially when the speaker or writer is asserting that one thing is equivalent to another thing.

Look at the slogans on the right. Do you recognise them? This is George Orwell, whose writings and ideas you met in Chapter 4, making interesting use of the human tendency to dislike being told what to do or believe. The slogans are from his novel *1984*.

The book, which was published in 1948, is set in an imagined future where the government tries to control how people think by making enforced changes to the language. A new language called "Newspeak" has been devised.

War is peace
Freedom is slavery
Ignorance is strength

Newspeak was the official language of Oceania and had been devised to meet the ideological needs of Ingsoc, or English Socialism …

The purpose of Newspeak was not only to provide a medium of expression for the world-view and mental habits proper to the devotees of Ingsoc, but to make all other modes of thought impossible. It was intended that when Newspeak had been adopted once and for all and Oldspeak forgotten, a heretical thought – that is, a thought diverging from the principles of Ingsoc – should be literally unthinkable, at least so far as thought is dependent on words. Its vocabulary was so constructed as to give exact and often very subtle expression to every meaning that a Party member could properly wish to express, while excluding all other meanings and also the possibility of arriving at them by indirect methods. This was done partly by the invention of new words, but chiefly by eliminating undesirable words and by stripping such words as remained of unorthodox meanings, and so far as possible of all secondary meanings whatever.

To give a single example. The word *free* still existed in Newspeak, but it could only be used in such statements as 'This dog is free from lice' or 'This field is free from weeds'. It could not be used in its old sense of 'politically free' or 'intellectually free' since political and intellectual freedom no longer existed even as concepts, and were therefore of necessity nameless. Quite apart from the suppression of definitely heretical words, reduction of vocabulary was regarded as an end in itself, and no word that could be dispensed with was allowed to survive. Newspeak was designed not to extend but to *diminish* the range of thought, and this purpose was indirectly assisted by cutting the choice of words down to a minimum.

1984 by George Orwell

Activity 9.3

Orwell here puts forward the idea that if you prevent people from using the words which refer to certain ideas, then the ideas will cease to exist. He suggests this can be done by "cutting the choice of words down to a minimum".

This is an attempt to interfere with the natural processes of semantics which we looked at in the section on semantic change in Chapter 7. Newspeak would try to halt semantic broadening and get rid of connotations and synonyms.

We're going to consider how that would work with a number of adjectives and abstract nouns in the table below. Copy it and see how much you can add from your knowledge of semantics.

word	connotations	synonyms
free	given permission not limited needing no payment	open unenclosed released unlimited
happy		contented carefree
equal	fair	identical
memory	influence	reminiscence
truth	virtue	honesty
strength	dependability	power endurance

Synonyms/antonyms and the paradox

As you know, synonyms are pairs of words with similar meanings, while antonyms are pairs of words with opposite meanings. Where opposite meanings are paired in a sentence as if they were the same, a paradox is created.

The dictionary definition of "paradox" is "a seemingly absurd or contradictory statement or proposition which when investigated may prove to be well founded or true".

Writers use verbal paradoxes in different ways.

Orwell offers the paradoxical slogans "WAR IS PEACE … FREEDOM IS SLAVERY … IGNORANCE IS STRENGTH" to show how the government is trying to make people believe absurd things.

Oscar Wilde uses verbal paradoxes in a more humorous way, most famously in his play *The Importance of Being Earnest*.

Firstly, when Algernon has come to visit Jack in his London flat.

Algernon:	Well, what shall we do?
Jack:	Nothing!
Algernon:	It is awfully hard work doing nothing. However, I don't mind hard work where there is no definite object of any kind.

And later, when Jack wants Lady Bracknell's permission to marry her daughter.

Lady Bracknell:	A very good age to be married at. I have always been of opinion that a man who desires to get married should know either everything or nothing. Which do you know?
Jack:	[*After some hesitation.*] I know nothing, Lady Bracknell.
Lady Bracknell:	I am pleased to hear it. I do not approve of anything that tampers with natural ignorance. Ignorance is like a delicate exotic fruit; touch it and the bloom is gone.

Activity 9.4

In the following extract from the opening chapter of *1984*, Winston Smith (the central character in the novel) is looking out at London from the window of his flat.

When you've read the extract, you're going to do the following directed writing and comparative commentary task.

1. You are a spokesperson for the Ministry of Peace. You are going to deliver a speech at the end of the evening television news

broadcast, explaining the three slogans of the Party:

WAR IS PEACE

FREEDOM IS SLAVERY

IGNORANCE IS STRENGTH

Write the opening of this speech in about 150 words.

2. Compare the style and language of your speech with the style and language of the extract by Orwell.

The Ministry of Truth — Minitrue, in Newspeak — was startlingly different from any other object in sight. It was an enormous pyramidal structure of glittering white concrete, soaring up, terrace after terrace, 300 metres into the air. From where Winston stood it was just possible to read, picked out on its white face in elegant lettering, the three slogans of the Party:

WAR IS PEACE

FREEDOM IS SLAVERY

IGNORANCE IS STRENGTH

The Ministry of Truth contained, it was said, three thousand rooms above ground level, and corresponding ramifications below. Scattered about London there were just three other buildings of similar appearance and size. So completely did they dwarf the surrounding architecture that from the roof of Victory Mansions you could see all four of them simultaneously. They were the homes of the four Ministries between which the entire apparatus of government was divided. The Ministry of Truth, which concerned itself with news, entertainment, education, and the fine arts. The Ministry of Peace, which concerned itself with war. The Ministry of Love, which maintained law and order. And the Ministry of Plenty, which was responsible for economic affairs. Their names, in Newspeak: Minitrue, Minipax, Miniluv, and Miniplenty.

Descriptive writing

Activity 9.5

Before we leave this extract by George Orwell, let's have another look at how he describes the scene Winston is looking at.

Think about how and why Orwell – or indeed any writer – might use a description of a scene near the start of a novel.

The easy and obvious answer is to give the reader a picture – which of course film-makers can do in a single shot. It can also be to plant ideas in the reader's head about things which might happen later on.

Can you come up with any other ideas?

Now, pick out 10 of what you think are the most distinctive words and/or phrases used by Orwell to establish a scene and/or an atmosphere. For each word or phrase that you've picked out:

- make sure you know what word class(es) is (are) being used
- think about literal and figurative meanings
- look at how/where the word/phrase is placed in the sentence construction.

TIP

Remember that adjectives are not the only class of words which can have a descriptive effect. Look back at the extract from *The Big Sleep* by Raymond Chandler in Chapter 4.

Discussion

Orwell creates a description and in doing so establishes an atmosphere with careful choices of:

- verbs
  - "*soaring* up, terrace after terrace, 300 metres into the air" – a verb with connotations of being effortless and unstoppable, like a powerful bird
  - "So completely did they *dwarf* the surrounding architecture" – a noun which shifts word class and becomes a verb, with connotations of one larger and superior object among smaller, inferior ones, like Gulliver in Lilliput

- syntax
  - "normal" word order in English has the grammatical subject of the sentence before the verb, but twice in successive sentences Orwell fronts the verb: "*Scattered* about London there were just three other buildings of similar appearance and size. So completely did they *dwarf* the surrounding architecture …"

- nouns
  - "ramifications" is an interesting choice (an abstract noun) because it's normally used in modern English in a metaphorical sense to refer to the many possible consequences (usually complex and unwelcome) of an action or event. But Orwell uses it here in its older, more literal sense of "branches" – the building is a structure (like a tree) with roots that spread underground
  - "architecture" is also an abstract noun, used here instead of the (very!) concrete noun you might expect: "buildings"

Why does Orwell use these two abstract nouns? He's breaking his own rules (seen in Chapter 4) about good writing. In particular, he's ignoring his advice: "Never use a long word where a short one will do."

You need to think about this!

By using abstract nouns which, as you know, are intangible, Orwell may be suggesting that you can't quite get hold of things in the society of *1984*. You can't be sure what's underground. You can't know for certain how far the roots of the Party reach: at any moment you might find that they have reached right into what you thought was your private space. And this is what happens in the novel. (If you want to know exactly how, read it!)

Description into narrative – or not

In Chapter 2, you met the famous opening words of the "play for voices" *Under Milk Wood*, by Dylan Thomas. Thomas was an author who at times took descriptive writing to extremes, for example, creating new compound adjectives like "sloeblack" and "crowblack" to emphasize the darkness of the sea.

Descriptive writing of such an imaginative sort can be very enjoyable on its own. Both writer and reader can derive pleasure from the effect of well-constructed description.

But there's usually a further and more long-lasting purpose to the description, often leading into some kind of narrative.

Multi-purpose texts

The Department of Education and Training of New South Wales offers pupils the following simple distinction:

> *Factual texts inform, instruct or persuade by giving facts and information.*

> *Literary texts entertain or elicit an emotional response by using language to create mental images.*

But, as we know, this is a simplification. For example, travel writing, diaries and journals, and biographies/autobiographies are often very "literary" – they are factual to some extent, but they are much more than just informative.

Here's the opening of a book which the author describes as having begun as a "history and a description" of a historic city in the Middle East.

> **TIP**
>
> Remember that very few texts fit neatly into just one text type or genre. Narrative itself may only be one element in a text, and one text may have different purposes and audiences.

We kept climbing up and up. Soon, it seemed, I would be able to stretch out a hand and touch the cloud above the hill. Every now and then the man's foot disturbed a stone, which escaped down the slope in ugly leaps, drawing a dust of pebbles after it. Saffron butterflies fidgeted among the rocks and settled on shrubs whose substance had been blown out by wind and sun.

Everywhere up the hill these ghosts attended us: clumps of colourless thistles; filmy-leaved plants whose violet stalks fingered each other obscenely over the stone; bushes which threw up thorns and noxious berries.

The sun had drunk up almost all life. The weeds themselves only flowered by miracle. Men had left rubbish behind, familiar objects which assumed a curious importance among the rocks: tendrils of rope, warped shoes, tins, shreds of cloth, corn cobs, broken plates decorated with sad flowers.

Mirror to Damascus by Colin Thubron

Activity 9.6

1. Imagine you work for the tourist board of the area that Colin Thubron describes in the extract above. Write the voice-over for a short television advertisement (50–75 words) aimed at encouraging wildlife enthusiasts to visit the area.

2. Compare the style and language of your voice-over with the style and language of the original account.

Hint: Select five negative details from the original which you can "re-position" as positive and encouraging details, slanted to appeal to wildlife enthusiasts.

Discussion

This activity required you to carry out an extreme transformation. The original passage describes a hostile landscape and is full of unpleasant images. Even the butterflies seem uncomfortable: first they "fidgeted", and then when eventually they "settled" it was on shrubs that were withered. Where natural forms have been given human characteristics, these are even more unpleasant: "plants whose violet stalks fingered each other obscenely". And man-made objects have started to develop characteristics of the natural: "tendrils of rope".

So what could you possibly have found that you could "spin" as an advantage?

1. Weeds that only "flowered by miracle" could be presented as a unique feature: "Come and see the miraculous flowering weeds!"

2. Saffron butterflies could be "re-positioned" as a marvel of nature: "Be amazed by the dazzling sunshine-yellow butterflies!"

3. Slant the rubbish as an advantage: "Man has made his mark on the area. Even the most familiar *objets trouvés* assume a curious importance among these barren rocks." (A touch of French can work wonders, and not just on restaurant menus!)

A brief language-change detour

Lynda Mugglestone (Professor of the History of English at Oxford University) wrote on "spin" in an Oxford Dictionary blog from 2011.

Spin is one of those words which could perhaps now do with a bit of "spin" in its own right. From its beginnings in the idea of honest labour and toil (in terms of etymology, spin descends from the spinning of fabric or thread), it has come to suggest the twisting of words rather than fibres – a verbal untrustworthiness intended to deceive and disguise. Often associated with newspapers and politicians, to use spin is to manipulate meaning, to twist truth for particular ends – usually with the aim of persuading readers or listeners that things are other than they are. As in idioms such as to put a "positive spin on something" – or a "negative spin on something" – one line of meaning is concealed, while another – at least intentionally – takes its place. Spin is language which, for whatever reason, has designs on us.

Activity 9.7

See if you can do the opposite – that is, adopt a negative rather than a positive angle – with the following text, an extract from a website originating in Bangalore. The writer is describing a National Park.

Tryst with Nature – Bannerghatta National Park

If you keep your eyes and ears open, you will be treated to the delight of exotic species of both flora and fauna. There are gigantic and overwhelmingly beautiful trees that will make you stand and stare in awe. These trees also provide shelter all round the year, helping maintain the temperature and humidity of the park to tolerable levels. The monsoon brings refreshing showers, covering the place in a blanket of lush green so that it is both soothing and pleasing to visit. Bamboos can be seen dotting the park and a small portion of it is dedicated to Eucalyptus plantations.

A diversity of wildlife can be seen in this park. To say so would be something of an understatement indeed. Elephants, cheetal, slow loris, wild boar, fox, squirrels, porcupine, muntjac, bonnet macaque, gaur, leopard, wild pig, sambar, barking deer, langur, bison, white tiger, Bengal tiger, panther and sloth bear can be found in abundance to name a few. These animals have been preserved in their natural habitat so as to allow them to propagate. If you wish to visit the park to spot wildlife, then doing so between November and June would be a good idea. The collection of wildlife here is sure to spark your interest.

A visit to the Bannerghatta National Park can be aptly described as a Tryst with Nature.

The entire area of the park includes 10 reserve forests from the Anekal Range. The forests are lined with hills abounding in ancient temples. The vegetation is mainly scrub land and dense dry and moist deciduous forests. The Suvarnamukhi stream, originating from the Suvarnamukhi Hill, cuts through the park. At a distance of 2km from this hill, the Suvarnamukhi pond is believed to have curative powers.

The Bannerghatta National Park boasts of a snake park that houses a unique collection of these scaly and slithering beauties. You will encounter innumerable species of snakes here. Other major attractions are a crocodile farm, aquarium and museum.

1. Imagine you recently visited this National Park, but you did not enjoy the experience. Many of the features which are described in such positive terms here were a big disappointment to you and your family.

   You decide to send an email to the director of the tourist board responsible for publicity for the National Park, pointing out how your experience of the attraction fell far short of what it promised.

   Write the text of this email in 120–150 words.

2. Compare the style and language of your email complaint with the style and language of the original website description.

Hints:

- Think about your *audience*. Students doing directed writing tasks that involve letters or emails of complaint or protest often lose sight of who they are writing to: they assume that the recipient is personally responsible, and will be able to put right whatever has been wrong. Here, you are not writing to the author of the website description; but you *are* writing to someone who you might reasonably expect to take some action.

- Think about the *purpose* of your email. Do you just want your disappointment to be recognized and acknowledged? Or are you asking for something more specific?

- Think about the *context* of language use for our text and the original text. Email is often brief and *transactional*; an article about a place to visit is likely to be more expansive and *expressive*.

Discussion

The simplest level of commentary is to recognize broad patterns and tendencies of language use. For example, the lexical choices in the original passage are likely to be positive, as the writer wants to construct a favourable impression of the National Park. But at A Level you need to go further and deeper than that: you need to analyse and explore.

We'll look for two particular linguistic species:

1. You would expect to find description, and *positive evaluative adjectives*. These are not difficult to locate in the passage, but you need to think more precisely about how they are used.

   Linguists refer to the process by which one word affects the meaning of another as **modification**. (You came across the term "modifier" in Chapter 2.) Most often, nouns are modified by adjectives and verbs are modified by adverbs. And, most of the time, the modifying word comes first.

   So we can analyse the following sentence from the end of the first paragraph: "The monsoon brings *refreshing* showers, covering the place in a blanket of *lush* green so that it is both *soothing* and *pleasing* to visit".

   All of the highlighted words are positive evaluative lexical choices. The first two provide *adjectival pre-modification*: they tell us what kind of showers and what kind of green to expect. The next two provide *adjectival post-modification*: they tell us what "it" (the place) is like once it's been bathed by the refreshing showers.

2. The use of *active* and/or *passive verb constructions* is always potentially interesting.

   As you'll remember from Chapter 2:

   – verbs used in the active voice involve the grammatical subject of the clause or sentence performing some action

   – verbs used in the passive voice involve the grammatical subject of the clause or sentence having some action done to them.

   Think about what you would expect to find in a description of a visitor attraction.

In an article about an activity holiday or a place where you would pursue a particular interest, you might expect lots of active verb constructions, used to draw attention to what you would be doing. You would be the *agent*.

In an article about a place where you would receive some kind of treatment – beauty therapy, for example – you might expect lots of passive verb constructions, used to draw attention to what you would have done to you! You would be the *recipient*.

What do we find in this article?

Right from the start, a mixture of active and passive verb constructions:

"*If you keep your eyes and ears open, you will be treated to* the delight of exotic species of both flora and fauna."

So, the visitor has to do something (active verb: *keep* your eyes and ears open), but it's something fairly natural and easy, and will lead to a pleasurable experience (passive verb: you will *be treated* to the delight of exotic species).

Now look back at your directed writing task, your email. How helpful would it be to analyse your own choices of active/passive verbs and your own use of pre- or post-modification?

It may be that neither of the tools illustrated here is of any use for the next do-it-yourself job I need to do. If the tap is dripping, I'll need a spanner and a pair of stilsons.

Similarly, if there are no significant instances of active as opposed to passive verbs or pre-/post-modification in your writing, there's no point wasting time locating insignificant instances, and then wasting more time in trying to prove that they're important.

Why is that?

- Because, as you'll remember, the answer to the question "What's not red?" is "No tomatoes" – and that's no use to anyone.

- Because identification of language features is a basic skill – it's useful, but it's only a start. The real work comes in analysing the workings and effects of what you've found.

TIP

Bear in mind, this is quite a literary description: it's not a "hard sell", full of facts and figures and prices.

TIP

Examiners say that the feature of language on which students waste most time is completely unimportant examples of pronoun use. The fact that you can recognise a feature of language doesn't make it significant.

Activity 9.8

One master of literature whose use of adjectival pre-modification is well worth studying is F. Scott Fitzgerald.

Here's an extract from his most famous novel *The Great Gatsby*. You may have studied the novel at some stage. If you have, you probably noticed how inventive and original this author is in his lexical choices.

At this point in the novel, Nick (the narrator) has invited Daisy to tea, with the intention that she should meet Gatsby. Daisy arrives in her car in the pouring rain.

The pre-modifying adjectives have been removed from the passage and replaced with the numbers 1 to 13. Try to fill the gaps with adjectives of your own choice which you think make sense and are consistent with the tone/style/register of the rest of the passage. (You can check your version with the original, which is at the end of this chapter.)

Under the (1) (2) lilac-trees a (3) (4) car was coming up the drive. It stopped. Daisy's face, tipped sideways beneath a (5) (6) hat, looked out at me with a (7) (8) smile.

"Is this absolutely where you live, my dearest one?"

The (9) ripple of her voice was a (10) tonic in the rain. I had to follow the sound of it for a moment, up and down, with my ear alone, before any words came through. A (11) streak of hair lay like a dash of blue paint across her cheek, and her hand was (12) with (13) drops as I took it to help her from the car.

Discussion

Some of the missing lexical items are *high-frequency* words – that is, they are common and often used.

The last two, however, are *low-frequency* adjectives, which is not to say that we would never come across them, but we might have to stop to think about their meaning.

And you will have noticed that the missing adjectives in the first paragraph all come in pairs. For a student with an inquiring mind – that's you! – this raises the interesting question of the order in which we use adjectives in English.

Adjective order

Fluent speakers and writers of English instinctively sequence adjectives in a particular order.

(When you have read Chapter 11, especially the sections on language acquisition, you might want to quarrel with my use of "instinctively" there.)

An inquiring mind

And as I write this, the lead story in the education section of today's *South China Morning Post* begins: "A thoroughly inquisitive mind is essential for students aspiring to enter top universities … Top candidates are also expected to demonstrate a deeper level of thinking."

Some highly accomplished writers whose first language is not English occasionally deviate from that order. For example, the novelist Joseph Conrad (1857–1924, born Józef Teodor Konrad Korzeniowski) was Polish, and did not speak English until he was in his twenties, yet managed to write some of the most admired novels in the English language.

He introduces one of his characters in *The Secret Agent* with the following words.

> The footman threw open a door, and stood aside. The feet of Mr Verloc felt a thick carpet. The room was large, with three windows; and a young man with a *shaven, big face*, sitting in a roomy armchair before *a vast mahogany writing-table*, said …

Does that adjective-order, "shaven, big face", sound right to you? On the other hand, "vast mahogany" does sound right …

Try the following exercise, and get several of your classmates to do the same. You are likely to find – unless you cheat! – that you all sequence adjectives in much the same way.

Activity 9.9

Students often claim in their analysis of a text that the basic sentence type in English contains a subject, a verb and an object. This is oversimplified, but works for **transitive** verbs – verbs which take a direct object.

So, for this activity, let's try creating some basic sentences, then decorating and embellishing them with multiple adjectives, one at a time, and putting them in order.

You can personalize these sentences, if you like, by using your own name as the subject; and you can make it much harder for yourself by insisting on alliterative adjectives! If this makes finding more adjectives impossibly difficult (for example, if your name begins with the letter z) then don't do it!

Here's an example:

Saeed bought soaps.
(add an adjective)

Saeed bought scented soaps.

(add another adjective)

Saeed bought sickly scented soaps.

(add another adjective)

Saeed bought six sickly scented soaps.

(add another adjective)

Saeed bought six sizeable sickly scented soaps.

(and so on …)

Now try your own. If you get stuck with the alliterative method, start again with a different item as the (grammatical) direct object and a different verb. You could even abandon the verb and concentrate simply on adding adjectives to pre-modify a noun.

The more examples you generate, the more linguistic data you will have to use. You are putting together a mini corpus which you can then investigate.

What "rules" of adjective order can you deduce from your data?

Hint: Think about putting the adjectives into groups or categories.

In my soap example above, I started with "scented", an adjective to do with the sense of smell. You could call that a *sensory* adjective, or you could be very precise and say it was *olfactory* – the technical term for anything to do with the sense of smell.

Then I added "sickly", an evaluative adjective with negative connotations. You could call this an adjective of opinion.

Next I added "six". Grammarians might argue over whether **cardinal** numbers (one, two, three) are adjectives or determiners, or even a word class of their own. There's greater agreement about **ordinal** numbers (first, second, third), since they seem to describe a quality as well as providing a way of counting. For the purposes of our activity here, "six" behaves like an adjective – it pre-modifies the noun "soaps" so it can be part of the investigation about word order.

"Sizeable" is an adjective of size (obviously!) though rather an imprecise one. It suggests that an object is fairly large in relation to other similar objects.

I'm going to stop at four adjectives, and invite you to see whether you can deduce (or "extrapolate") any rules about adjective order from our very limited data, and to ask yourself whether what you deduce matches your own mini corpus of linguistic data.

It looks as if categories of adjectives go in this order:

number ➜ size ➜ evaluative ➜ sensory

What if we added colour? Saffron is a nice shade of yellow, just right for sickly scented soaps.

Saeed bought six sizeable sickly scented saffron soaps.

This word order would also work if saffron were a material or a substance rather than a colour – which in some cases it might be – as with saffron rice.

So now we have an order which goes:

number ➜ size ➜ evaluative ➜ sensory ➜ colour/substance

Look through your own data to see how well it matches the pattern above. There may be some slight variations, but adjectives of material/substance are usually last, and adjectives of number are usually first.

One more simple example, without the limits of alliteration, then we'll look at a more obviously literary text:

I could see, waving high on top of each building, seven large rectangular red-white-and-blue British flags.

number ➜ size ➜ shape ➜ colour ➜ nationality

Activity 9.10

You're going to read two passages from fictional literary texts, written a little more than 100 years apart. Each one contains some description and some narrative, and the first also has a short snatch of dialogue.

As you read each one, jot down what seem to you *genuinely significant* aspects of style and language. Your analytical toolkit is now fairly full and heavy: you need to choose your methods with care. The instructions for the task are at the end of the second passage.

Here's the first passage. It's from the second chapter of a novel published in 1899. (This chapter is called "The Strange Lady".) You might notice how, like Joseph Conrad, the author – an American called Booth Tarkington – tells us how one of the men is "shaven".

Suddenly there was a hum and a stir and a buzz of whispering in the room. Two gray old men and two pretty young women passed up the aisle to the platform. One old man was stalwart and ruddy, with a cordial eye and a handsome, smooth-shaven, big face. The other was bent and trembled slightly; his face was very white; he had a fine high brow, deeply lined, the brow of a scholar, and a grandly flowing white beard that covered his chest, the beard of a patriarch. One of the young women was tall and had the rosy cheeks and pleasant eyes of her father, who preceded her. The other was the strange lady.

A universal perturbation followed her progress up the aisle, if she had known it. She was small and fair, very daintily and beautifully made …

Mrs. Columbus Landis, wife of the proprietor of the Palace Hotel, conferring with a lady in the next seat, applied an over-burdened adjective: "It ain't so much she's han'some, though she is, that – but don't you notice she's got a kind of smart look to her? Her bein' so teeny, kind of makes it more so, somehow, too."

And here is the second extract. It comes from near the beginning of a novel published in 2005. The narrator has moved to a different town in the United States, and this is her first day at a new school.

They were sitting in the corner of the cafeteria, as far away from where I sat as possible in the long room. There were five of them. They weren't talking, and they weren't eating, though they each had a tray of untouched food in front of them. They weren't gawking at me, unlike most of the other students, so it was safe to stare at them without fear of meeting an excessively interested pair of eyes. But it was none of these things that caught, and held, my attention.

They didn't look anything alike. Of the three boys, one was big – muscled like a serious weight lifter, with dark, curly hair. Another was taller, leaner, but still muscular, and honey blond. The last was lanky, less bulky, with untidy, bronze-colored hair. He was more boyish than the others, who looked like they could be in college, or even teachers here rather than students.

The girls were opposites. The tall one was statuesque. She had a beautiful figure, ... the kind that made every girl around her take a hit on her self-esteem just by being in the same room. Her hair was golden, gently waving to the middle of her back. The short girl was pixielike, thin in the extreme, with small features. Her hair was a deep black, cropped short and pointing in every direction.

Compare the style and language of the two passages, paying particular attention to how the two writers use contrast.

Discussion

You probably noticed the following features of *style*:

- Passage 1 was in the third person; Passage 2 in the first person.

- Both passages employ a variety of sentence lengths and structures.

- Passage 1 employs one notable simple sentence and places it, for effect, at the end of the first paragraph: "The other was the strange lady".

- Passage 2 employs four notably simple sentences. What can you say about their structure and where they are placed?

- Pronoun use genuinely is interesting in both passages.

  - In Passage 1, the characters are either referred to by fairly vague noun phrases ("Two gray old men and two pretty young women") or by third-person pronouns.

  - In Passage 2, the narrator first refers to the five characters as a group, using the third-person plural pronoun "they", then describes them individually, referring to each with fairly vague determiners or noun phrases with simple adjectives ("Another ... The last ... The tall one ...").

What about the *language*?

Most students find it easiest to comment on lexical choices, and these are likely to be more obvious in a passage written at some time in the past. But it's never enough to identify a few lexical items and just dismiss them by commenting that they are **archaic** ("no longer in everyday use but sometimes used to impart an old-fashioned flavour").

Which lexical items in Passage 1 might be seen as archaic?

- Most people would say that "universal perturbation" is a collocation we no longer use in even the most literary of texts. It means more or less the same as "general disturbance".

- "Stalwart" and "cordial" are low-frequency lexis in modern English. "Patriarch" more often appears in its adjectival form "patriarchal" in the collocation "patriarchal society", which almost always has pejorative connotations.

- "Handsome" in modern English almost always connotes masculine appearance, or it can have a more figurative meaning of "generous in a gentlemanly way", as in a "handsome gesture" or a "handsome present".

- When Mrs Columbus Landis uses the "over-burdened adjective" "han'some", she clearly intends feminine attractiveness.

- Otherwise, the lexis of Passage 1 is mostly simple, and in modern English would be high frequency.

So, if you found Passage 1 harder to follow than Passage 2, why is that?

I suggest it's for the same reason that most students find Shakespeare difficult at first. Individual words are not the problem most of the time, but the order in which they are placed (the syntax) is different from modern syntax, and therefore off-putting.

Let's look at just one sentence. It is compound-complex, consisting of two coordinating clauses followed by a (subordinated) relative clause:

> "One of the young women was tall and had the rosy cheeks and pleasant eyes of her father, who preceded her."

Two elements of thought have been combined here: the description of the young lady, and the link between her and her father. *Four* elements of grammatical/syntactical meaning are present, however, and in modern English we might have had them presented to us in four separate simple sentences:

1. One of the young women was tall.
2. She had rosy cheeks and pleasant eyes.
3. Her father had rosy cheeks and pleasant eyes too.
4. Her father was walking in front of her.

In Passage 2, the syntax is mostly easier to unravel. Here's a compound-complex sentence from Passage 2, longer than the one we've just analysed from Passage 1 but very similar in structure. It is compound-complex, consisting of two coordinating clauses followed by a (subordinated) "concessive" clause beginning with "though":

"They weren't talking, and they weren't eating, though they each had a tray of untouched food in front of them."

Most people would find it easier to follow the meaning of the Passage 2 sentence. Can you explain why?

Hint: In the sentence from Passage 1, the final (subordinate, relative) clause involves a shift of the grammatical subject from one of the young women to her father.

Conclusion

In the previous chapter on media texts, we considered some quite literary material.

In this chapter on literary texts, we've considered some features of spoken language and investigated texts which shift between genres. You've done a number of directed writing tasks, including shifts of genre and text type from literary material to a party political broadcast, a tourist board voice-over, and an email complaint.

You've also done a "cloze" procedure exercise, replacing missing pre-modifying adjectives, and a mini corpus linguistics study into adjective order in English.

The final section of this chapter involved some highly detailed analysis at a complex level. If there were parts you didn't understand, come back to them after you've worked through the next two chapters.

In the next chapter, on spoken texts, we are quite likely to find just as much overlap as we have in the previous two between what might at first seem separate text types. We will also explore a quite different meaning of the word "overlap".

Follow-up to activities

For Activity 9.8: original version of extract from *The Great Gatsby*.

> Under the dripping bare lilac-trees a large open car was coming up the drive. It stopped. Daisy's face, tipped sideways beneath a three-cornered lavender hat, looked out at me with a bright ecstatic smile.
>
> "Is this absolutely where you live, my dearest one?"
>
> The exhilarating ripple of her voice was a wild tonic in the rain. I had to follow the sound of it for a moment, up and down, with my ear alone, before any words came through. A damp streak of hair lay like a dash of blue paint across her cheek, and her hand was wet with glistening drops as I took it to help her from the car.

Advanced textual analysis: spoken texts

Introduction

Peter Elbow, Emeritus Professor of English at the University of Massachusetts Amherst, wrote a book in 2012, *Vernacular Eloquence: what can speech bring to writing*, in which he defines speech and writing as different linguistic products.

> People commonly assume that spoken and written language are different. But strictly speaking, there is no real difference between them. Linguists like to create huge "corpora" of millions of strings of spoken and written language. When they jumble together all the strings, they find they can't usually identify which ones were spoken and which were written. That is, when we look at spoken and written language that was produced in a full range of human contexts and purposes, we find that almost any kind of language can be found coming out of a mouth or from a hand.
>
> … People tend to assume that writing is more formal than speaking, but that's not always the case. Some writing (such as what people write in some diaries and letters) is more "speechy" than some speech (such as what people utter in some carefully planned lectures, announcements, and interviews).
>
> But after linguists are done demolishing the distinction between spoken and written language, they turn around and start using it again – but in a careful way. They recognize that it's useful to distinguish what they call "*typical* speech" and "*typical* writing." That is, they distinguish between two common *kinds* or *genres* or *registers* of language: everyday conversational *spoken* language versus the written language that's common in careful informational or expository prose – "essayist" writing.

Activity 10.1

Re-read the three paragraphs above and summarize in note form (in your own words) the main points the writer is making.

No excuses! You know how to make notes.

Discussion

The author helpfully sums up his own argument about the differences between speech and writing at the end of the article, saying that:

- they are not different if we look at the full range of spoken and written language produced in the full range of situations and contexts

- they are, however, very different if we restrict our view to easy, conversational, casual chat versus essayist writing

- it is usually this restricted view that people have in mind when they talk about spoken and written language.

This argument supports what we've found throughout the last three chapters. Most texts shift between different registers, and it's risky to jump to conclusions about the language which will be used to construct any particular text type.

We noticed in Chapter 9 that it's better to use the term "utterances" than the word "sentences" when discussing spoken language because in casual conversation people rarely speak in what would be considered grammatically perfect sentences in a piece of writing.

However, some interactions involving speech are more prepared and less spontaneous, and thus (probably) more formal, for example, presentations and interviews.

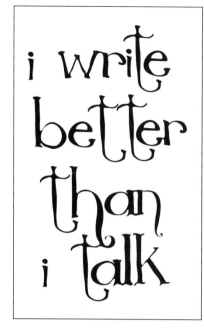

Spoken language and politics

In many situations involving spoken language, the audience will be relatively private and immediately present. In the world of public life and politics, however, speakers have to imagine possible distant and future audiences.

We will now see how audience affects language in a range of texts.

Activity 10.2

The following text is a transcript of the beginning of an audio broadcast made in 2000 by Tony Blair, then Prime Minister of the United Kingdom.

What differences can you find between the language used here and the language you might expect in a written text?

Hello and welcome to what I am sure will be the first of many direct broadcasts from the Downing Street website. I'm sitting here at my desk in Downing Street in front of my PC terminal, which I'm just getting to use after many years of not really wanting to come to terms with the new computer technology. I did a course. I'm coming to terms with it. I'm using the new PC terminal and it really brings me to reflect upon what I wanted to say to you this week, which is of course the importance of education and skills – the importance of education and skills for everyone including adults but most particularly for our children. My children, like others, are having to learn the new technology. They have to become expert at it and they are going to be leaving school and going to work in a world in which skill and talent and ability is not just their route to personal fulfilment, it is their route to prosperity. They will need those skills and talents if they have got any chance of succeeding. And the country needs them to be highly skilled as well.

In Britain, we've always been excellent at educating an elite well. The top 20 per cent have always been pretty well educated. But for the majority, the standards just haven't been high enough. We've had a poverty of ambition and aspiration which has meant that large numbers of people leave school either without qualifications or without nearly the qualifications they need. Our vision for the education system is really like this. We need education throughout life. Everyone understands that.

It has to begin at a young age so the first stage is nursery education for the four year olds and three year olds. And we're pretty well on the way to achieving that. The four year olds have now got the chance of decent nursery education. We've doubled the numbers of three year olds who get the chances of nursery education and will extend that further over time.

Then after that, at the second stage, we need primary schools that really focus on the basics – getting literacy and numeracy right – and I'll come back to that in a minute.

Audio broadcast by Tony Blair

You could probably find a few examples of "typical" features of spoken language.

- Tony Blair breaks the rule of formal written language that decrees you should never begin a sentence with a conjunction: "*And* we're pretty well on the way to achieving that."

- There are some short simple sentences: "I did a course. I'm coming to terms with it."

- He uses the **present continuous tense** to give the impression this is happening now: "*I'm sitting* here at my desk in Downing Street in front of my PC terminal, which *I'm just getting* to use after many years of not really wanting to …"

But otherwise there are few signs of genuinely spontaneous speech. What explanations can you suggest for that from the context?

Look back at Chapter 2 where you encountered speeches made by two American presidents, Abraham Lincoln and John F. Kennedy. As you noticed then, both were trying to conjure up a presidential voice to match the seriousness of the occasion, and to do that they used a range of rhetorical devices. (You also saw in that chapter how, more recently, Barack Obama employed rhetoric on a historic occasion.)

Here (and in the Nelson Mandela speech you looked at in Chapter 5) the speaker is conscious of the need to create a particular impression. Blair's purpose is nowhere near as serious as Mandela's, nor is the occasion so historic, although Tony Blair is creating a "first" of a less momentous kind. The audience is less immediate: anyone logging on to the 10 Downing Street website can access the broadcasts/podcasts.

During his time as Prime Minister, Tony Blair was seen as a very skillful public speaker. One of his particular skills was the ability to make a prepared speech sound spontaneous. Why would this be useful to a politician?

"No education, no skills, no experience, no character references... I'm afraid the only thing left for you is politics."

A linguistic joke

(When you come to think of it, all jokes are linguistic.)

In the 17th century, the verb "to lie" was used in most of the same ways as it is today – mainly in the senses of "lying down" and "telling a lie" – but was also used (semantic broadening) to mean "to live" somewhere for long enough that you would have your own bed to sleep in (to lie on). The English diplomat Sir Henry Wotton made a famous joke out of this ambiguity when he was made ambassador to Venice. Commenting on how one of the skills of a politician was the ability to tell people what they want to hear, he said that an ambassador was a man "sent to lie abroad for his country".

Semantic amelioration has taken place with the common noun "politician". Although few people might admit to admiring politicians, the term itself in modern times is not pejorative. However, when the word first emerged – probably in the 1580s – it rapidly acquired negative/pejorative connotations.

Shakespeare certainly uses the word in pejorative ways:

In *King Lear*:

> Get thee glass eyes,
> And like a scurvy politician seem
> To see the things thou dost not …

And in *Hamlet*, when Horatio and Hamlet consider a skull which has been thrown up by one of the grave-diggers:

> It might be the pate of a politician … one that would circumvent God, might it not?

Euphemisms, a way of saying something to make it seem less unpleasant, have often arisen from situations in which politicians were accused of telling lies (or were trying to avoid doing so).

In 1906 Winston Churchill used the term "terminological inexactitude": "that word in its full sense could not be applied without a risk of terminological inexactitude" rather than say something was a lie.

Another phrase that has come into common use is being "economical with the truth", an expression which gained currency when used by Sir Robert Armstrong, British cabinet secretary, in a trial in 1986:

- Lawyer: What is the difference between a misleading impression and a lie?

- Armstrong: A lie is a straight untruth.

- Lawyer: What is a misleading impression? A sort of bent untruth?

- Armstrong: As one person said, it is perhaps being "economical with the truth".

As well as employing euphemisms, politicians have often been accused of using **circumlocution**, "the use of many words where fewer would do, especially in a deliberate attempt to be vague or evasive".

Activity 10.3

Many authors have satirized circumlocution. The character who speaks or writes in unnecessarily complex and roundabout ways is often used for comedic effect by novelists, playwrights, and scriptwriters. In the novel *Little Dorrit* (1855), Charles Dickens invented a government department which he called the Circumlocution Office. (As Tony Blair said: "And I'll come back to that in a minute …")

The extract below is part of a satirical sketch from "Monty Python's Flying Circus", a television comedy show from 1970. Read it, make a note of features of lexis and syntax which show signs of circumlocution, then give yourself an hour to do both parts of the following task.

1. Imagine you watched this comedy sketch, but you didn't find it funny at all. You are angry at the way Mr Pudifoot was treated by the interviewer, and you have decided to send an email to the producers of the comedy series, complaining about a member of the public being exploited in this way. Write the text of your email in 120–150 words.

2. Compare the style and language of your reply with the style and language of the original comedy sketch.

Interviewer: Good evening. Well, we have in the studio tonight a man who says things in a very roundabout way. Isn't that so, Mr. Pudifoot?

Mr. Pudifoot: Yes.

Interviewer: Have you always said things in a very roundabout way?

Mr. Pudifoot: Yes.

Interviewer: Well, I can't help noticing that, for someone who claims to say things in a very roundabout way, your last two answers have had very little of the discursive quality about them.

Mr. Pudifoot: Oh, well, I'm not very talkative today. It's a form of defensive response to intense interrogative stimuli. I used to get it badly when I was a boy – well, when I say "very badly," in fact, do you remember when there was that fashion for, you know, little poodles with small coats …

Interviewer: Ah, now you're beginning to talk in a roundabout way.

Mr. Pudifoot: Oh, I'm sorry.

Interviewer: No, no, no, no. Please do carry on because that is in fact why we wanted you on the show.

Mr. Pudifoot: I thought it was because you were interested in me as a human being. (*gets up and leaves*)

Monty Python's Flying Circus

Discussion

There are several layers of register and context to cut through here.

Firstly, the sketch is satirizing television programmes in which people with unusual skills or habits are interviewed. How is this done?

Secondly, the writers began the sketch by constructing Mr Pudifoot as the victim of an interviewer who just wants to exploit him for the sake of the programme, but ended the sketch by having the "victim" refusing to join in. His final utterance – "I thought it was because you were interested in me as a human being" – is a complete shift of register.

Thirdly, the sketch is not meant to be taken seriously, but the directed writing task puts you in the position of someone who *is* taking it seriously. That means shifting your point of view, and consequently shifting your register.

In their television series, the writers of the Mr Pudifoot sketch used to signal a **topic-shift** at the end of every sketch with the words …

> **TIP**
>
> Mark schemes for directed writing tasks always emphasize the importance of understanding audience, form, purpose, conventions, and effects. Although your grasp of these aspects will be demonstrated in an explicit way when you do the second (comparative commentary) half of this kind of examination question, you can't do the first (re-cast) part of the task without at least an implicit grasp of how to shift the point of view and the register.
>
> We'll keep coming back to this!

Features of spontaneous speech

The individual speaker

It is always a bad idea to consider spoken language as an inferior version of written language, that it is full of "mistakes". Students who adopt a "deficit" approach to spoken language data and concentrate on what's wrong with it tend to do very badly in responding to tasks.

As we noticed earlier, some spoken texts are not spontaneous. Speeches are normally prepared, even if the speaker deliberately uses some features which are normally associated with unprepared, spontaneous speech.

Verbal fillers

Verbal fillers are one example. These are words and phrases which, in the particular context, have very little lexical or grammatical function. They act instead as a way for the speaker to **hold the floor** – that is, to signal that they intend to continue speaking, but they haven't quite got their thoughts in order yet.

The novelist Kingsley Amis makes use of this for comic effect in his novel *Lucky Jim*. Jim Dixon is about to give a public lecture. He is reluctant and nervous, and has had quite a few glasses of sherry and whisky in the belief that they will help him give a confident performance. When he starts speaking, he realizes that he's been imitating the lecturing style of his boss, Professor Welch.

When he'd spoken about half a dozen sentences, Dixon realized that something was still very wrong. The murmuring in the gallery had grown a little louder. Then he realized what it was that was so wrong: he'd gone on using Welch's manner of address. In an effort to make his script sound spontaneous, he'd inserted an 'of course' here, a 'you see' there, an 'as you might call it' somewhere else; nothing so firmly recalled Welch as that sort of thing. Further, in a partly unconscious attempt to make the stuff sound right, i.e. acceptable to Welch, he'd brought in a number of favourite Welch tags: 'integration of the social consciousness', 'identification of work with craft', and so on. And now, as this flashed into his labouring mind, he began to trip up on one or two phrases, to hesitate, and to repeat words, even to lose his place once so that a ten-second pause supervened.

Lucky Jim by Kingsley Amis

The effect in this fictional example is the opposite to the impact politicians aim for when they try to sound spontaneous even when they are prepared.

Turn-taking

Turn-taking is the mechanism by which conversations and other spoken interactions are carried on. One speaker who has been holding the floor gives way – **yields the turn** – to another speaker.

In fictionalized or scripted conversation, this happens neatly: one speaker finishes and another takes over. If you look back at the extracts in Chapter 9 from *The Importance of Being Earnest*, you can see how each speaker provides a cue for the next. Obviously, the dramatist (Oscar Wilde in this case) has done this deliberately in order to help the audience follow the ideas in the scene.

Activity 10.4

Here is a longer extract from the scene in *The Importance of Being Earnest* in which Jack Worthing wants Lady Bracknell's permission to marry her daughter. Lady Bracknell has a high social position – and a high opinion of herself – which allows her to "interview" Jack.

- Read the extract. I'm going to refer to it as an "interaction", which is not a very literary term, but which will focus our attention on how the conversation works in terms of types of utterance. I'm also going to invite you to ignore Oscar Wilde's very witty paradoxes and social commentary, in favour of concentrating on turn-taking.

- Make a note of each utterance which provides a cue for the other speaker, and try to explain how that works.

Lady Bracknell: (*pencil and note-book in hand*) I feel bound to tell you that you are not down on my list of eligible young men, although I have the same list as the dear Duchess of Bolton has. We work together, in fact. However, I am quite ready to enter your name, should your answers be what a really affectionate mother requires. Do you smoke?

Jack: Well, yes, I must admit I smoke.

Lady Bracknell: I am glad to hear it. A man should always have an occupation of some kind. There are far too many idle men in London as it is. How old are you?

Jack: Twenty-nine.

Lady Bracknell: A very good age to be married at. I have always been of opinion that a man who desires to get married should know either everything or nothing. Which do you know?

Jack: (*after some hesitation*) I know nothing, Lady Bracknell.

Lady Bracknell: I am pleased to hear it. I do not approve of anything that tampers with natural ignorance. Ignorance is like a delicate exotic fruit; touch it and the bloom is gone. The whole theory of modern education is radically unsound. Fortunately in England, at any rate, education produces no effect whatsoever. If it did, it would prove a serious danger to the upper classes, and probably lead to acts of violence in Grosvenor Square. What is your income?

Jack: Between seven and eight thousand a year.

Lady Bracknell: (*makes a note in her book*) In land, or in investments?

Jack: In investments, chiefly.

Lady Bracknell: That is satisfactory.

The Importance of Being Earnest by Oscar Wilde

Discussion

Lady Bracknell asks the questions – you might say she is conducting an interview – and Jack responds each time with a short declarative answer. Did you notice that some of these show signs of **ellipsis**? Words which are unnecessary in the context of the conversation are left out. These are mostly grammatical-function words, and this is typical of natural unscripted speech too. For example, when asked "How old are you?" most people would simply reply (as Jack does here) with a number, leaving out the personal pronoun ("I") and the corresponding part of the verb "to be" ("am").

Cooperative principle and Grice's maxims

A relevant theory which you may have come across is the idea that there is an underlying cooperative principle in all conversational interactions. Paul Grice is the theorist most associated with this idea, and it can be helpful to refer to some or all of his four maxims.

- Maxim of quantity: only say as much or as little as you need to in a situation
- Maxim of quality: only say what you know to be true
- Maxim of relevance: only say what's relevant to this situation, here and now
- Maxim of manner: avoid being unclear/obscure or ambiguous

Like all theories, the cooperative principle and Grice's maxims can be useful if you apply them carefully, but they don't explain all interactions, and they are not a set of "rules" which people have to follow.

However, it can be useful to use the term **flout** to describe ignoring one of the maxims. As you will see below, an apparent flout might turn out not to be a flout at all.

Activity 10.5

The partly completed table below explores a range of responses to the question "How old are you?" for different situations and contexts. Complete the table, and add as many more examples as you can think of.

Tip: Remember to apply what you've learned about spoken language, and always to think about how function and context affect choices of language.

Context	Response	Linguistic analysis
Trying to buy an alcoholic drink	"I've got my student card here. It shows I'm 19."	The implicature of the question is: "You don't look old enough to be allowed to buy alcohol." The reply seems at first sight to be flouting the maxims of relevance and manner, but it's actually an entirely relevant answer in this situation.
Filling in a form at the dentist's office		
Chatting with friends		Might be sarcastic implicature, for example, if you've just done something childish or silly.
Being interviewed for a job		
Meeting someone for the first time	"None of your business!"	Elliptical construction. Deliberate flouting of the maxims of quantity and manner, in order to communicate that this is an impolite question in this situation.

Non-fluency

Sometimes called "dysfluency" or "disfluency", this term refers to the accidental features of spoken language that occur because in spontaneous speech we don't have the time to plan our utterances before we start to speak them. As a result, we hesitate, sometimes in silence and sometimes with some sort of sound to signal that we still want to talk but haven't yet worked out what we want to say.

In real-life, real-time interaction, turn-taking is likely to be much less clear cut than when it is represented by writers of fictional dialogue. Watch or listen to a few minute of dialogue from a film, play, or soap opera: the chances are that the speakers will be extremely fluent.

In natural spontaneous speech, speakers still provide each other with cues – they ask questions (interrogatives) or offer suggestions – but they are quite likely to interrupt or overlap each others' utterances since it's often not clear when/whether someone has finished speaking.

Speakers vary in how fluent they are in conversational interaction. But, as with everything in language use, the context makes all the difference. When I am teaching a lesson to a group of students in a classroom, I will be more fluent than if I am giving one-to-one tuition to an individual student who is struggling to understand.

TIP

It's always unhelpful to make assumptions about a speaker's level of education or social class on the basis of fluency/non-fluency!

Activity 10.6

The following passage is a transcription of an individual speaker who is relatively fluent. Nigel has just been asked about his "pet hate" – an idiomatic collocation that you may not have seen before meaning something for which you feel a strong dislike.

As this is a subject he has thought about, Nigel is able to talk about it at some length, and you'll notice he uses some low-frequency lexis. Even so – and even though no-one interrupts him – Nigel still pauses, uses verbal fillers, repeats himself unintentionally, hesitates, re-formulates, and repairs his utterance.

- Pick out what you think are significant features of language.

- For each one, try to explain how the context here – an individual speaker invited to give his opinion – leads to these particular linguistic features and structures.

Transcription key:	(.) = micro-pause	(1) = pause in seconds
	<u>underlined</u> = emphatic stress	

Nigel: I have a pet hate at the moment about football (1) professional (.) professional footballers (.) premier league (.) it's dis<u>gus</u>ting (.) you know they (.) some of those players should be taken off for abuse when they (.) when they go on at the referee for a bad decision the way they er (.) actually att<u>ack</u> um not actually <u>phys</u>ically but very intimidatingly (.) attack the referee's decisions (1) that is <u>abys</u>mal and that is maybe something that's (.) that's en<u>dem</u>ic (.) right throughout and it's a lack of respect if you like for authority isn't it (2) now those top professional footballers are showing no respect whatsoever for the (.) for the runner of the game

You probably noticed pauses, sometimes with unintentional repetitions ("professional (.) professional footballers"). There are voiced pauses ("er … um") and verbal fillers ("you know").

Nigel re-formulates and repairs one particular complex construction: "when they go on at the referee for a bad decision the way they er (.) actually att<u>ack</u> um not actually <u>physically</u> but very intimidatingly (.) attack the referee's decisions". Why do you think he does this?

He uses some complex low-frequency lexical items. The three adverbs he uses to pre- and post-modify the verb "attack" show him trying to express his thoughts precisely. The footballers don't literally attack the referee – they don't physically assault him – but Nigel wants to express his strong disapproval for this behaviour. He ends up using one adverb to modify the next – "not actually <u>physically</u>" – and then goes on to an unusual adverbial, the adverbial form of the adjective "intimidating".

The adjectives "disgusting" and "abysmal" are strongly pejorative. And while the adjective "endemic" is not directly pejorative in its denotative meaning, it has connotations of disease, as it comes from a lexical field of infection control.

He acknowledges his audience – although we don't know who that audience is – when he says "it's a lack of respect if you like for authority isn't it". The term for expressions such as "if you like" is a **hedge**: the speaker is softening or weakening the force of what he has just said by suggesting that the listener has some choice about how to receive the meaning.

Nigel also recognizes his audience when he ends his utterance with "isn't it". This kind of question, typically used at the end of an utterance to invite the listener to agree, is called a **tag question**. Like hedges, tag questions are thought to be used more frequently by women than by men, and suggest that the speaker is less than 100% certain of what she or he has just said, so is inviting speaker support from her or his audience. (We don't know from our transcript evidence whether Nigel received any support: it may have come in a paralinguistic way, with a nod of the head from the listener, or some back-channel noise like "uh huh" or "mm hmm".)

Lastly, you may have noticed how Nigel ends with a rather vague noun phrase to refer to the referee, and how he hesitates and repeats himself before he gets to it: "now those top professional footballers are showing no respect whatsoever for the (.) for the runner of the game".

Activity 10.7

Imagine you are a sports journalist writing an article about respect for authority in a number of sports.

1. Write the first paragraph of your article in 120–150 words, using as many of Nigel's ideas as you can.

2. Compare the style and language of your article with the style and language of the transcription of Nigel's speech.

Other hedges some speakers use include: "as it were", "if you see what I mean", "it seems to me", "maybe", "sort of", "kind of", and "like". When we come to consider ideas about gendered language in the next chapter, we'll consider research into "typical" male and female speech styles, some of which suggests that women use more hedges and other softeners than men do.

Interactions between speakers

Nigel's spoken utterance in the example above was, as we noticed, unusually fluent. It was also uninterrupted by any other speakers. Once we start to look at spontaneous interactions involving two or more speakers, we encounter a wider range of features in the transcript evidence.

Activity 10.8

The following passage is a transcription of part of a committee meeting held in London in 2010. The four speakers are from the London Organizing Committee of the 2012 Olympic and Paralympic Games. Here they are discussing the number of tickets to be made available to particular age groups.

With the help of the transcription key below, pick out what you think are significant features of spontaneous interaction. Try to account for each one by thinking about how the context affects the language.

Transcription key
(.) = micro-pause (1) = pause in seconds
CAPITALS = speaking with raised volume

// = speech overlap
<u>underlined</u> = emphatic stress

Paul: let's look at those numbers (.) but (.) before we do (.) London 2012 will be the first summer games in (.) certainly in
//
Dee: in living memory

Paul: CERTAINLY (.) in living memory where there are special prices for (.) for young people and for elderly people
//
Vicki: it hasn't been done

Paul: it certainly hasn't been done in the last thirty years (1) we followed that through directly from the Singapore promise (.) when we said we

//
Len: well we were en<u>trusted</u> with
//
Dee: we want to engage with YOUNG people (1) we want to make sure <u>they</u> can get to the games (.) the pay-your-age scheme that we have devised
//
Paul: one point three million tickets (.) and if you're <u>sixty</u>
//
Dee: as you said (.) one point three million tickets (.) anyway (.) the pay-your-age scheme means that a twelve year old pays twelve pounds

Len: (*laughs*) and a five year old pays five pounds

Paul: and if you are sixty (.) or over (.) you pay sixteen pounds (.) SIXTEEN POUNDS at two hundred and twenty sessions out of out of the six hundred and fifty at the games

Vicki: well (.) it's a major part of our (.) our ticketing pro (.) provision (.) and
                                             //
Paul: and and certainly our our leading way to engage with young people

Len: those two point five million tickets which cost (.) what (.) twenty pounds (.) or less
                                                      //
Paul: about one million of those are in football and about (.) about
                    //
Vicki: so about one point five million of those are not in the football (.) they're in the wide range of Olympic sports

Dee: including the one point three million?

Paul: the one point three million are split across the football and the (1) across the other twenty five sports

Discussion

It's important to consider the context of this interaction.

As this is part of a committee meeting, the participants are likely to be sitting down, and to have some information on paper (or computer screen) in front of them. The interaction is not completely spontaneous: speakers are likely to have prepared some of the things they might want to say, and will not have to rely entirely on memory for information. You would therefore expect to find some non-fluency features, but not as many as you would find in a completely spontaneous interaction.

Although we are not told the exact roles (or job titles) of the participants, we might expect that one speaker would be the chairperson of the committee, and would therefore be dominant.

In this interaction there are overlaps which can sometimes indicate one speaker interrupting another in order to seize the floor, but if you look carefully at the dynamics here you can see that the overlaps are cooperative rather than competitive. For example, Paul overlaps Dee when Dee refers to "the pay-your-age scheme that we have devised" by mentioning the "one point three million tickets". Dee then regains the floor: she acknowledges Paul's point – "as you said (.) one point three million tickets" – then uses a discourse marker to resume her point: "anyway (.) the pay-your-age scheme …".

TIP

Issues of dominance, status, and role are sometimes relevant in spoken interactions, but you must be careful not to overstate power dynamics. If you're always looking for a power struggle, you're likely to misread the transcript evidence and miss signs of cooperation.

There are frequent micro-pauses and some one-second pauses. The easy way to account for a micro-pause is to say that it allows for thinking time; speaking spontaneously requires us to think in the future while speaking in the present.

TIP

This sort of mental processing is actually quite a complex thing to do, but we take it for granted in our ordinary everyday interactions. When you look at a section of transcribed spoken language, be careful not to assume there's something "wrong" with an utterance because it includes pauses and

Activity 10.9

Here's a transcription of the next section of that Olympics committee meeting. Look back through the section above on features of spontaneous speech, then read the transcription and trace the **dynamics of interaction**, the way speakers hold or yield their turn, and the ways in which they cooperate to make sense of the topic of their conversation.

Paul: the one point three million are split across the football and the (1) across the other twenty five sports (.) so about six hundred thousand to seven hundred thousand
//
Dee: where does the six (.) the six hundred thousand come from
//
Paul: six to seven hundred thousand of those are in football and about six hundred thousand of those are in other sports (.) that leaves us with
//
Dee: sorry (.) you're totally confusing me now (1) if there are one million tickets for football where does the six hundred thousand come from?

Paul: six hundred thousand of the pay-your-age tickets are in football

Dee: the <u>chi</u>ldren tickets

Paul: YES (.) they are in football (1) the rest of those pay-your-age tickets are in non-football

Len: in the one point five million

Paul: YES (.) in the one point five million (.) okay?

Len: okay

Paul: right (.) so (.) you've got two point five million tickets which split into football and into non-football (.) within those tickets
//
Vicki: children or not children? (1) because I think this is really confusing (.) well (.) I thought I understood and now (.) and now I'm confused

Len: okay (.) let's try again

Dee: we've got two point five million less one point three million
//

Paul: NO (1) we have two point five million which splits into one million football and one point five million non-football

Vicki: of all ages?

Paul: of <u>all</u> ages (2) within the one million football (.) two thirds of those are for <u>chil</u>dren (.) within the one point five million <u>non</u>-football (.) six hundred thousand of those are children (.) that leaves us nearly <u>nine</u> hundred thousand tickets (.) in non-football (.) which are ADULT twenty pound tickets (.) and a further thirty thousand in football which are adult twenty pound tickets (.) we are (.) we have (.) we (.) just over one point one million adult twenty pound tickets across the pay-your-age which

Len: AH (.) so that gets us up to the two point five million

//

Paul: that gets us up to the two point five million

Dee: RIGHT (1) well (1) that's better than two hundred thousand (.) MUCH better than the two hundred thousand (1) but it's still nothing like enough (.) ABSOLUTELY NOTHING LIKE enough

Conclusion

In this chapter we set out to look at features of spoken texts. As we've noticed throughout our journey so far, texts don't always fit into neat categories. They normally contain a range of features, and even the shortest texts can vary in register from one line to the next, even from one word to the next.

We had already encountered transcriptions of spoken language and theories from the study of spoken language. In Chapter 7, we looked at two individual speakers – two athletes talking about being "in the zone", with minimal intervention from a radio interviewer. In Chapter 9, we used theories and terminology from the study of spoken language to help us with a more advanced analysis of literary texts.

Now, in this chapter, we have looked at a range of spoken texts. Some were natural and spontaneous, or semi-spontaneous, while others were "crafted" – planned in advance, and used for a particular rhetorical or literary purpose.

In the next chapter, we will look at a number of topics of particular interest to students of English Language. Among them will be at least three more aspects of spoken language as we consider how children acquire language, how particular social groups use language (for example, to include or exclude others), and how far a person's language use depends on gender.

Language topics

Introduction

We have already come across a number of current issues and debates in the field of English Language. Since almost all speakers and writers of a language have some right to consider themselves experts, people are likely to have strong opinions on what we will call "language topics".

Every day we see language use discussed in the news. As television news bulletins and newspaper articles are usually written for a wide general audience, they are often not very precise in their linguistic knowledge and understanding. Students and teachers of English Language will be more precise – for instance, about the confusion between **grammar** and **punctuation** in the example below.

Later in this chapter we will explore a wider range of topics that create interest, debate, and disagreement among people who care about language use.

But first let's remind ourselves of topics we've considered earlier in this book. (And you can give yourself a special prize if you can find a spelling mistake – one depending on a **homophone** – as well as understanding the joke in the cartoon below.)

Look at the cartoon above. The joke is obvious – that you have to use semi-colons to express the opinion that people no longer need to use semi-colons – and this is a nice example of irony.

Activity 11.1

But semi-colons are a feature of punctuation, and the caption refers to *endangered grammar*. To a linguist, **grammar** is the system of rules which govern how words combine to create clauses and sentences; **punctuation** is the system of standard marks and signs used in writing and printing to signal the separation of groups of words into clauses and sentences. So, although grammar and punctuation are obviously connected and interdependent, they are not the same.

For example, if a teacher asked a young child of seven or eight to write a description of the night sky, that child might write:

> The stars shining brightly. The moon appearing from behind a cloud. I watched from my window.

Here we have three sentences marked and divided by the use of full stops. But our knowledge of grammar tells us that the first two are both **minor sentences**: neither has a **finite verb**, though both have **present participle verbs** (*shining, appearing*).

It would be difficult to explain that to a seven year old, so the teacher might just encourage the child to change the order of the ideas and alter the punctuation. (It's easier to identify a full stop than it is to identify a finite verb.)

Your task now is to do the following.

1. Rewrite the three sentences above in three different ways. You may combine them into one sentence or use separate sentences, but you must use "correct" grammar – that is, your sentence(s) must be grammatically complete.

2. For each of the three versions you've composed, write a short explanation of how your choices of punctuation and grammar have worked.

> **TIP**
>
> Before you do this task, look back over the sections on grammar and sentence structure in Chapter 2.

Correctness

In Chapters 2 and 7, we touched on the debate about "correctness" between descriptivists and prescriptivists.

People have a range of attitudes to correctness in the use of the English language. At one end of the scale are language **purists**, who want English to remain unchanged so that a system of rules can always be applied and there can be no argument about what is correct.

The Queen's English Society is one organization that promotes attitudes close to those at the purist end of the scale. The society sets out its intentions in the following words:

The Society campaigns to encourage high standards of written and spoken English, which have been found to be lamentably low among school-leavers and even university graduates. One of its principal campaigns is for better and explicit English language education and regular constructive correction of errors in English language in schools.

Activity 11.2

Here is an extract from the *Frequently Asked Questions* section of the website of the Queen's English Society. Read it carefully, making notes in two columns, one column for what the society does believe and the other for what it does not.

Q.   Does the QES want to police or govern the language?

A.   No. That is not seen as our role, as our language will always continue to evolve just as it has done through the ages. We would, however, comment on any alterations to the language that are felt to be not in keeping with clarity and elegance in written or spoken English.

Q.   If the QES does not want to police or govern the language, why does it claim to be 'prescriptive'?

A.   The Society prefers the prescriptive approach to the descriptive approach, as we do not want the language to lose its fine or major distinctions. We believe that descriptive linguistics, which declares anything anybody said or wrote to be 'correct' caters to mass ignorance under the supposed aegis of democracy and political correctness. Indeed some changes would be wholly unacceptable as they would cause confusion and the language would lose shades of meaning.

Q.   Does the QES tolerate deviations from the rules that exist?

A.   The Society believes that the rules of Standard English should be adhered to in formal written communication as far as possible and where the context demands it. We do not believe, however, that the rules should be adhered to blindly at the expense of literary impact. Indeed, the Society encourages rich and imaginative English where appropriate, as in poetry, drama, fiction and some non-fiction. Schools should teach pupils to suit their style of writing to the context.

Q.   Does the QES want to police or govern the language?

A.   No. That is not seen as our role, as our language will always continue to evolve just as it has done through the ages. We would, however, comment on any alterations to the language that are felt to be not in keeping with clarity and elegance in written or spoken English.

TIP

Look back at the last question and answer in the Queen's English Society extract. Notice what it says about accent, and how the word "accent" is pre-modified (or not) each time it is used.

Speech sounds and accents

Everyone who speaks a language, speaks it with an accent. A particular accent essentially reflects a person's linguistic background. When people listen to someone speak with a different accent from their own, they notice the difference, and they may even make certain biased social judgments about the speaker.

The quotation above is from the introduction to a speech accent archive maintained by a university in the United States. The archive contains a large collection of speech samples. A wide range of people from a variety of language backgrounds – native and non-native speakers of English – were recorded reading the same paragraph, and these recordings were then carefully transcribed using phonemic symbols. The archive is used by people who wish to compare and analyse the accents of different English speakers.

If you are interested in studying English language – or indeed any language – at a higher level, you will need to learn more about transcription and the use of phonemic symbols to represent speech sounds.

For the purposes of studying English Language at A Level, you need to be familiar with the kinds of transcriptions you will have to deal with in examination questions.

The transcriptions you have looked at so far in Chapters 7 and 10 only gave you simple information about aspects of the dynamics of speech: pauses and stresses/emphases used by individual speakers, and interruptions made by other speakers. For example, in Chapter 10 we had the following transcription key:

(.) = micro-pause	(1) = pause in seconds	// = speech overlap
CAPITALS = speaking with raised volume		underlined = emphatic stress

If we want more information about what speech sounds like, we would have to use more technical symbols, for example, the symbols of the International Phonetic Alphabet (IPA). These are easily available on the Internet, and there are many helpful websites that link the symbols to audio samples.

In general, vowel sounds vary more than consonant sounds from one accent to another. One simple example is the *a* sound in the word bath.

Pronunciation and accent

Accent is the technical term that linguists use to refer to the sound of speech used by a certain group of people. These people may form a group because of their nationality or because they live in a particular area.

Accents are made up from the pronunciation of particular sounds and words. The accent in which non-native speakers pronounce English words is likely to be influenced by their native language, and this effect may be continued over many generations. For example, the vowel sounds of English-speaking people in the northern area of the American Midwest (an accent sometimes called North-Central American English) may have been influenced by the Scandinavian and German ancestors of these people.

It's important not to confuse **accent** and **dialect**. Accent refers to the sounds of speech, so it's a *phonological* feature; dialect refers to the choice of words, so it's a *lexical* feature.

Of course, the two generally appear together. If someone speaks English in a local accent, they are likely to use local dialect words.

Activity 11.3

Using your own knowledge of speech sounds and any Internet resources you can find, complete the table below. An **orthographic transcription** uses the normal English alphabet to suggest how a word is pronounced by spelling it as it is said; a **phonemic transcription** uses a special alphabet:

Variations in pronunciation of the vowel sound in simple words

Word, speaker	Orthographic transcription	Phonemic transcription
bath, north of England	bath	/bæθ/
bath, south of England	barth	/bɑ:θ/
bath, American English		
bath, South Africa		
tune, British English	tyoon	/tʊən/
tune, American English	toon	/tu:n/
tune, your local accent		
fish, British English	fish	/fɪʃ/
fish, Australian English	feesh	
fish, your local accent		

Discussion

Sometimes variations in accent and pronunciation can be amusing. Here is a humorous account of some supposed differences between British, Australian, and New Zealand accents.

The scene is North Africa, at the height of fierce battles in World War 2. An Australian junior officer meets a British senior officer on the front line. "Good morning young man," says the British officer, "Did you come here to die?"

"No Sir," replies the young Australian, "I came yesterday".

To British ears, our heroic young Australian would sound like he said "Oi kime yester-die". The butt of the joke here is how, to British ears, Australians (and New Zealanders) pronounce "day" as "die" and "lay" as "lie," etc so that "today" becomes "to die". Of course, British people with a Cockney accent also come close to pronouncing "day" as "die" and the Cockney influence is certainly the source of the sound in Australian and hence New Zealand English.

The way in which 'i' becomes 'oi' is very much more an Australian pronunciation than a New Zealand one. Some New Zealanders can sound very Australian in this regard. I'm not quite sure why New Zealanders vary so much in this – it doesn't seem to be a regional variation.

Finally, the true clincher to decide whether you are listening to an Australian or New Zealander lies in the pronunciation of the letter "i" in the famous fish and chips test.

If your companion likes eating "feesh and cheeps," he or she is Australian.

If, on the other hand, they prefer "fush and chups," you are undoubtedly dealing with a New Zealander.

Source: http://www.enz.org/Accent NewZealand.html

But accents and pronunciation are often taken very seriously. At a basic level, people need to be able to understand each other: if you can't distinguish the speech sounds another speaker is making, you won't be able to make sense of what is being said.

At a more complicated level, accents can be seen as a marker of social status, education, intelligence, or any combination of those things. If a speaker uses local dialect forms of syntax and lexis as well as having a local accent, listeners in some contexts might be prejudiced against that speaker.

Activity 11.4

Think of the way you speak with your friends and family. Focus on:

- ways in which you speak with friends
- features of dialect and accent you use when speaking to members of your family
- sayings and idioms which particular family members or friends use.

Make lists of all of these.

Now, imagine you've been asked to make a radio documentary about your local accent and dialect. This documentary will be broadcast on the BBC World Service, so you will have an international audience.

Write the script for the opening two minutes of this documentary. (Hint: You might want to use several different "voices" – perhaps one main presenter and several speakers giving examples.)

Discussion

Once again, as you did in Chapter 9, you began by compiling a mini corpus of linguistic data. This time it was data related to spoken language used by particular social groups. And this is a very important topic in current linguistic research.

Your script probably included some or all of the following:

- local **idioms** – figurative expressions which people in your area or family use, but which might not make sense to someone outside your group

- **field-specific lexis** – jargon that belongs to a particular interest, such as a sport which you and your friends enjoy, and which might have to be explained to someone who doesn't share that interest

- **colloquial** language/**slang** – words you would use in conversation but which you might not write in a more formal text

- jokes and (perhaps) taboo language which you might not use outside your familiar social and family groups because of the risk that they might offend someone.

What do all of these features have in common?

All of the features listed above – and others that you came up with – tend to *include* some people and *exclude* others. They create an in-group ("us") and an out-group ("them").

It's simple- you can't have an in-crowd unless you leave somebody out of it – without uncool, there is no cool. So basically, you're nothing without me. HA!

Suzie would later win a Nobel Prize for her Theory of Special Social Relativity.

Activity 11.5

The following text is a transcript of part of an interview broadcast on a music radio show in 2000. Rock star Noel Gallagher (NG) is being asked by interviewer Tim Lovejoy (TL) about the latest album he has recorded with his band Oasis. The album features the first song written by NG's brother, Liam.

Read the transcript. Make notes on:

- features of spoken language which show how TL and NG have shared knowledge and understanding of the topic of conversation
- how the two speakers cooperate to share ideas with each other and with the listeners to the radio show.

Transcription key		
(.) = micro-pause	(1) = pause in seconds	// = speech overlap
CAPITALS = raised volume	[laughs] = paralinguistic feature	

TL: [laughs] all right (.) now (.) Liam's got a song on this album (.) called
                                                                //
NG: yeah

TL: called (.) erm (.) Little James (.) erm (1) quality (.) I think

NG: yeah (.) we thought it was
                      //
TL: quality (1) did you know he had it in him?

NG: erm (1) we sort of sensed that he did (.) but he never (.) you know (.) he would never play me anything because he (.) he must have thought(.) being the way I am (.) I was just gonna dismiss it anyway

TL: because you're brothers [laughs]

NG: [laughs] because we're brothers (.) and all that stuff (.) you know

TL: but erm you've (.) since (.) you've mellowed over the last couple of years

NG: and it is a great song (.) you know (.) but Liam (.) he's a strange cat [laughs]

TL: [laughs] so (.) is he gonna do it? solo?

NG: I (1) well (.) if I was him (.) I'd do it (.) because he's (.) you know (.) he's an oddball character anyway (.) and his music's quite odd (.) that (.) that (.) the song that you hear on the album is (.) is quite a straightforward erm you know pop song
                        //
TL: but some of the stuff that I've heard

NG: //
                                              oh some of the stuff that he does write is just
      plain bonkers (.) it's just weird (.) it's got no place on an Oasis album (.) I have to say

TL: [*laughs*] but when he was a kid he wasn't into music (.) I read the other day (.) it was YOU
      that was into music (.) HE thought it was just a bit of
                                              //
NG: HE was into (.) no (.) no (.) he was into football
                                                                          //
TL: footy

NG: yeah (.) well (.) we were all into football (.) cos we're from Manchester innit? but I think
      his first musical experience was (.) you know (.) travelling around on the bus with his mates
      (.) doing all the break-dancing nonsense

Discussion

The conversation in the interview transcript has a number of features which suggest shared understanding.

To start with, TL sometimes seems to be telling NG things which NG obviously already knows, such as that "Liam's got a song on this album". Why is he doing this? Well, TL and NG both know about this song, and they both know its name (*Little James*) but the radio audience might not know, so TL makes sure that he mentions it.

Each speaker overlaps the other three times, but these are *cooperative overlaps* rather than *competitive interruptions*. Research studies into spoken language suggest that men tend to interrupt much more often than women do, and that they tend to compete for the floor more.

But here, when TL overlaps to say "but some of the stuff that I've heard", he is showing that he has been listening carefully and following NG's previous utterance.

And that previous utterance is interesting, because NG talks for over three lines, making a contrast between Liam's usual music ("quite odd") and his new song ("quite a straightforward erm you know pop song"). However, he doesn't give a direct answer to the simple question that TL asked: "is he gonna do it? solo?"

TL laughs several times and NG joins in the joke. When TL suggests that the reason NG was "just gonna dismiss it" was "because you're brothers", NG uses the *echo utterance* "because we're brothers" to show agreement.

The two speakers don't just cooperate. They also **converge** – that is, they use similar features of language, which is a natural thing for people to do when they are getting on well with each other and feel comfortable. They both use **contractions**, saying "gonna" instead of "going to" and "cos" instead of "because", and **vague language** like "all that stuff". These are also features of colloquial language – casual and informal choices of lexis which you wouldn't find in a formal interview or speech.

TIP

Before you go on with this chapter, look back at the sections in Chapter 2 on lexis and diction, and style, register, and tone.

Activity 11.6

Before we leave the Tim Lovejoy/Noel Gallagher interview, you're going to do the following directed writing task based on that transcript. (You should find that the notes you made and the discussion above will help you to do this.)

1. Write the text for a short television news item about the new Oasis album (110–150 words). Use the material in the transcript. Make sure your choices of language and style are suitable for the purpose and audience.

2. Compare the style and language of your news item with the style and language of the transcription of the Tim Lovejoy/Noel Gallagher interview.

Spoken language and gender

In the discussion in Activity 11.5, the issue of possible differences between male and female speech styles was mentioned briefly.

Let's look again at how I expressed this point:

> Research studies into spoken language suggest that men tend to interrupt much more often than women do, and that they tend to compete for the floor more.

How can you tell from my choices of language here that I'm trying to be careful not to sound too definite? How have I avoided committing myself on this controversial topic?

- A simple definite statement would have been a compound declarative sentence with un-modulated verbs: "Men interrupt much more often than women do, and compete for the floor more."

- I added *modality* by placing "tend to" before each of the verbs: "tend to" introduces the idea that this *sometimes* happens with *some* people.

- I began by making "Research studies" the *grammatical subject* of the sentence. Because the verb "suggest" is in the *active voice*, the grammatical subject of the sentence is also the **agent** – the do-er or initiator of the action.

- And we all know that the agent is always to blame for what's going on in the sentence! I shifted the responsibility for this comment away from myself and onto the researchers.

- Even then, it's not certain: the research only "suggests" that men interrupt more.

Some of these strategies for giving the impression of uncertainty are called **hedges**. People often hedge in conversation: they say "sort of" or "kind of"; they preface their comments with "I guess" or "probably".

Often this can be part of a politeness strategy to avoid giving offence or committing a **face-threatening act** – we'll come back to these ideas later in the chapter.

But why was I being so careful not to commit myself over the issue of gendered differences in speech styles?

The answer is that it's important not to "go overboard" about any research study in English language. Read the box on the right for an example.

Many research studies which were influential when they first appeared have been questioned later on. It's important to investigate research studies yourself, and not to rely on vague references to concepts which you really haven't understood properly.

Most importantly, if you have some real linguistic data in front of you – for example, a transcript of spoken language – then you must deal with it as it really is and not try to use it to "prove" a theory. The usual view is that women are more cooperative than men in conversational interaction, but if you're looking at an interaction that suggests the opposite then you need to mention the research but point out that this example doesn't support it.

Verb-phrase idioms

"Go overboard" is an idiom made up of a simple verb plus an adverbial.

For non-native speakers of English, phrasal verbs are often very difficult – or sometimes very amusing. One summer when I was at university, I taught English to Spanish students, who found it very funny when one of them tried to get on a bus without having the correct fare. The bus driver said to him: "Come on! Get off!"

There are many idiomatic expressions involving phrasal verbs. See how many you can think of using the very simple verb "*go*".

Activity 11.7

Below is a table of features thought to be typical of language used by women. Study the ideas and examples in the columns, then add your own.

Linguistic features which characterize women's speech

(according to *Language and Woman's Place* by Robin Lakoff, 1975[1])

Feature	Example	Effect
lexical hedges or fillers	you know, sort of, well, you see	"softens" the meaning: a way of avoiding causing offence or confrontation by being less direct
tag questions	she's very nice, isn't she?	invites the **interlocutor** – the other speaker – to agree
rising intonation on declaratives	I was walking past the cinema ↗ … (invites the interlocutor to identify and locate that cinema from their shared knowledge)	reduces certainty – suggests that the speaker is inviting agreement by adding an *interrogative* tone to a *declarative* utterance (thought to be more prevalent among young speakers)
back-channel support/ feedback	mm hmm, uh huh, yeah, I know (can be verbal or paralinguistic – e.g. a nod or a squeeze of the speaker's arm)	shows understanding and/ or agreement; provides "speaker support"; often a response to a tag question or rising intonation
cooperative overlaps		
intensifiers	really, extremely, so e.g. "I like him soooo much"	
"empty" adjectives	nice, lovely, sweet, brilliant	

Feature	Example	Effect
emphatic stress	it was a FANTASTIC performance	
precise colour terms	lilac rather than purple	
"hyper-correct" grammar	consistent use of standard verb forms	shows desire to "fit in"?
"super-polite" forms	indirect requests – e.g. "I don't suppose you could … ?" euphemisms	
avoidance of taboo terms and obvious swearing		

TIP

At this point, you need to do some research of your own. See what you can find out about ideas and research studies by Robin Lakoff, Zimmermann and West, Jennifer Coates, Deborah Cameron, Dale Spender, Deborah Tannen, and others.

Remember to proceed with caution!

As with many aspects of English language study:

- some of the research findings contradict each other
- some of the linguistic data you will come across will not clearly support any particular theories of gendered language
- your own experience may confuse the picture.

Even so, your own experience will be useful. Pay attention to the way you hear English language used around you, in everyday life and on radio, television, and other media. If you can get their permission, record your friends and family talking, play back the recordings and try to transcribe exactly what you hear.

You may find that making people aware of their own language – and the fact that you are recording it – will change their linguistic behaviour. I have found this happen to me on more than one occasion when I've been running teacher-training sessions. After I suggested to the participants that they might want to listen to each other's use of politeness strategies, tag questions, and intensifiers, a lively and chatty group became almost silent during the coffee break!

Language acquisition

We have looked at how people speak and write but we haven't yet investigated in depth how they develop their abilities with language. So now we will go back to those early stages of language acquisition.

In Part 1 of this book – at the very start of Chapter 1 – you were congratulated on your expert language skills. And these skills will have gone on developing in the time it's taken you to progress from that introductory chapter to now, as you moved from the start of AS Level to part of the way through the second year of your A Level course.

But how do humans acquire language?

"WHAT'S THE BIG SURPRISE? ALL THE THEORIES OF LINGUISTICS SAY WE'RE BORN WITH THE INNATE CAPACITY FOR GENERATING SENTENCES."

The acquisition of language "is doubtless the greatest intellectual feat any one of us is ever required to perform." (Leonard Bloomfield, 1933)

Activity 11.8

Below is a transcription of part of an interaction between a three-year-old child (Tamsin) and her mother. They are playing a game in which Tamsin is putting her toy bear to bed. She has given the bear a smaller toy bear of its own!

Transcription key
(.) = micro-pause   (1) = pause in seconds   // = speech overlap
CAPITALS = raised volume   [*shrugs*] = paralinguistic feature

[*Tamsin puts pillow under bear's head*]

Tamsin: lift your head up

[*Tamsin tucks bear in*]

Tamsin: there (.) lay down (.) here's YOUR bear (.) there (.) now

Mother: cover his feet up too (.) his feet are sticking out (1) there you go (1) I know what he needs now

Tamsin: what?

Mother: a story (.) better get him a storybook over there and read him a story

Tamsin: no [*but Tamsin gets a book*]

Mother: come over here and sit [*mother holds book*]

Tamsin: i just don't know how to read it

Mother: here (.) what (.) what's the ducky saying to the birds?

Tamsin: quack quack

Mother: and what are the birdies saying to the duck? (1) what do birdies say?

[*Tamsin shrugs*]

Mother: what do birds say?

Tamsin: tweet tweet.

Mother: yeah

Look at how Tamsin's mother speaks to her in the extract, and make a note of:

- the different utterance types she uses – declarative, interrogative, imperative
- features of child-directed speech.

TIP When we look at evidence of how children speak, we also need to look at how adults (and other children) speak to them.

Discussion

When a parent speaks to a child, there's often an underlying attempt to help the child develop her or his language skills. Here Tamsin's mother combines different utterance types in order to engage and interest her daughter and to encourage her to respond.

She gives Tamsin instructions, either as straightforward imperatives ("cover his feet up too", "come over here and sit") or indirect suggestions ("better get him a storybook over there and read him a story").

Then she asks a series of **"closed" questions** – questions to which she already knows the answer. Tamsin responds immediately (and "correctly") to the first of these questions ("what's the ducky saying to the birds?") but not to the second ("and what are the birdies saying to the duck?") so her mother has to prompt Tamsin to respond with the "right" answer.

Child-directed speech

You can't help noticing that people speak to young children rather differently from the way they speak to their peers or to older children.

The range of ways in which we vary our language when speaking to infants has been the subject of much research, and is sometimes called "caretaker/caregiver speech", "parent-ese" or "mother-ese".

We'll look at the research findings a little later, but first you need to explore your own language use and the language use of those around you.

Three little kids and their first words. Can you find out which one is the British kid?

Activity 11.9

Collect as many examples as you can of language used to speak to babies and young children.

Use a table like the one below to apply your linguistic knowledge to the data you collect. A few ideas have been provided for you.

Strategy/technique	Example	Intention
speaking slowly in short utterances with lots of pauses		
	birdies moo-cows	
playing "peek-a-boo"		
		teaching child new words

Theories of language development

The following text is taken from an article that reviews some of the most important theories of child language acquisition. It follows the usual practice of referring to a researcher by name, followed by the date of publication of the study, for example, "Chomsky (1965; 1975)". This is a convention of writing academic articles, and it allows you to look up the original research for yourself.

Activity 11.10

1. Read the first five paragraphs of the article and make notes on what you understand of the concepts which appear in bold.

The earliest theory about language development assumed that children acquire language through **imitation**. While research has shown that children who imitate the actions of those around them during their first year of life are generally those who also learn to talk more quickly, there is also evidence that imitation alone cannot explain how children become talkers. For example, in the English language, young children will say 'We goed to the shops' – they are very cleverly inventing the past tense of 'go' based on the rules they have absorbed.

Skinner, the Behaviourist theorist, suggested that children learn language through **reinforcement**. In other words, when a parent or carer shows enthusiasm for something a child tries to say, this should encourage the child to repeat the utterance. But again, even though reinforcement may help, this theory cannot account for children's inventions of language.

Some argue that it is not just hearing language around them that is important, it is the kind of language – whether it is used responsively (for example, following a baby's input, such as the baby making a noise or doing something). It is also clear that babies need to hear language to develop this themselves. This point is of great importance in relation to young children with impoverished language experience (see for example Ward 2000). The idea of **motherese** (Snow and Ferguson 1977; Trevarthen 1995) – using tuneful, accentuated speech to babies, and repeating their own language (often extended) back to young children – was put forward as a basic human requirement.

However, other research (see Bee 1989) indicates that while motherese can be used to explain how aspects of individual children's environments help or hinder them from talking, it does not explain the underlying causes of language acquisition. We can at least suggest that talking in motherese attracts and holds babies' attention and that it allows the infants themselves to take part in enjoyable **turn-taking** exchanges, the beginnings of conversations.

Chomsky (1965; 1975) proposed that babies are born with an inbuilt **Language Acquisition Device** (LAD). He suggested that language then simply emerges as the child matures. Slobin (Ferguson and Slobin 1973; Slobin 1985) continued this line of thought, proposing that just as newborns come into the world 'programmed' to look at interesting, especially moving, objects, so babies are pre-programmed to pay attention to language. Research has shown that treating babies as if they understand talk and involving them in conversational exchanges are essential experiences on which later abilities are founded.

2. Now read the last three paragraphs (below) of the article. There are some very complex ideas here about how the human brain works and how children develop various abilities. Try to think of examples from your own experience of the processes that are being explored here.

Piaget argued that language is an example of symbolic behaviour, and no different from other learning. One of his colleagues, Hermine Sinclair (1971), proposed that a child's ability to nest a set of Russian dolls uses the same cognitive process as a child needs for understanding how sentences are embedded in one another. Nelson (1985) and others, using this **cognitive processing** explanation, think language is an extension of the child's existing capacity for making meaning. This seems to fit with the fact that children will generally begin to engage in **pretend play** at about the same time as their first words are expressed, indicating that they are using symbols in the form of words and also symbolic pretend objects (for example using a block as a pretend cake).

Following on from Vygotsky's social learning tradition, Bruner (1983) stressed the importance of opportunities for babies and children to interact with, and observe interactions between, others. As we explained above, this idea is supported by research showing that mothers who behave as if their babies and young children understand language right from the start, make eye contact with them and engage in dialogue, responding to their babies' reactions (kicking, waving arms, smiling, etc) are laying the foundations of conversation.

Karmiloff and Karmiloff-Smith (2001) argue that none of these theories about language is, on its own, adequate in explaining language development and learning in the first three years of life, and that we need to take account of each of them for their ability to explain part of the story.

Source: https://czone.eastsussex.gov.uk/sites/gtp/library/core/english/Documents/language/
Theories%20about%20language%20develpment.pdf

Discussion

Did you find that difficult? It would be very surprising if you didn't. But perhaps if you are studying human biology, psychology, or child development as well as English Language, you might have come across these ideas before.

You can probably see how the ideas of the different theorists connect with each other:

Imitation ➡ Reinforcement ⬅Motherese➡Turn-taking

The child interacts with a parent or other adult or older sibling, and hears examples of motherese (or child-directed speech). The child then imitates some of these words and phrases, and receives positive reinforcement ("that's it!" "well done!") from the older speaker. Turn-taking begins to emerge as the child and adult respond verbally to each other.

The adults and older siblings in the child's environment act as a **Language Acquisition Support System** (LASS).

TIP

Don't worry if you did not understand all of the concepts in that text! You can't expect to understand every idea in every text you meet. You will have the chance to come back to all of these ideas and the theorists who are associated with them.

Language acquisition device → Pretend play ← Cognitive processing

As the child learns about the world from playing, concepts such as size and shape and time – which you will recognize as *abstract nouns* – begin to make sense.

Piaget suggested that language emerges at the same time as understanding. For example, a child playing a shopping game might be able to put into words the idea that the shopping bag had become heavy; a child playing with a shape-sorting toy might be able to identify colours or shapes, and eventually will recognize both. ("It's that one!" → "Oh, it's the big square yellow one!")

> (How awake are you? Did you notice that in the example above the child is also learning about the right order in which to put adjectives? Shape (square) comes before colour (yellow), but size (big) comes before all of them. Look back at Chapter 9, after Activity 9.7.)

Activity 11.11

Like almost all theories, ideas about child language acquisition make better sense when we look at specific examples.

So here is some more data to examine. This is a transcription of an interaction between Amit, a three-year-old boy, and his mother. They have been playing with his toy train set.

Transcription key

(.) = micro-pause	(1) = pause in seconds	// = speech overlap
CAPITALS = raised volume	[*shrugs*] = paralinguistic feature	

Mother: is that a piece of the bridge as well?

Amit: yeah (.) don't matter

Mother: shall we put that one on (.) yeah?
//

Amit: that

Mother: there we go (.) there

Amit: here.

Mother: where're you gonna put the bridge (.) the tunnel? (1) that's it (1) we'll have to try and get you some more of these pieces (.) won't we (.) to match this train? (1) see if auntie sue can get you some for christmas and go to father christmas

//

Amit: yeah

Mother: what would you like? (1) what else do they do?

//

Amit: father christmas got this (.) birthday (.) got this

Mother: got that

Amit: who put the heater on?

Mother: I did (.) earlier (1) it was cold

Amit: hot

Mother: mm hmm?

Amit: these ones (1) these ones like (1) these ones are (1) these ones are

Mother: what?

Amit: these ones are a car ones

Mother: there? (1) shall we put them there?

Amit: yeah (1) leave the tunnel up

Mother: leave it up a bit?

Amit: yeah (1) LOOK (1) both trains coming (.) can put it that way

Mother: okay

Amit: done that (.) hother one?

Mother: other one? (1) behind you (.) there it is (1) put that one like that (1) yes .

Amit: got no trains

Mother: what darling?

Amit: got no trains (.) that one pushing that one is pushing that bit (.) cause that bit (1) got no trains

Mother: you have got lots of trains (.) haven't you?

Amit: I go get some more

Read through the transcript, paying attention to how Amit's mother helps her son to communicate as well as to play. Look especially at how she uses different utterance types.

Discussion

Just a quick look at this transcription shows you that there is regular *turn-taking*. Amit's turns are mostly shorter: his mother's *mean length of utterance* (MLU) is greater.

She asks him a range of questions or interrogatives. Some of these are closed questions inviting just a yes/no answer ("is that a piece of the bridge as well?"). Others are suggestions or prompts to encourage Amit to respond, for example, the tag question "won't we?" One question is quite open ("what would you like?") and is followed almost immediately by another open question ("what else do they do?") perhaps because his mother thinks Amit needs more prompting.

Most of the time, Amit's mother sets the agenda. She is the topic manager, directing the conversation in ways which will help Amit to enjoy his playing time and help him to develop his language and his thinking. At one point, Amit introduces a new topic – "who put the heater on?" – and shows he understands the concept of hot and cold.

Amit's next utterance shows him struggling to convey a new idea: "these ones (1) these ones like (1) these ones are (1) these ones are …" And when his mother prompts him with "what?" his reply is not in standard grammatical English, "these ones are a car ones". But his mother does not correct him – perhaps she judges that it will be too difficult for him to learn a more grammatically complex way of saying what he means here.

She does correct Amit when he adds an unnecessary **initial aspirate** (an *h*-) to the beginning of a word ("hother"), but she does it tactfully by simply repeating the correct pronunciation "other", thus modelling the correct form of the word and acting as his Language Acquisition Support System.

You should also have noticed examples of **deixis** – simple words like *this* and *that* which refer to objects or actions in their immediate environment. When his mother asks "shall we put them there?", Amit can see what "them" refers to and where "there" is. These are therefore examples of **context-dependent language**: if you are present in the situation, you can understand their meaning.

TIP
You need to look at *linguistic* features. A general understanding of how a parent helps a child is a good start, but you must apply what you've learned about language.

Activity 11.12

1. Look back at the table in Activity 11.11. If there are any gaps you could fill them with examples from the interaction between Amit and his mother.

2. Look also at the following table. Add to it with examples from the interaction between Amit and his mother

Theorist/ theory	Concept and how it works	Examples
B.F. Skinner "operant conditioning"	• Behaviourism • Imitation and Reinforcement (with repetition)	Child: I falled down the step. Adult: You fell down the step, did you? Child: Yes, I fell down the step.
Piaget "cognitive development"	• Stages of development • Idea that language development depends on psychological maturity	Abstract ideas, e.g. times and future occasions, like Christmas and birthdays
Chomsky "language acquisition device"	• Innate ability to acquire language • Grammatical/ syntactic structures are innate: child only has to learn vocabulary	Errors arise from over-generalizing a rule, e.g. the rule that plurals are formed with -s and past tenses are formed with -ed, so child says "I goed to see the sheeps"
Vygotsky "Zone of Proximal Development"	• Actual (unaided) developmental stage as opposed to • Potential (assisted) developmental stage	Teachers and parents provide help for children to progress beyond their current stage, e.g. by modelling a structure
Bruner "Language Acquisition Support System" (LASS)	• Adults provide "scaffolding"	The "peek-a-boo" game as an early introduction to conversational turn-taking.

Main stages of early child language development

The table below outlines the main stages of a child's language development.

Pre-linguistic	Parents sometimes infer/ imagine that the child is trying to communicate a particular meaning.	Cooing and babbling sounds.
Holophrastic	Single words – often concrete nouns – used to stand for whole phrases.	"Drink!" could mean "I would like a drink" or "I have spilled my drink". What else could it mean?
Telegraphic	Elliptical utterances: *function* words (*grammatical items*) left out, *content* words (*lexical items*) used.	"Want drink juice" could mean "I want to drink my juice" or "Do you want me to drink my juice?" Can you think of other possible meanings?
Post-telegraphic	Beginning to use utterances with more than one clause. Words which were missing in the telegraphic stage are now present: determiners, auxiliary verbs, personal possessive pronouns.	

Functions of language

As well as looking at the stages of child language acquisition, we can also examine language development from a different angle.

The linguist Michael Halliday in a very influential book called *Learning How to Mean: Explorations in the Development of Language* (1975)[2] identified seven functions that language has for children in their early years. He argued that a child is motivated to develop language because it serves certain purposes or functions for her/him.

The first four functions help the child to satisfy physical, emotional, and social needs:

- **instrumental** function: language used to fulfill a need such as obtaining food, drink, and comfort
- **regulatory** function: asking, commanding, requesting
- **interactional** function: language that develops social relationships
- **personal** function: language that expresses personal opinions.

The next three functions are to do with helping the child to come to terms with her/his environment:

- **representational** function: relaying or requesting information
- **heuristic** function: language that is used to explore the world and to learn and discover, for example, by asking questions, especially the question "Why?"
- **imaginative** function: using language to tell stories and create imaginary worlds.

Activity 11.13

Look back at all the transcript evidence of children's talk in this chapter and look for as many examples as you can find of each of the functions above.

Discussion – and a warning

If you read carefully – and you should always read carefully! – you should be able to *identify* examples of each of Halliday's functions.

But being able to find, identify, and label features of language is only ever the start of useful linguistic analysis. One danger with applying Halliday's "framework" is that (because it is quite complicated) you may feel you have done your work when you finish what I'm calling the "labelling" stage.

This is a risk with any theory or framework that you use. If you work through a text carefully making a catalogue of features, you won't have discussed the effect that they have on meaning.

As an example let's look at the first 15 lines of the interaction between Amit and his mother in Activity 11.11 and try to avoid the danger I've outlined above.

In answer to his mother's first question – "is that a piece of the bridge as well?" – Amit gives first of all a *minimal response* ("yeah") but then goes on to employ the *personal* function to express an opinion ("don't matter"). The effect is that his mother can tell if he understands her question but is prepared to go on with the game.

Amit offers another minimal response to his mother's next long utterance – "where're you gonna put the bridge (.) … see if auntie sue can get you some for christmas and go to father Christmas". Then he follows it up by mentioning Father Christmas and birthday, combining the *interactional, personal* and *representational* functions. He is thus engaging with his mother's topic on a *personal* level by *interacting* with her in terms of the ideas of times when children receive presents, all the time building their relationship and *representing* his understanding of the world.

Amit's sudden topic-shift – "who put the heater on?" – shows signs of the *heuristic* and *regulatory* functions, because his response to his mother's explanation ("it was cold") is the holophrastic utterance *"hot"*, which may imply a request that the heater be turned off again.

I've tried to use knowledge of Halliday's functions in the discussion above to reach a deeper understanding of the dynamics of interaction between mother and child.

You may think that this framework has only had limited success here. Other approaches/concepts/theories might have been more fruitful. For example, you might analyse the lengths and types of utterance (such as one-word responses and interrogatives).

Or you might consider the **pragmatics** – the meanings which are implied. When Amit's mother explains that she put the heater on, she seems to think it's necessary to defend herself by adding (after a pause) "earlier", and then (after a longer pause) a justification: "it was cold".

Further independent study: other child language acquisition theories

You might want to explore Jean Aitchison's stages of **labelling**, **packaging**, and **network-building**. Like many other internationally renowned English language experts, Professor Aitchison has her own website, which is well worth exploring.

Jean Aitchison gave a series of lectures for the BBC in 1996, one of the annual sequences of Reith Lectures, on the subject "The Language Web". Podcasts and transcripts from these lectures, and indeed for all the Reith Lectures going back to 1976, can be downloaded from the BBC website.

TIPS

As we said in Chapter 9, the analytical toolkit is becoming fuller and heavier. You need to choose your tools, methods or approaches with care.

Think of the old English saying – don't use a sledgehammer to crack a nut.

Extracts from the articles and lectures of Professor David Crystal, probably the most versatile linguistics expert working today, can be found on his website and elsewhere.

Resources like these are widely available. All of the public radio broadcasters in English-speaking countries have similar archives of their broadcasts and are well worth searching. The Internet provides access to all sorts of useful material.

On the other hand, the Internet also offers easy access to some very poor material, and you need to be careful what you read and believe. It's a very good thing for students like you to be able to set up or contribute to online discussion of English language topics. Many A Level students are doing that in blogs and through the Virtual Learning Environment of their school or college. But there are also many commercial sites offering "student essays" – these are often of very poor quality and badly written.

If it's by David Crystal or Jean Aitchison, you can trust it! If it's from the website of a respected university, you can probably trust it too. But, as with so many aspects of further study, you need to be selective.

Language acquisition and development in older children and teenagers

> Becoming a native speaker is a rapid and highly efficient process, but becoming a proficient speaker takes a long time. (Berman, 2004)

Language-learning is a lifelong activity. We learn new words for new objects and activities, and we develop new ways of expressing our old ideas.

As you were reminded on the very first page of this book, you were probably speaking quite fluently by the age of five. After a year or so of school, you would have had about 2,500 words in your **active vocabulary** (words you could use to *express* yourself) and over 20,000 words in your **passive vocabulary** (words you could *understand* but didn't normally use).

Of course, you have learned to read and write as well as to speak in the years since you started school. During all of that time, the relationship between your spoken and written language has become more complicated.

For many people, and especially for teenagers, the boundaries between spoken and written English are becoming increasingly blurred. Prescriptivists (see page 206) worry about this tendency; descriptivists look for evidence and explanations.

1. Some linguists suggest that societies in general are becoming less formal, and that written language is likely to absorb more influences from spoken language since the spoken mode is usually more informal.

2. But the main influence for language change is the rise of computer technology and electronic communication. We will come back to this later in this section; and you will find further discussion in the section on Global English.

> **TIPS**
>
> Older children and teenagers go on learning language in all of the ways we have studied for language acquisition in younger children. These processes – cognitive processes – continue to develop as young people are exposed to a wider range of influences, and their linguistic environment grows more diverse.

Activity 11.14

This activity is going to take some serious thought, and you may find it easier to share your thinking with a partner.

1. Think about the influences on your own language development from the age of 5 until the present.

2. Using a format that gives you plenty of space, construct a chart, dividing that time into stages. (Some of these stages may match transferring from one school-stage to another.)

3. Work out some significant *"milestones"* – points of development when you can identify some change in how you used language.

For example:

- Think about how **stories** which you have had read to you – or have read for yourself – have affected your language.

- You might remember the point at which you started to listen to **jokes** and tell your own jokes with friends. Jokes mostly depend on understanding something about how language works – **puns** are a good example, because they depend on homophones and ambiguous meanings.

- You might remember a time when you didn't understand that a particular usage of language was figurative and not literal. Understanding **metaphor** is a significant milestone in a child's language development.

- Other "milestones" might be to do with your ability to use **electronic communication devices**. Make lists of words and phrases which have come into your vocabulary from web-sites, chat-rooms, e-mail, instant messaging.

Discussion

Your language has been developing for all of the time that you can remember, and long before that. It will go on developing.

One point which your chart may have picked up is to do with the stages at which you learned **politeness strategies** – see pages 220 and 223.

Young children are encouraged to use language to *make their meaning clear*: the point is to be understood.

But we all know stories about situations where young children have said things which are true but which older children and adults would know are not polite: sometimes the point of language is to *avoid making our meaning too clear*!

When one of my daughters was about 4 years old, we were walking to her school. I could see a lady coming towards us whom we knew – a very pleasant and friendly person, but someone who always wanted a long conversation, and we were in a hurry. I muttered a quick explanation to my daughter and led her across the road and down a side-street. She said, very loudly, "Why are we avoiding that lady, Daddy?"

Activity 11.15

On page 220, you were introduced to the idea of *avoiding a face-threatening act* (FTA) as part of a politeness strategy.

Face is a concept in spoken language theory which refers to how people want to maintain their status and self-esteem in interaction with other people, and how (most of the time) they want to avoid offending other people.

This is similar to – but not exactly the same as – the English idioms *"saving face"* or *"losing face"*.

The concept of Face has two aspects:

- **Positive face** is our wish to have our self-image approved of by others.

- **Negative face** is our wish not to let other people impose upon us.

A face-threatening act is any form of words which creates a risk that our own **face needs** – or the face needs of anyone with whom we are interacting – will be damaged.

Younger children sometimes have to be told and taught what to do in order to avoid causing a FTA; they also have to learn how to deal with FTAs from others.

But you are a sophisticated and skilful user of language, so you will manage the following activity very well …

Here is a list of situations in which **face needs** may be threatened. For each one, think of a specific example and write two brief exchanges: one which includes FTAs, and one which avoids FTAs by using politeness strategies.

- Making a request – for information, for a product or service, for a change in plans, for clarification or even for money.

- Saying 'No' – which may suggest you don't care about the concerns of the person who made a request to you.

- Disagreeing / Stating a preference / Offering contrasting ideas.

- Making complaints / Demanding explanations.

- Making suggestions / Giving advice.

- Offering Help – this may seem the opposite of a FTA, but we may risk giving the impression that we think we have superior skills to the person to whom we offer our help.

- Giving Warnings.

(If you're struggling, read the Discussion below, then come back to the Activity.)

TIPS

Grice's Maxims can be useful again here. Look back at Chapter 10 (Activity 10.4) for a reminder of them. You will have another chance to apply the Maxims in Chapter 12 (Activity 12.2).

TIPS

It may help to think of situations which you would have found difficult when you were younger. Or you may have younger sisters, brothers, and other junior relatives and friends whose politeness strategies are not so well-developed.

Discussion

In most of the situations above, you can modify your language to avoid FTAs. One way is to use **hedges** – as explained in page 203, these are words and phrases used to *soften the force* of an utterance, particularly if it's an order (*imperative*) or a question (*interrogative*).

So, when asking a stranger to tell you the way to the station, you will probably not issue an *imperative*: *"Tell me the way to the station!"*

This would be very **direct** – too direct for the context. It would be more polite to use a more **indirect** request, an *interrogative* utterance with a *modal verb* and a *hedge*: *"Could you perhaps tell me the way to the station, please?"*

If you're interested in pursuing ideas about politeness strategies and face needs, you can look up research findings on negative and positive politeness.

All of these ideas about politeness apply to your work on spoken language and social groups, and to your study of language and gender.

In addition, there are connections with Global English. Different varieties of English employ different levels of politeness strategies. Standard British English, for example, is thought to be excessively polite when compared to Standard American English or Standard Australian English.

As with language and gender, there are popular stereotypes (like those in the last paragraph) which don't always match the research. The next section, on language and thought, considers a particular example of how stereotypes can be created and altered by language.

But first, as promised, we will look again at the influence and effects of what we will call Computer-Mediated Communication (CMC). The next activity will also include the use of language in instant messaging.

> **TIPS**
>
> Remember, you are a *Digital Native*! You have grown up using the technology, so you will have to make an effort to imagine what a non-user would need to have explained.

Activity 11.16

Keep an e-communication diary for a week. Each day, record all the interactions you have by e-mail, text, the internet, smart-phone, and any other communication medium or device you use.

Imagine you have to explain to someone who doesn't use any of these media how you adapt your uses of language to suit each situation – for example, by using abbreviations or non-standard punctuation and/or grammar.

Then, working on your own or with a partner, compile a mini-research paper on how students of your age use language in electronic media.

Language and thought

Understanding the process of first-language acquisition in older children and teenagers is complicated by ideas about *the relationship between language and thought*.

We saw in Chapter 9 (page 170) how George Orwell used the theory that we can only think about ideas for which we have corresponding words – that is, the theory that *language governs thought*. This is sometimes called **linguistic determinism**.

Another theory - **Linguistic relativism/relativity** – suggests that the **structure** of a person's native language will influence how that person sees the world. For example, in the sentence you've just read, I repeated the noun "person" when it might have been neater to use an **anaphoric** pronoun – that is, a pronoun that refers back to a noun which the writer or speaker has just used. But in English this causes a problem, because there are three singular third-person pronouns – **he/ she/it** – two of them "gendered" and one neutral.

Activity 11.17

Let's try the relevant part of my sentence again: "The structure of *a person's* native language will influence how *that person* sees the world."

If we replace the second use of the noun "*person*" with a pronoun, we might get: "The structure of *a person's* native language will influence how **he** sees the world."

But this is a gender-biased way of using language: 50% of the human race is female, and I've just used the male pronoun to represent "*person*", who could equally well be female as male.

Linguists would be able to demonstrate that for centuries this is what happened in the English language. The male pronoun was used whenever the person to be referred to might be male or female. Traditionally, laws and other legal documents assumed that the male "included" the female.

Even today, this is sometimes the case. The International Football Association Board (FIFA) introduces its 2011-2012 document "Laws of the Game" with the following statement:

> *Male and Female:*
>
> *References to the male gender in the Laws of the Game in respect of referees, assistant referees, players and officials are for simplification and apply to both men and women.*

Your task now is to make a list of *occupation titles*, then divide them according to whether they are "marked" for gender – that is, whether the job-title includes an indication or assumption that the job will be done by a male or a female or neither.

For each term, note down what you think is the effect of the gender-marking.

Marked: male	Marked: female	Un-marked
policeman (assumes that a figure of authority will be male)	cleaning lady (assumes that a domestic job will be done by a woman)	doctor (BUT is there an assumption that most doctors are male?)

Discussion

You probably found more examples of stereotypes – situations where we assume that men or women are more suited to a particular occupation, and where our language reflects that belief.

For example, it's common to refer to a *business**man***, to mean (in the dictionary definition) *"a person who works in commerce, especially at executive level"*. This is a male-gender-marked term, and it includes the *connotation* of being senior and successful.

Language and identity

It's likely that children will pick up most of their language habits by **imitation** from their immediate environment and **reinforcement** from parents and carers of 'good' language use.

So as they grow older and spend more of their time at school and with friends, other influences may take over.

It's likely that lessons in school and interactions with adults in educational settings will favour "correct" and "formal" uses of language. Children will learn to seek **overt prestige**: this is the respect or status given by society to a particular variety of language. Children may **upwards-diverge** to more formal choices of lexis/grammar/syntax and accent. In English-speaking countries, the variety which has overt prestige will be a form of Standard English: it may be British Standard English or American Standard English or Australian Standard English or South African Standard English or any other local Standard.

This **dialect** may be reinforced by a matching **accent** which also has overt prestige. Traditionally in the United Kingdom this was **Received Pronunciation** (RP) which was often said to be the accent of the Queen and the BBC. However, this has changed over time, as you can clearly hear by listening to sound-clips of broadcasts from twenty, thirty, forty, fifty, sixty years ago.

At the same time as they are being influenced towards a Standard with overt prestige, children are likely to be influenced in the opposite direction by social and friendship groups which they belong to. It's natural for humans to **downwards-converge** to the 'norms' of their peers, and to modify their choices of words and speech-sounds to match the more casual aspects of their environments. Colloquial language has **covert prestige**: older children and teenagers use **slang** to demonstrate their membership of social groups and to separate themselves from parents and teachers.

So, for example, some white teenagers in the United States converge to aspects of African-American Vernacular English (AAVE) because it has associations with rap and hip-hop music and allows them to assert their identity against other groups in society.

English as a global language

Like some of the other cartoons and signs which I've borrowed to illustrate points about English language, the notice above is an example of *paradox* (or *oxymoron*). It's a serious joke. One famous saying of Oscar Wilde's was 'I can resist anything except temptation'. Depending on the context in which this line is uttered, it might be a heartful cry or just a smart remark. For example, someone trying to give up smoking for the tenth time is more likely to be serious than joking.

And the idea of English as a global language is a topic worthy of study.

Borrowing

The term **borrowing** is used by linguists to refer to the process by which words from one language are used in another. This usually happens at the same time as another interesting linguistic process: language contact.

> **Activity 11.18**
>
> The Language Contact Working Group at the University of Manchester has this to say about borrowing.

TIP

Look back at Chapter 9 and the sections on paradoxes used by George Orwell and Oscar Wilde.

While speaking in our own language, sometimes we use words which originally derive from other languages. These words are called "Borrowings". Another term for borrowing is "Loanword". Words can be borrowed because a language needs to designate new objects, products, or concepts; an example are the English words for "coffee" (originally from Arabic *qahwe*) and for "tea" (originally Chinese *cha*). Sometimes words are borrowed to introduce finer distinctions of meaning which are not available in native words; for example in English, French-derived words such as *beef* and *pork* are used to refer to dining terms, while the English words *cow* and *pig* refer to the corresponding animals. Smaller languages tend to borrow many words from more dominant, majority languages. This is because of the role that "major" languages have in technology, media, and government institutions, and in public life in general.

Content words – words representing certain concepts, or objects, or products – are usually borrowed most easily and most frequently. But borrowing can also affect the grammar of a language. Words such as *and* or *but* are often borrowed by smaller languages in contact with majority languages. These are what we call "Function words"; you cannot for instance draw a picture of what they represent, and yet they play an essential role in the structure of sentences and especially when we combine sentences into conversations.

Language Contact Working Group

Your task is to do some research into loanwords. You can start by looking into your own knowledge and memory.

1. If your first language is not English, make a list of words from your first language that are used in modern English.

2. Make a second list of words from other languages which you are aware of as being used in English. When you've used all the examples you know of, ask friends and family for their ideas.

3. Now you can do an Internet search for further examples.

4. Look at the lists you've compiled. You have another mini corpus of linguistic data. What are you going to do with it?

   You could organize your data according to:

   - word-classes – I would guess that most of the words will be nouns, and more concrete nouns than abstract nouns

   - origin – you'll probably find that those words which were borrowed a hundred or more years ago were from countries and cultures which were part of the British Empire

   - mode of transmission – the route the word travelled from its origin into English usage. You'll probably find that those words which were borrowed more recently have been communicated by computer technology.

Discussion

By examining your data and considering how you've chosen to use it, you'll be able to see how far my predictions above are supported (or not) by the evidence.

The second and third of my predictions raise two more language topics closely connected with the rise of English as a global language:

1. **cultural imperialism** – the way in which a more powerful civilization imposes its values (including language) on a less powerful civilization

2. **electronic/computer technology** – the effects of the Internet and mobile communications technology on the development of the English language.

We'll see in the following pages some of the ways in which each of those factors has produced variation and change in the English language, and how these effects arouse strong feelings.

Activity 11.19

The following text is from an article written about the issue of Global English.

Read the text carefully, then:

● use the table below it to make a list of possible advantages and disadvantages of having a language which can act as a *lingua franca* – a language which can be used by different groups whose native (first) languages are different

● add the ideas which are put forward in the text about English as a global language. They might not be obviously advantages or disadvantages.

English developed remarkably as a global language in the late 20th and early 21st centuries. For the first time, a single language became sufficiently universal that it could be considered a lingua franca for communication around the world between speakers of different languages.

Traditionally the history of the English language has been divided into three main phases: Old English (450 -1100 AD), Middle English (1100 -circa1600 AD) and Modern English (since 1600 AD). However, it appears that Global English represents a new, fourth phase in which its main use is between non-native speakers around the world. This new phase in the history of English has only just begun and both the linguistic form and status of the language are rapidly developing.

Since the nineteenth century many people have discussed the possibility that the majority of the world's population could speak English. We may be witness to this occurrence in the next few years. Economic globalisation and recent developments in communications technology have both contributed to the development of Global English (and it has helped accelerate both), however the roots of English as a world language lie much further in the past. Some suggest that the first English colonies in Ireland and Wales in the 11th century, or the English-speaking settlements in North America in the 17th century that brought cheap labour from Africa are the earliest origins of Global English. But British colonial expansion in the 19th century contributed the most to the large communities where English is used as a second language: West and East Africa and South and South-East Asia.

New Englishes, as new varieties of English are known, arose rapidly from contact with local languages in these areas and, by the end of the 19th century, there was concern that they were diverging so much from native-speaker varieties of language that English would become a series of related but unintelligible languages, in the same way that Spanish, French and Italian had evolved from Latin. In that way Global English could have become only a celebration of diversity, similar to World Music, instead of the lingua franca it is today.

English as a global language

Advantages	Neutral	Disadvantages
"mutual intelligibility" from having a *lingua franca*	borrowing of lexical items and syntactic structures from local language into dominant language	damage to local language(s) – even language death
culture (e.g. film and popular music) becomes more "portable"	possibility that soon the majority of the world's population may speak and/or understand English	loss of cultural variety

	helps to accelerate economic globalization and developments in communications technology	
	new varieties of English ("New Englishes") emerge from contact with local languages	

Discussion

There are many articles, research papers and indeed books on the subject of English as a global language or "Global English". Sometimes the terminology varies – the term used may be "World English" or "International English" – and each of these terms may carry connotations with it. These associations may be ameliorative, pejorative or neutral. (If you've forgotten the meaning of these terms, look back at Chapters 8 and 10.)

As well as a variety of terminology, there is a range of attitudes in the many texts written (and spoken) about Global English.

This text is fairly neutral in tone. Is it balanced in content? And how far can you explain its tone, style, and content by looking at the context in which it was produced?

An example of the neutral/balanced stance is that "the British colonial expansion in the 19th century" is mentioned, but no opinion is expressed or implied about its effects.

Yet I told you in the opening of this chapter that language topics usually give rise to strong opinions. We'd better have a look at some.

Activity 11.20

You're now going to be presented with a wide range of texts from different sources which offer a variety of views and a good deal of information about Global English. You will need your wits, plus a pen and paper, and some reading stamina.

> **TIP**
>
> You can read all of the following texts at one sitting; or you may prefer to deal with them one at a time. Choosing a study strategy is part of your growing independence as a student.
>
> As you read, you need to be taking notes and/or making annotations. The "two-column" method might help: you will probably find as many points in favour of English as a global language as you find against.

Text A

We will start with a section from the Open University website.

The Politics of Global English

The spread of English around the world was historically a colonial process. Does the emergence of Global English represent a form of neo-imperialism, serving the economic and cultural interests of the English-speaking countries - especially the United States of America?

Undoubtedly, there has been an economic advantage for English speakers during recent decades. Individual native speakers have found themselves with a skill much in demand overseas.

Multinationals based in English-speaking countries have found it easier to outsource manufacturing and services to parts of the world with cheap labour. But Global English has not arisen because of a conspiracy between English-speaking governments or multinationals.

Learning English is now seen as being of economic benefit to individuals and national economies in every part of the world.

In fact, the continuing spread of English may no longer be in the economic and political interests of English-speaking countries. Universities across the world are now able to attract international students who might otherwise have gone to English-speaking countries by teaching their courses through the medium of English.

And in future, monolingual English-speaking graduates will find it difficult to compete, even in their own countries, with job applicants from other countries who speak several languages - including English - fluently, who are more internationally mobile and more experienced in intercultural communication.

For many centuries, Latin served as a lingua franca between educated elites in Europe. Global English may be the new global Latin but just as the use of Latin gradually faded away, so Global English may not prove to be a permanent phenomenon.

It took centuries for Global English to develop and, like Latin, it may take centuries for its influence to decline. The global linguistic future is already looking more complex. Language learners in some parts of the world are already queuing for classes in Chinese, Spanish and Arabic.

Source: http://www.open.edu/openlearn/ history-the-arts/culture/english-language/ global-english

Text B

This is part of an article (2010) from the *New York Times*.

As English Spreads, Indonesians Fear for Their Language

JAKARTA, Indonesia — Paulina Sugiarto's three children played together at a mall here the other day, chattering not in Indonesia's national language, but English. Their fluency often draws admiring questions from other Indonesian parents Ms. Sugiarto encounters in this city's upscale malls.

But the children's ability in English obscured the fact that, though born and raised in Indonesia, they were struggling with the Indonesian language, known as Bahasa Indonesia. Their parents, who grew up speaking the Indonesian language but went to college in the United States and Australia, talk to their children in English. And the children attend a private school where English is the main language of instruction.

"They know they're Indonesian," Ms. Sugiarto, 34, said. "They love Indonesia. They just can't speak Bahasa Indonesia. It's tragic."

Indonesia's linguistic legacy is increasingly under threat as growing numbers of wealthy and upper-middle-class families shun public schools where Indonesian remains the main language but English is often taught poorly. They are turning, instead, to private schools that focus on English and devote little time, if any, to Indonesian.

For some Indonesians, as mastery of English has become increasingly tied to social standing, Indonesian has been relegated to second-class status. In extreme cases, people take pride in speaking Indonesian poorly.

The global spread of English, with its sometimes corrosive effects on local languages, has caused much hand-wringing in many non-English-speaking corners of the world. But the implications may be more far-reaching in Indonesia, where generations of political leaders promoted Indonesian to unite the nation and forge a national identity out of countless ethnic groups, ancient cultures and disparate dialects.

The government recently announced that it would require all private schools to teach the nation's official language to its Indonesian students by 2013. Details remain sketchy, though.

"These schools operate here, but don't offer Bahasa to our citizens," said Suyanto, who oversees primary and secondary education at the Education Ministry.

"If we don't regulate them, in the long run this could be dangerous for the continuity of our language," said Mr. Suyanto, who like many Indonesians uses one name. "If this big country doesn't have a strong language to unite it, it could be dangerous."

New York Times

Text C

This is the "abstract" (a summary) of a university research paper (2005).

English in China: The Impact of the Global Language on China's Language Situation

The language situation of today's world is drastically different from that which existed in the past. English has become the global language – it is used more and is more widespread than any other language has ever been. At the same time we are faced with large-scale language endangerment which could result in the extinction of half or more of the world's languages.

While not the only reason for language endangerment, the status of English as the global language has important consequences for all other languages and therefore deserves to be studied carefully. However, exactly what English means for other languages and cultures is far from simple and there is no general agreement on this issue. English has been seen as a destructive language, a pluralistic language and as an irrelevant language.

This thesis explores the issue of global English as it applies to China. English language learning and teaching has been, and by all indications will continue to be, an important part of China's reform and modernisation. China is also an ethnically and linguistically diverse country with 55 minority nationalities and over 80 languages. What does the spread of English mean for China's language situation?

Drawing on data gained through fieldwork and published sources, I argue that English in China is multifaceted, that it has destructive, pluralistic and irrelevant elements. English is now used more and has higher status in China than at any time in the past and this has raised some concerns. However, English is not displacing Chinese language or culture. English is actually taking on Chinese features in both form and function. The Chinese language, far from being threatened, is currently expanding both in China and the world at large.

Much effort has gone into promoting *putonghua* and there is great interest in learning Chinese in many parts of the world. China's minority languages, like those elsewhere, are under varying degrees of threat. However, English is not the main reason for this situation. At the present time at least it has relatively little presence in minority areas. Despite the fact that it is not destroying China's languages and cultures, English remains a significant issue for China and must be dealt with thoughtfully and carefully, especially among the minority nationalities.

I argue that it is possible for China to acquire English without losing its linguistic diversity. Whether this can be achieved is a question of the resources and political will required to do so rather than any inherent difficulty with speaking two or more languages. To this end, the Context Approach is put forward as a possible way to improve English language teaching and learning among the minorities. In light of the results of this study, I suggest new directions for research, both on language issues in China and in general. I also argue for a new approach to our study of English as a global language and language endangerment.

We need to appreciate the complexities of English on a local level as well as a global level and focus our attention more on how English can be taught to speakers of endangered languages in such a way that does not lead to language loss.

Text D

This is part of an article from an online version of a magazine about contemporary art and culture.

Three artists – one Swedish, one American and one German – are talking together at an opening. The Swede says: 'We know we don't speak English so good.' The American disagrees while unconsciously adding a correction: 'I think you both speak English well!' And the German says: 'Not really, but we don't care because we have an understandment.'

That's no joke – nor is it a jab at these nationalities and their ability to master foreign languages. It's yet another conversation I've overheard where a native English speaker was outnumbered by non-native English speakers. And the non-natives are no longer embarrassed about making mistakes, precisely because they are speaking English primarily with other non-natives. What's important in these conversations is being understood, not being correct.

But what language are they speaking, if not bad English? Jean-Paul Nerrière might say 'Globish' (short for 'Global English'). In 2004 the French businessman wrote *Don't Speak English… Parlez Globish!*, a guide to learning, not the Queen's English or American English, but a simplified English with only 1,500 words to talk with people around the world, whatever their mother tongues. For Nerrière – and followers such as Robert McCrum, author of *Globish: How the English Language Became the World's Language* (2010) – non-native English speakers have developed their own English, which native speakers cannot always understand. With Globish, natives no longer have the last word.

from the article 'Speak Easy' by Jennifer Allen, frieze magazine, issue 137 March 2011

Text E

This is an account of Braj Kachru's model of World Englishes.

In this model the spread of English is imagined in terms of three Concentric Circles of the language:

- the Inner Circle – a spread from the United Kingdom to countries where native English speakers have settled down in large numbers (Australia, Canada, New Zealand, South Africa, and the United States) where English is a *first language* for many

- the Outer Circle – where English is a *second language* for many (e.g. Hong Kong, India, Singapore)

- the Expanding Circle where English is a *foreign language* (e.g. Germany, Hungary, Poland, China, and Japan)

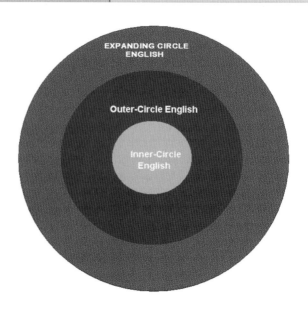

Discussion

As you have discovered from reading the texts above, there is considerable debate about the virtues of English as a global language.

Look back at your notes. It's quite likely that most of the arguments you have identified will have been about economics or education (for example, whether promoting English is good for business) or about how people feel about their local culture.

Some governments have language-planning policies to encourage or limit the spread of English. For example, the government of Singapore believes that the country's economic success depends on international communication in English. For that reason, it promotes a Speak Good English Movement, with an annual campaign.

There is an emphasis on correctness and on Standard English.

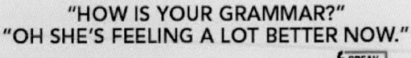

At the same time as promoting Standard English, the government discourages the use in formal situations of the local "variety", Singapore Colloquial English known as Singlish.

Activity 11.21

Think about your local context. Which of Kachru's concentric circles does your home country belong in?

Think also about your own consumption of English-language culture. Do you watch American films at the cinema, on DVD, or as downloads? Do you watch the television programme *The Simpsons*?

Not only has the scriptwriter been very skilful in using passive verb constructions – "your mother was involved in an incident. Mistakes were made …" – but the features of spoken language (a false start and hesitation/pause) also suggest regret and uncertainty. Bart tells the truth in the end by adding the *agent* of the mistakes: " … by me."

You've now had time to think about the impact on your local context of the international status of English.

Your task is the following.

1. Write a paragraph about your own country in terms of Kachru's "three circles" model.

2. Consider the status of English in your country. Is it an official language, for example, is it used in law courts or in parliament? Write a paragraph about your government's attitude to the status of any "local" varieties of English compared to Standard English.

TIP

If you don't watch *The Simpsons*, then you are missing a great opportunity to sharpen your skills as a serious student of English Language.

For example, here is an excellent example of the use of a verb in the passive voice to try to avoid responsibility for an action. Bart Simpson has been with Nelson (the local bad boy) playing around with a gun. Not realizing the gun has a crooked sight, Bart accidentally shoots and kills a bird. Now his mother is very angry with him, and he feels guilty. He climbs up to the dead bird's nest to apologise, and manages to sound like a politician shrugging off responsibility:

(*Bart climbs the tree*) Hi little eggs. I'm not sure how to tell you this, but … y-your mother was involved in an incident. Mistakes were made … by me. But don't worry, I'll take care of you.

In the Cambridge International A Level examination, you will be asked a question about English as a global language and given a text of some kind which will provide you with relevant material to discuss. You will, however, need to have prepared some ideas and examples of your own.

The questions in this section should have got you thinking along helpful lines. What you wrote in answer to the two parts of the task above will have depended very much on the individual circumstances of your local area and culture. However, the issues are common to many countries and cultures across the world.

Here are some views which should prompt you to further thought about English as a global language. They come from a question and answer webchat in which members of the public from across the world were invited to put their concerns to Professor David Crystal.

Marilena – Italy

Hello David, I'm reading your book "English as a Global Language". English is now the most important language, but the development of computer communication, artificial intelligence can replace this leadership?

David Crystal

Hello Marilena. It's very difficult to predict what Artificial Intelligence will bring. My next book is on 'Language and the Internet' - it's not out until September, but when I was researching it last year, I learned two things. First, all the AI people tell me 'you ain't seen nothing yet'! Second, the Internet is ceasing to be a purely English-language medium, as it was when it started. I found over 1500 languages on the Net. And my estimate is that the Net is now down to about 65% English, and still falling. That's much lower than the figure I give in EGL.

Gillian – Scotland

Do you consider that as world economic change and countries such as India or China begin to dominate that English will lose its place as the only global language?

David Crystal

If that happens, then yes. A language becomes a world language for one reason only - the power of the people who speak it. Power means political, economic, technological, and cultural power, of course. For historical reasons, English has achieved the position it has. But it could be knocked off its path if some major shift in world power were to take place. I think it's unlikely in the immediate future - but who dares predict very far ahead? Who would have predicted, 1000 years ago, that Latin would be negligible today?

Majika

What do you think about the trend of accepting faults of international English?

David Crystal

Depends what you mean by a fault. When English settles in a new part of the world, local people adapt it, and may speak it with errors. Some of these errors then come to be used by everyone, including the most influential people in the country. At that point, even the native speakers in that country start using those 'errors' - and they cease to be errors anymore. For instance, 'gotten' was thought of as an error a long time ago - but not any more. And when I was in Egypt last year, I found everyone said 'Welcome in Egypt' - a usage which is now recognised in one of the English grammars published there. I would be cautious about accepting a change until there is clear evidence that it is really widespread - including its arrival in the written language. But such changes will always happen.

Indira

Will the usage of Email all over the world impact on the language creativity?

David Crystal

Yes, and for the good, I feel. All domains of the Internet – e-mail, the Web, chat groups, and the fantasy games that people play - are introducing new styles and possibilities into the language. Every new technology does this. The arrival of printing brought an amazing range of new forms of expression. Broadcasting brought another. And now we have Internet technology, also adding a fresh dimension to language. And don't forget that e-mail is changing. It's only been around a few years, and its original 'speedy language' - lacking punctuation, capitals, careless spelling - is now being supplemented by more formal e-mail writing. Many people write to me these days and begin 'Dear David', and so on, just like a letter. Its style is changing.

Jack - USA

If English is to be considered a global language, why is there always a movement afoot to adulterate it here in the USA by allowing certain segments of our population to speak only their native tongues? A common language is the cement that keeps the arch of our democracy in place. David, can you tell us your feelings on allowing the use of multiple languages in a country?

David Crystal

I know there is a confrontation on this one in the US, probably because the rate of change has been so rapid this century. But there isn't any need for confrontation. Three-quarters of the world's population are naturally bilingual. It's perfectly possible to maintain the role of a standard language as a lingua franca and at the same time maintain local languages - the standard guarantees intelligibility; the local expresses identity. In my ideal world, everyone would be bilingual, with the two languages being used for different purposes. I'm speaking from Wales, and Welsh is my other language - but I wouldn't use that in this chat room!

Tony - Australia

OK - so we're now in the year 2101, and English has no more languages left to borrow from because it has powerfully permeated the globe. Ecologically we now know that diversity is critical for environmental health. Likewise, the creativity and innovation (social, economic, technology, political) that has been seeded by the world's diversity of cultures coming into contact with each other. The future is not inevitable - we can now be more conscious in our choices. A McDonald's world ain't that appealing. Is an English-speaking world, with all of a language's power to "see" meaning, any more desirable? Do you see a problem when this cultural and linguistic diversity disappears?

David Crystal

I believe in the fundamental value of diversity, as an evolutionary principle. Half the languages of the world are likely to die out in the next 100 years - and if this happens it would be a true intellectual disaster. The world is a mosaic of visions, expressed through language. If even one language is lost, it is awful.

Atnes - Slovenia

Professor Crystal, do you think that a 'lingua franca' of such an impact as is the case with English today can seriously threaten languages of limited diffusion - languages spoken by a relatively small number of people?

David Crystal

Yes - this has already happened in Australia and North America, where most of the indigenous languages have gone down under the English steamroller. But it isn't just English. In South America, Spanish and Portuguese have been the steamrollers. Any powerful language is a danger. Which is why smaller languages need our respect and often protection.

Bingley – Indonesia

Has the fact that you live in Wales influenced your work on language death?

David Crystal

Very much so. I've lived through a period when Welsh was on its way out, seen the activism which led to its turnaround. It now has two Language Acts protecting it, and a Welsh TV channel, for example. And we've now seen an upturn in the number of speakers, at the last census. So I do have a certain emotional sympathy which might otherwise have been lacking. On the other hand, the plight of languages which have only one speaker left, or very few, is nothing like the situation here in Wales. So I can see that there are many other stories out there.

Source: http://wordsmith.org/chat/dc.html

Language death

David Crystal's final point (above) was about language death – the final disappearance of a language as a "living" thing, when there are no native speakers left. This issue gives rise to perhaps the strongest feelings of all.

I was born in a village in Wales where almost everyone spoke Welsh, as either their first or their second language. When I was four, I moved to a town just a few miles away where hardly anyone spoke Welsh. At the time, the Welsh language was declining: road signs and place names and official letters were all in English.

In the years since then, the Welsh government has made sure that signs and letters are written in both languages. If you were to do an Internet search of news items and surveys on the use of the Welsh language now, you would find that people disagree: some would argue that the Welsh language was still declining, and others would put forward evidence for the opposite point of view. Is there a difference of opinion on such issues in your local area?

Here, to end this chapter, is how Jean Aitchison ended her Reith Lectures. As you read, look out for an interesting metaphor she uses to describe the diversity of languages.

Yet there is one extra worry to add in: language loss. Ninety per cent of the world's languages may be in danger. Around 6,000 languages are currently spoken in the world. Of these, half are moribund in that they are no longer learned by the new generation of speakers. A further 2,500 are in a danger zone in that they have fewer than 100,000 speakers. This leaves around 10 per cent of the current total as likely survivors a century from now.

Of course languages inevitably split, just as Latin split into the Romance languages – so some new languages may emerge, but the diversity will be much reduced. The splendiferous bouquet of current languages will be whittled down to a small posy with only a few different flowers. To take a random example, it is unlikely that Menya will survive. It is a language fairly unlike English, spoken in Papua New Guinea by only a small number of people. In 100 years time audio recordings may be our only record of it.

Source: http://downloads.bbc.co.uk/rmhttp/radio4/transcripts/1996_reith5.pdf

Conclusion

As we consider your own writing in the next chapter, think back to ideas of literal and figurative language.

Our English language experts, Professors Aitchison and Crystal, naturally used metaphors to convey their ideas. If they had been talking to each other, they might have used more technical linguistic terminology, so we see once again that audience matters.

All of the elements of the work you have done throughout this book are connected. The Cambridge International A Level syllabus and examinations recognize this by asking you to demonstrate your reading and writing skills and knowledge in combined, integrated ways. This was true at GCSE and at AS Level, and it's still true now.

As we speed towards the end of the course, remember this idea of things being connected. What you know about spoken language will be very useful when you analyse written texts. Ideas about the writing of professional authors will apply to your writing too.

References

1. Lakoff, Robin. 1975. *Language and Woman's Place*. New York, NY. USA. Harper Colophon Books.

2. Halliday, Michael. 1977. *Learning How to Mean:Explorations in the Development of a Language*. New York, NY, USE. Elsevier.

Your own writing

Introduction

It's really very simple. All you have to do is write clearly, accurately, creatively, and effectively for different purposes/audiences, using different forms.

"And that's the end of that chapter!", as Homer Simpson says.

Well, not quite.

It wasn't really Homer Simpson, not as we usually know him.

It was a (good-looking, athletic, successful) character named Homer Simpson in a (fictional) television show being watched by a (fat, lazy) character named Homer Simpson in a (fictional) cartoon.

But you understand all that without even having to think about it.

We understand all these layers of reality and imagination, and it's only when we stop to think about them that we appreciate how complicated they actually are, and how sophisticated we are to be able to cope with them.

That's how it is with your writing as well. As with your speaking which you were congratulated on in Chapter 1, you deserve great praise for having reached the stage you have. You have mastered some extremely complex skills.

Are you waiting for the "but"?

Back in Chapter 7, we looked at how top athletes thought about themselves as being "in the zone" when all their training came together and they performed automatically. But (there it is!) there are also interesting examples of athletes who were quite successful but not world champions until they stopped and took time to analyse their style and change it.

This is hard to do: if you've been doing something for a long time and it works, you probably won't want to change it. We are inclined to believe the common-sense advice in the colloquial American saying "if it ain't broke, don't fix it".

But thinking about how you approach your writing can make a big difference to what you can achieve.

Planning

If you are one of those annoying students – I've taught quite a few! – who say they don't need to plan their writing, you need to change your ways right now.

Each Cambridge International A Level examination paper lasts 135 minutes. In this time you have to read and understand several texts which you will not have seen before. Your writing time will be at most 55 minutes for each question.

If you think this seems a lot, believe me – it isn't!

It's enough time to do well if you plan and enough time to go badly wrong if you don't plan. It isn't enough time to recover from a disaster caused by not planning.

> **TIP**
> Look back at the advice on writing a commentary at the start of Chapter 4. Reading and annotating the question as well as the text you're dealing with is the essential first step to good planning.

The features of style and language which you identify in the text(s) will provide your answer with a structure. For example, if you find that the most significant feature of a text is the presence of a large number of words in a particular lexical field, it makes good sense to start your analysis with examples of these.

Writing in Paper 3

Look at the general advice given at the start of Chapter 4. The types of writing tasks you have in Paper 3 for Cambridge International A Level are the same as for Cambridge International AS Level, but the order is different.

At AS Level in Paper 1 you had to write a commentary of someone else's writing and then produce your own in response. At A Level in Paper 3, you do the response first and then a *comparative* commentary in which you discuss the style and language of your writing in relation to the style and language of the original text.

Although the word "imagination" is not on the syllabus for Paper 3, you have to make a strong effort of imagination where you think yourself into the context of the original text as you're reading it, then think yourself into a different context – the one defined by the purpose and audience you're given for your own writing in the wording of the question.

For example, you might be given a news item – from a printed newspaper, an online news source, or from radio or television – and invited to *transform* it for a different purpose and audience. It might be transformed into something more permanent like an information sheet or leaflet, an advertisement, or a review.

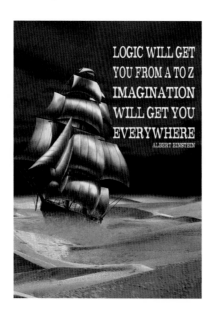

It's rather like the transformations which occur in the natural world: we believe that the flower is there in the seed, although we can't yet see it; we know that the butterfly or moth is already there in the caterpillar.

So, the seed of your transformed text is in the original.

And this is where the effort of imagination comes in. You need to ask yourself: What is the exact nature of the transformation task?

TIP

Look back at Chapter 4, and remember the acronym RAPP.

- Register
- Audience
- Purpose
- Point of view

Activity 12.1

Here's an extract from a news item in the online edition of a newspaper. The residents of part of Eastern Australia are being given a weather warning.

Severe thunderstorm warning has been issued for parts of southern Queensland.

The warning, issued at 3.59pm on Monday, forecasts damaging winds and large hailstones in the Cunnamulla, St George, Bollon, Dirranbadi, Goondiwindi and Wyandra areas.

The Bureau of Meteorology has advised residents in the affected areas to:

- move cars under cover or away from trees

- secure loose outdoor items and furniture

- seek shelter, preferably indoors and never under trees

- avoid using the telephone during a thunderstorm

- beware of fallen trees and powerlines

Source: http://www.couriermail.com.au/news/queensland/severe-weather-warning-issued-for-southern-queensland-including-hailstones-strong-winds/story-fnihsrf2-1226720368602

Imagine you were living in the area when the severe weather arrived, and you hadn't taken the advice issued by the Bureau of Meteorology. Now you're standing in front of the wreckage of your house and car, with the rain still pouring down and bits of debris flying through the air, being interviewed by a television news reporter about what happened to you.

Write the opening of the interview (120–150 words). Then compare the style and language of your writing with that of the original text. Plan your answer in note-form first.

Discussion

What is the exact nature of the transformation task here? (Remember to make sure that you're discussing it from a linguistic angle.)

Well, it's a transformation from an informative and advisory tone to a personal – and probably emotional – tone. You need to shift the point of view to the first person as you will be speaking directly to a reporter and a television camera. You will be describing what happened in the past tense, and you might use conditionals too: "If only I had paid more attention to the warnings, I could have saved my car … "

Your register is likely to be less formal than the original news item. It used a series of declarative sentences to provide information, then it moved into a series of polite imperatives to give the public the advice of the Bureau of Meteorology. You are more likely to use exclamatives ("Oh my goodness!") and maybe interrogatives such as rhetorical questions ("Why didn't I take it more seriously?")

The purpose is the same as it always is with television news: to entertain the public! There may not be many laughs from the television audience as they listen to you. But your immediate audience – the interviewer – may give you some supportive verbal or non-verbal feedback; and the structure of your interaction might show features of adjacency pairs or overlapping speech.

All of the above are predictions about the types of language you might have used. You can now look back at what you wrote and comment on specific examples of style and language. For example, you should pick out and comment on lexical choices that you made, and compare them with the lexis of the news item, such as the choice of four verbs with connotations of taking precautions: "secure … seek … avoid … beware".

Further practice

A very effective way of practising your writing skills is to invent further transformation tasks for yourself. You can start with any text, and the more unusual your transformation is the more your skills will be extended. You could do this with a fellow student, taking it in turns to find texts and invent transformation tasks for each other.

You don't need to complete whole answers. It would be enough to make notes, plan the piece, and write just the opening few sentences. In any case, the directed writing task that appears at the start of the exam paper is only intended to be a short one. The important thing is to start well with a clear sense of the purpose and audience.

What is required in the examination?

Now to remind you of what you need to do in the examination.

In Question 1(a) you have to write:

- for a specific purpose and/or audience
- using appropriate vocabulary, tone, and style.

The material on which your writing is based is on the question paper, so you don't have to invent any of the content. What you do have to do is imagine yourself into the situation that the question sets up for you.

In Question 1(b) and in Question 2, you have to:

- identify and analyse distinguishing features of written and spoken language in the text(s), such as vocabulary, word order, and the structure of sentences/utterances, figurative language (for example, use of metaphor and simile), formality/informality of tone, and the communication of attitudes, bias, or prejudice
- relate these features to the function and context of the text(s)
- organize information coherently in your answers.

If you've followed the rule RAPP, then you're on target to cover the function and context of the text(s).

There are many ways of organizing an answer, and none of them is automatically the best way with every piece of writing. As we've discussed above, the annotation/note-making stage will usually choose a structure for you because it will show you the most important features of language in the material.

Writing in Paper 4

The types of writing tasks in Paper 4 are *not* entirely the same as for AS Level.

This paper deals with language topics and for each question you will be given one of two sorts of text to deal with:

- texts offering you linguistic *data* – for example, a transcript of spoken language, which you will be expected to analyse and use to provide support for your essay answer
- texts which put forward *ideas and theories* about language – for example, articles about trends and fashions in language use, or extracts from research papers about a linguistic issue, which you will be expected to discuss in relation to your own studies.

TIP Look back at Chapter 11 and the warning about only identifying features. That's just the first step: the real work is in the analysis.

TIP Use the question paper to do your planning. It will be open in front of you all the time you're writing, so you won't need to turn over pages of an answer booklet to look back at your plan, and you can tick each point off as soon as you've dealt with it. For more ideas about planning, look back at Chapter 4.

Your response will be an academic essay in which you discuss the topic in the terms of the question, referring to ideas and examples from the textual material on the question paper as well as to ideas and examples you have covered during the course.

The techniques for answering any of the questions on this paper will be similar. The texts for both of the spoken language topics – "Spoken language and social groups" and "Language acquisition by children and teenagers" – are likely to be transcripts of speech.

As we've looked at a range of speech transcripts throughout Part 2 of this book, we'll now try a question on English as a global language. The text(s) offered with a question on this topic might involve speech data, but you are more likely to be offered textual material which contains ideas, opinions and/or concepts.

Activity 12.2

Here is an extract from an article which appeared recently in an academic journal based in India. The author is discussing the difficulty which some African countries experience when they choose to use English as their "official" language.

For instance, in Africa, countries such as Ghana, Gambia, Sierra Leone, Nigeria, Kenya, Uganda, Zambia, and Zimbabwe use English as their official language. In these situations, English serves as a *lingua franca* and so defuses ethnic conflicts, and yet questions the authenticity and identities of these users. This has always resulted in arguments about the choice of indigenous languages for official and national purposes. The use of English as official or national language strikes at the root of national pride since English is a colonial language. In other words, the fight against English has mostly been part of the struggle for total independence.

Discuss some of the advantages and disadvantages of having English as a global *lingua franca*. You should refer to ideas and examples from your wider study as well as to ideas and details from the extract.

Everywhere in the world, there appears to be one language problem or another. "Every country ... has its language problems ... All the former British colonies ... were left with the English language on the departure of the colonial government, and this legacy has turned out to be an ambiguous one."

Planning your answer

In any question like this, you could start with the extract, or you could start with your own ideas. The risk of starting with your own ideas is that you may spend too long in setting out all that you know on the subject and then find that you haven't time to discuss the main points of the question or to use the material you've been given.

This is always a danger with an examination which involves learning material and examples as part of your preparation: you've worked hard to learn the information, so now you want to use it. But dumping a lorry-load of information straight into an essay answer doesn't work. You have to sort through the contents carefully and only unload the items you really need for the question which you've been asked.

Over a number of years, many students who have been disappointed with their examination grades have later seen their examination answers and realized that this is what they had done: they'd written everything they could remember about Global English or child language acquisition, but ignored what the question had asked them to do.

Traditionally, witnesses in court cases swear an oath to be truthful. They promise that their evidence will be "the truth, the whole truth, and nothing but the truth." It can help to apply this guidance to what you write in an examination answer: you should answer "the question, the whole question and nothing but the question."

When planning an essay answer like those required in Paper 4, I would always advise starting with the extract(s).

- Make sure you know exactly what the question is asking you to do.

- Read and annotate the extract.

- Underline or highlight key concepts, and jot down links to examples from your own studies as soon as you think of them.

- Decide on a helpful order in which to discuss the ideas, then start writing.

Looking back at the question and extract, I'm hoping you would have picked out a number of useful ideas.

Since the question asks you about "advantages and disadvantages of having English as a global *lingua franca*", you could immediately start your planning in two columns – almost always a helpful strategy. Where the extract offers just an idea, try to find examples from your own studies to support it. Look at the example below.

Advantages and disadvantages of having English as a global **lingua franca**

Advantage	Disadvantage
"defuses ethnic conflicts" (examples from your studies?)	"questions the authenticity and identities" of non-native speakers who use English (examples from your studies?)
	"arguments about the choice of indigenous languages for official purposes" (examples from your studies?)
	"use of English as official or national language strikes at the root of national pride since English is a colonial language"

TIP

Clever readers – that's you! – will have noticed that this guidance is very close to Grice's maxims, which we discussed in Chapter 10. The maxims are excellent advice for anyone writing an examination essay!

➤ Be clear and unambiguous.

➤ Be relevant.

➤ Write what you know to be true – and if you add some possibilities, make sure you support them with evidence.

➤ Only write as much or as little as you need to – go into detail where it's necessary; make briefer references where detail isn't needed.

See how useful spoken language theory is!

Conclusion

Athletes and their preparation have been a theme of Part 2 of this book. Racehorses are an interesting reference point too! Both human and equine runners aim to "peak" at the right moment: the Olympic final or the biggest steeplechase of the horse-racing calendar.

They want to be ready …

… but they don't want to be exhausted.

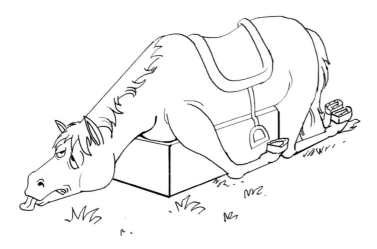

The same goes for English Language examinations. Making sure you're ready but not jaded will be the purpose of the remaining short chapters.

Exam preparation and technique

Introduction

As we said at the end of the previous chapter, you want to reach the day of the examination feeling prepared but not exhausted. It's good – and sensible – to feel a little nervous, but not paralysed by fear.

You'll have gathered that I'm quite interested in sports psychology, and I've suggested to you a number of times that "performing" in the pressurized situation of an examination room is in some ways similar to a sporting performance.

Top performers in a range of sports "visualize" themselves succeeding. Sometimes they prepare by going into the arena or stadium when it's empty, so that they know what it feels like and are familiar with the surroundings. Then when they come to the real performance they can concentrate on what they're doing and forget everything and everybody else.

Can you prepare yourself for an English Language examination in this way?

You want to avoid:

- being surprised or shocked by anything you're faced with
- feeling underprepared
- being distracted.

You want to feel:

- ready to perform, but not in a panic
- reasonably prepared for any question, but flexible enough to respond to what's put in front of you
- in control of your time and able to organize your work.

How can you help yourself to feel "in the zone"?

I'm **IN THE ZONE** Baby!

"If you fail to prepare, you prepare to fail."

One of my sporting heroes is the former England cricket captain Graham Gooch. When he began his career he was quite light-hearted, and perhaps didn't make the most of his opportunities. Later when he became the team captain, he took a more responsible attitude and was always the best-prepared player. He kept himself fit so that he was still playing international cricket when he was in his 40s.

Now he coaches younger players, and his favourite advice is, "If you fail to prepare, you prepare to fail." Even so, you have to be flexible and react to the current circumstances. One of Gooch's most impressive batting performances came in a Test match against India on a very dry and dusty pitch. He decided that the conditions meant he would need to use the "sweep", a batting shot he hardly ever employed. So just before the game he spent a number of hours practising just that shot. He batted very well.

This is a nice story with an obvious moral, but how does it apply to you?

Well, however well prepared you are, you must respond to what you're given.

Imagine for Paper 4 you've prepared yourself for a question on "Spoken language and social groups" and you've learned a lot about the theories of gendered language (see Chapter 11). You read the question on the examination paper, and the accompanying textual material: neither of them have anything to do with gendered language! What do you do?

You look in your toolbox! You look for the tools – ideas, approaches, concepts, theories – that are relevant to that question and that material.

Timing

Another person whose advice I have found valuable is the teacher who taught me economics. (I won't say how long ago.) He taught his classes some very useful lessons about timing, and he pointed out that it's always easier to get the first 50 per cent of the marks for any question than to get the second 50 per cent.

Again this is nice simple advice but how does it apply to you?

Well, if you plan carefully and divide your time according to the number of marks for each question and part-question, it won't apply to you.

But occasionally things might go wrong: you might be struggling to understand a text and then realize you've spent too long on that part of the question.

If time is really short – if the exam is nearly over, or if you still have another question to do – it's all right to finish your answer in note form. It's also all right to leave some space at the end of the answer so that if you do finish with time to spare you can come back and add to your unfinished response.

So, using the 50 per cent rule, if your timing does go wrong, it's better to do two half-questions than one whole one.

But your timing won't go wrong, will it? Because you're well prepared and calm! (And I bet you noticed my tag question there, didn't you? Oh! And again!)

> **TIP**
>
> Look back at the opening of Chapter 4 for serious words about watching the clock.

Finally, think about *checking*.

At every level, in every situation, you must be in the habit of checking what you have written. It's so easy to leave out a "not" (or put one in where it wasn't intended) and write the opposite of what you meant.

You need to allow at least five minutes for each answer to check every word that you've written – not what you *meant* to write, but what you actually *did* write. The examiner will be impressed, not irritated, by a crossing-out and correction which improves the sense.

Don't expect to understand everything

At A Level, you shouldn't be surprised to meet complicated texts, and you shouldn't expect to understand every word. If you do understand every word, that's a bonus, but you can do very well in an examination without total comprehension.

It's all right in an English Language examination to admit that you're not sure of a meaning, and you will always be given credit for exploring (sensible) possible alternative interpretations. Start with what you do know, and work towards what you can find out.

For example, here's a sentence from a text you encountered near the start of Chapter 4, the text that begins: "But I did not want to shoot the elephant."

> I watched him beating his bunch of grass against his knees, with that preoccupied grandmotherly air that elephants have.

You know what a grandmother is, but here the noun has been turned into an adjective. And you might not have come across the word "preoccupied" before, or the noun "air" in its metaphorical sense of a style or fashion of doing something. But you can use your linguistic knowledge to get close to the writer's intended meaning.

How does the clause which takes up the second half of the sentence relate to the main clause in the first half of the sentence? Well, it post-modifies the verb "beating" – it tells us *how* the elephant was performing this action, and if it answers the question "how" then it's adverbial.

So it means performing an action like a grandmother would do.

And this is a curious way of describing an elephant, because the connotations of "grandmother" are not like the connotations (or the denotations) of "elephant".

All of this means that we've been able to comment in plenty of detail on the writer's use of language without knowing the meaning of "preoccupied".

If you look back at the rest of that passage in Chapter 4, you'll be impressed at how much more you understand now.

Don't let yourself be surprised and flummoxed by a text

Just as you can't expect to understand every word of every text, you also can't expect to have encountered every possible type of text that you might be given in an examination.

The syllabus lists many text types. For Paper 3, for example, you could be asked about advertisements, brochures, leaflets, editorials, news stories, articles, reviews, blogs, investigative journalism, letters, podcasts, biographies, diaries, essays, and narrative/descriptive writing.

In a way, the text type (or genre) doesn't matter, because we know from all the preceding chapters that any text (spoken, written, or multi-modal) can exhibit characteristics from any other text type. The important thing is to apply what you've learned to what's actually in front of you.

Even so, you will feel more comfortable and confident if before the exam you have encountered as wide a range of text types as possible.

Luckily, in this age of access to the Internet, it's easy to find a huge variety of texts. Almost all printed texts exist in some online form, and you can research all the text types above. Don't waste time reading *about* types of texts: read the texts themselves.

What types of texts cause students most difficulty in examinations?

In my experience, the aspect of style or language which students find hardest to deal with is **irony**. At its simplest level, irony just means some kind of opposite or reversal.

Sarcasm is verbal irony. We say the opposite of what we mean in order to make a joke, to avoid (or cause) embarrassment. My son drops his buttered toast onto the kitchen floor, and I say "Well done!" Someone opens their car door as I'm cycling past, nearly knocking me off my bike, and I yell "Brilliant! Thanks very much!"

Some sarcasm is more complicated!

Authors use irony in many ways. You need to be aware of the possibility that a writer's surface meaning is not quite the same as his or her intended meaning. The *audience* is very important: if an author believes that the likely readers will be able to identify a gap between obvious and implied meaning then he/she is more likely to employ an ironic tone.

Journalists often employ irony when reporting on stories which are not completely serious. A good exercise for you would be to choose one of the day's top news stories and look at the different ways in which it is reported by different news agencies and newspapers. For example, *The Guardian* newspaper in the UK often adopts an ironic tone and uses puns in its headlines.

At the other end of the scale, some Asian newspapers maintain a "straight" reporting style which treats news in a respectful rather than light-hearted way.

Conclusion

We've considered four areas in which you can give yourself the best opportunity to do yourself justice in the exam.

1. Being well-prepared, but also being flexible.

2. Timing and checking: what you do before you start writing and after you finish.

3. Making the most of what you know, and using your skills and knowledge to work out what seems difficult.

4. Being determined not to be put off by any textual material you meet.

In the next chapter, we'll see some sample answers which follow the above advice.

Sample question
and answers

There are many possible ways of approaching examination questions. No one way is automatically better than any others, so there is no "formula" to follow.

However, it is interesting to look at a couple of possible responses to see particular approaches that work well or not so well. The examples here are in response to a question that requires you to do a directed writing task followed by a commentary because this type of response shows most clearly what you need to do in order to improve.

Sample question

This task is comparable to what you will need to do for Question 1 in Paper 3. It is similar in style to the one at the start of Chapter 12 and is followed by two possible responses to the question.

> The following text consists of part of a story from the online edition of the *New York Times* newspaper, published when Hurricane Sandy was about to hit the East Coast of the United States.
>
> (a) Imagine you are employed by the Emergency Management Agency. You have been asked to produce a brief information sheet, advising people what to do when the hurricane arrives.
>
>   Write the text for this information sheet in 120–150 words.   [10 marks]
>
> (b) Compare the style and language of your response with the style and language of the original article.   [15 marks]

Sharp Warnings as Hurricane Churns In

Hurricane Sandy, a menacing monster of a storm that forecasters said would bring "life-threatening" flooding, churned toward some of the nation's most densely populated areas on Sunday, prompting widespread evacuations and the shutdown of the New York City transit system.

Officials warned that the hurricane, pushing north from the Caribbean after leaving more than 60 people dead in its wake, could disrupt life in the Northeast for days.

New York went into emergency mode, ordering the evacuations of more than 370,000 people in low-lying communities from Coney Island in Brooklyn to Battery Park City in Manhattan and giving 1.1 million schoolchildren a day off on Monday. The city opened evacuation shelters at 76 public schools.

The National Hurricane Center said it expected the storm to swing inland, probably on Monday evening. The hurricane center reported that the storm had sustained winds of almost 75 miles an hour.

"We're going to have a lot of impact, starting with the storm surge," said Craig Fugate, the administrator of the Federal Emergency Management Agency. "Think, 'Big.'"

The subway closing began at 7 p.m. to darken every one of the city's 468 stations for the second time in 14 months, as officials encouraged the public to stay indoors and worked to prevent a storm surge from damaging tracks and signal equipment in the tunnels. A suspension of bus service was ordered for 9 p.m.

The closing this year seemed more ominous. The shutdown before Tropical Storm Irene last year began at noon on a Saturday, and service resumed before the workweek started on Monday. This time, officials warned, it might be Wednesday before trains were running again.

Another fear in the Northeast was that winds from the storm might knock down power lines, and that surging waters could flood utility companies' generators and other equipment.

Forecasters said the hurricane was a strikingly powerful storm that could reach far inland. Hurricane-force winds from the storm stretched 175 miles from the center, an unusually wide span, and tropical storm winds extended outward 520 miles. Forecasters said they expected high-altitude winds to whip every state east of the Mississippi River.

President Obama, who attended a briefing with officials from FEMA in Washington called Hurricane Sandy "a big and serious storm." He said federal officials were "making sure that we've got the best possible response to what is going to be a big and messy system."

"My main message to everybody involved is that we have to take this seriously," the president said.

The hurricane center said through the day on Sunday that Hurricane Sandy was "expected to bring life-threatening storm surge flooding to the mid-Atlantic Coast, including Long Island Sound and New York Harbor."

The storm preparations and cancellations were not confined to New York.

Amtrak said it would cancel most trains on the Eastern Seaboard, and Philadelphia shut down its mass transit system.

In the New York area, the Metropolitan Transportation Authority's commuter rail lines, which suffered the heaviest damage during Tropical Storm Irene, were suspended beginning at 7 p.m. on Sunday.

New Jersey Transit began rolling back service gradually at 4 p.m., with a full shutdown expected by 2 a.m.

The Staten Island Ferry was scheduled to stop running by 8:30 p.m., PATH trains at midnight.

The nation's major airlines canceled thousands of flights in the Northeast. The Port Authority of New York and New Jersey, which operates the three major airports in the New York City area, said it expected major carriers to cease operations entirely by Sunday evening. The Coast Guard closed New York Harbor — cruise ships were told to go elsewhere — and the Northeast faced the possibility of being all but shut down on Monday.

New York Times

Sample responses

Student A

(a) Directed writing

<u>An announcement from the Emergency Management Agency</u>

Hurricane Sandy is expected to arrive Monday evening, preparedness is vital; sixty people have been killed. Those to the south will be first hit. It's going to be high impact and will begin with a possibly life threatening storm surge, flooding the mid-Atlantic coast.

Those living in low-lying areas from Coney Island, Brooklyn to Battery City Park, Manhattan will need to evacuate the area; evacuation shelters have been opened at 76 public schools, so make your way there now while you can.

The subway will close at 7 p.m Sunday, if you can't make it to a station by then, bus services will not be suspended until 9 p.m. The harbour is closed.

Airlines have cancelled flights and Amtrak is cancelling services along the Eastern Seaboard and Philadelphia.

Hurricane Sandy is dangerous; stay inside once it hits.

Take it seriously and stay safe.

(b) Commentary

The original article is mostly written in the past tense and does not address the reader personally which is different to my response, which directly addresses those in danger. The original includes many facts and quotes that are not relevant to an information sheet and therefore those have been excluded.

While the original "Sharp Warnings as Hurricane Churns In", almost sensationalises the event to make it a noticeable headline that will attract readers outside of the danger zone, my response does not, a safety announcement has nothing to prove and therefore does not require dramatics as they are inappropriate for the reader. Those living within the area of impact would not wish to hear exaggerated accounts that could further alarm them; instead sticking to brief, informative sentences is wiser.

The response also solely focuses on the events at hand in a way the original does not; because the original is an article from an online newspaper, giving background to the reader is important, comparing the events of the present hurricane and the previous tropical storm is logical, for an announcement informing the population about the steps they should take to keep themselves safe it is not vital.

My response is also far briefer than the original article, to ensure that the key facts are not forgotten amongst an ocean of extraneous writing - especially important as the intended audience is everybody, regardless of reading level, whereas readers of a newspaper article will come seeking information, not all those receiving an announcement like this would be so willing.

The language used much more personal and informal, to create a sense of community within those reading it, as when such catastrophes occur, people can either band together or the attitude can be the entirely different, 'every man for themselves' mind set, which in this situation benefits no one. By removing the section about the enormous population, the announcement attempts to minimize this risk.

Comments on Student A's response

Part (a), the directed writing task, works well. The student has a clear sense of the audience and purpose, shown by the mixture of declarative sentences to impart information and imperatives to give warnings and advice. There is also a mixture of verb tenses to explain what has already happened and to forecast what will happen. High modality suggests a reliable forecast and the certainty of danger: "Those to the south *will* be first hit. It's *going to be* high impact and *will* begin …".

Choices of lexis are suitable, with "preparedness" being a particularly neat abstract noun to summarize the attitude the public needs to adopt.

The structure is good. Advice and information are skillfully combined, and the piece ends well: "Hurricane Sandy is dangerous; stay inside once it hits. Take it seriously and stay safe."

Part (b) is only slightly less successful overall. It begins well by commenting on the differences in verb tense and mode of address to the reader. There's a good understanding of the need not to sensationalize. The student appreciates the difference in genre/purpose/audience, commenting on how a newspaper can use drama and exaggeration while a safety announcement must not.

The rest of the commentary concentrates on the content, and the focus on style and language is not so sharp. Even so, a very proficient appreciation is evident.

With a little more analysis of specific details of language, this would be an excellent answer for both parts of the task.

As you read Student B's attempt at the two parts of the task, think about how this student might have made different or better choices of style and language.

> **TIP**
>
> Remember that what you do in one part of the question directly affects what you do in the other. You can turn this to your advantage: if you realize that you haven't made a very good job of the part (a) directed writing task, you can explain how you might have made better choices of style and language when you come to do part (b), the commentary.

Student B

(a) Directed writing

Emergency Management agency – Hurricane Sandy emergency action

Citizens of the eastern coast of the USA are advised to stay indoors if at all possible this Monday due to the approach of Hurricane Sandy, a violent storm during which there is a severe risk of storm surge flooding across many areas of the mid-Atlantic coast.

The National Hurricane Center has predicted the storm to move inland on Monday evening.

Public transport in many areas including New York, Philadelphia and New Jersey will be completely shut down by Sunday evening, so citizens are urged to return home before this time.

For your safety, all travel is deeply discouraged unless in an absolute emergency from Sunday until the storm passes.

Most flights in the Northeast have also been cancelled.

President Obama urges the public to take this threat very seriously in order to prevent any loss of life.

(b) Commentary

In my response, I greatly condensed the information given in the original article, retaining only information which I deemed useful to the general public during an emergency situation, such as the time when the hurricane is predicted to move inland, the areas affected and the action that should be taken during the storm (stay indoors, do not travel). The information that has been kept is organized into separate, concise paragraphs in order to make the message conveyed as clear and easy to understand as possible.

The language used was originally a journalistic, dramatic style of writing, using words such as 'menacing monster' and strikingly powerful' to describe the hurricane and containing a lot of information which was not absolutely necessary, such as mention of Tropical Storm Irene, which added interest to the article. I have changed this style to a more official tone by dividing the information up into concise sentences and short paragraphs, and not using descriptive words which sound exaggerated as the article from the New York Times contained. The leaflet will therefore be taken more seriously by the public because the information is delivered in a way which they associate with authority, and therefore they are more likely to follow the instructions given.

The information leaflet is written as if I am a figure of authority addressing the public directly but not individually by use of the identifier 'Citizens'. The emphasis is on public safety, and instructions are given using words such as 'advised' and 'discouraged'. Human nature can often cause people to resist absolute instructions such as 'the public must stay indoors at all times on Sunday', and so by using language which makes the reader feel as if they are still in control, the public are more inclined to listen to the advice given.

The final sentence is a message from President Obama, a figure which many Americans respect and would look to in times of trouble for guidance, gives the leaflet some weight in the reader's mind as, although it is never suggested that the leaflet is written by Obama himself, the inclusion of a message from the President will help to link the instructions of the leaflet with a higher authority and, again, make the reader more willing to follow any instructions given within the information leaflet.

Comments on Student B's response

The tone and register of part (a), the directed writing task, work reasonably well. The mode of address to the reader is suitably formal: it shifts from third person at the start ("Citizens of the eastern coast of the USA are advised … ") to second-person direct address in the middle ("For your safety … ") and then back to third person at the end ("President Obama urges the public … ").

The selection of details is good, and the student explains immediately in the commentary how this selection was made. As pointed out in the tip above, it's very helpful to explain your choices from the part (a) writing task in your part (b) commentary, and the student does this very competently.

This student explains very well at a general level how the original text and the transformation work. There are some references to specific details ("The language used was originally a journalistic, dramatic style of writing, using words such as 'menacing monster' and strikingly powerful' to describe the hurricane … ") but there isn't any developed analysis using precise linguistic terminology.

> **TIP!**
> If you find yourself writing, as this student does, "words such as …", stop and think! You need to explain what these words are; you need to analyse their linguistic construction and their effect.

The student has missed the opportunity to show a developed attention to details of language here, although it is possible to tell that she/he understands the overall impact of the language choices. For example, the student makes useful comments about the structure of both texts, such as the order in which information is presented and the technique of ending with a message from the President.

But there aren't enough specific examples to support the understanding. The following comment would have been worth more marks if the student had quoted some examples and shown how they work: "I have changed this style to a more official tone by dividing the information up into concise sentences and short paragraphs, and not using descriptive words which sound exaggerated as the article from the New York Times contained."

There *is* some more detailed awareness of language choices in the third paragraph: 'The emphasis is on public safety, and instructions are given

---

Let's do that now: What can we say about the expression "menacing monster"? It's an example of alliteration, which is usually used to draw attention to a detail, and often used for partly comic effect in headlines. It's also an example of metaphorical language: the weather is being compared to an imaginary living creature. And what are the connotations of "monster" in the reader's imagination? It's something frightening that's chasing you and determined to catch you.

using words such as 'advised' and 'discouraged'. Human nature can often cause people to resist absolute instructions such as 'the public must stay indoors at all times on Sunday', and so by using language which makes the reader feel as if they are still in control, the public are more inclined to listen to the advice given."

But there's that "words such as …" again, and another missed opportunity of saying something about the lexical or semantic field of polite/gentle imperatives and the use of the passive voice ("travel is deeply discouraged") to suggest some impersonal authority that shouldn't be questioned.

Both parts of the answer are well written and fluent. If you are able to write as well as that under the pressure of time in an examination, you can be very pleased with yourself.

Student B's work is not quite as good as Student A's, but the student has still produced strong answers.

Conclusion

The main message which I hope you have seen from these two examples is that for the top-level grades you need to focus on specific details of language and explain how they work. Teachers and examiners often have two very simple questions in their minds as they listen to student responses in class or read student answers – *how* and *why*?

- If the effect of some feature of style or language is xyz, *how* does that work?

- If the writer – the writer of the original text or the student writing the transformation – has used techniques abc, *why* have they done that?

I should add that both of the students who produced these answers annotated the question paper carefully as they read it, and were able to use their very good notes to organize their answers.

You can do as well as that.

Conclusion

You probably felt you had achieved a great deal when you got to the end of Part 1 of this book. And you had: just look in Chapter 6 at the list of things you had done.

You've done many more now!

An interest in language doesn't stop when you come to the end of a book like this, or when you do your Cambridge International A Level examinations, or when you get the results. It's completely natural for an intelligent lively mind (like yours!) to be interested in language.

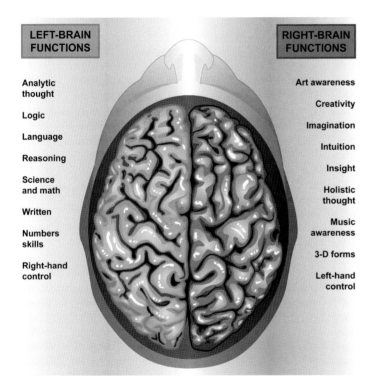

LEFT-BRAIN FUNCTIONS	RIGHT-BRAIN FUNCTIONS
Analytic thought	Art awareness
Logic	Creativity
Language	Imagination
Reasoning	Intuition
Science and math	Insight
Written	Holistic thought
Numbers skills	Music awareness
Right-hand control	3-D forms
	Left-hand control

You've practised and extended your capabilities in all the directions above.

In terms of the English Language syllabus, you have developed:

- a critical and informed response to texts in a range of forms, styles, and contexts
- the interdependent skills of reading, analysis, and research
- effective, creative, accurate, and appropriate communication skills
- a firm foundation for further study of language and linguistics.

With all this, you don't need luck in your examinations … but good luck anyway!

Index